SHOOTING BACK
FROM THE HEART

JIM HUBBARD
EDITED BY ALAN YUHAS

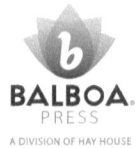

BALBOA.
PRESS
A DIVISION OF HAY HOUSE

ABOUT THE COVER

Cover Design by Marcel Menges
Photo by Jim Hubbard

I needed a photo for the cover of my book that would visually communicate what my story entailed. My family thought I should use one of my famous photos on the cover. I disagreed. I drove to South Los Angeles where ghettoes stretch for miles. I had a vague idea about the elements needed for the cover photo and brought a Bible and several cameras. I knew the area well as I had worked with many youth for years in these impoverished communities. Many of the sidewalks and alleys are strewn with discarded clothes and furniture and covered with shards of glass from broken wine and beer bottles.

There was a large, old wooden table, in front of one abandoned house. The windows were boarded and gang graffiti sprayed across the outside walls. Piles of debris were dumped next to the table. As I rummaged through the discarded items I found items that symbolized elements for my book's narrative. There were pieces of partially burned wood with the tips of rusty nails protruding. I propped the cameras, the Word Of God and the wood on the table and began taking pictures.

Two boys walked up and watched me for several minutes. One of the boys asked,"Will you put this in your picture?" He had taken his chain with the crucifix dangling from his neck and wanted me to place it near the Bible. They understood the context and symbols for the photographs I was taking. The cameras symbolized visual communication and my long career in photojournalism. The Bible symbolized God's grace and our faith. The rusty nails were symbols of Christ's painful crucifixion. Ironically, a shadow of a cross was cast on the right front wall of the house as the sun set and a utility pole formed the cross. The ghetto setting was a reminder of the two thousand verses in the Bible that address poverty and injustice.

Balboa Press books may be ordered through booksellers or by contacting:

Balboa Press
A Division of Hay House
1663 Liberty Drive
Bloomington, IN 47403
www.balboapress.com
1-(877) 407-4847

Printed in the United States of America.

ISBN: 978-1-4525-7767-8 (sc)
ISBN: 978-1-4525-7769-2 (hc)
ISBN: 978-1-4525-7768-5 (e)

Library of Congress Control Number: 2013912282

Balboa Press rev. date: 8/6/2013

To my daughters Priya, Hanna, and Sofie
and in memory of Brijin Marie

ACKNOWLEDGEMENTS

Marcel Menges, Alan Yuhas, Lydia Wills, Neal Baer, Dr. Stuart Fisher, Dennis Fitzgerald, Orson Bean, Alley Mills, Mike and Mary Hubbard, Lynn Warshafsky, Michael Andrew Hubbard, my daughters, Priya, Hanna, and Sofie. Grandson's Aiden and Dylan. Davidica Little Spotted Horse, Calvin Stewart, David Gusse, Geoffrey Cowan, former dean Univeristy of Southern California's (USC) Annenberg School for Communication, Larry Gross, Director, School of Communication, Pastor's Rankin Wilbourne, Marshall Browne and other pastoral staff at Pacific Crossroads Church (PCC) in Santa Monica, California, Wesley Theological Seminary (WTS), Washington, D.C., Hamline University, St. Paul, MN

TABLE OF CONTENTS

Part III

Part IV

Part V

PROLOGUE

By the time I turned twenty, I had little hope. I didn't consider myself very smart, especially since my dad judged me off my report cards and he would compare me to my older brother, who was academically brilliant. I don't remember ever taking an IQ test, but I suspect I would have flat-lined the score. Had there been a test to measure street smarts, however, I'd have tested off the charts.

My senior year in high school, I was assured my doom. Mr. Schumacher, the principal, said sternly, "You are a retard. You will be dead or in prison by the time you're twenty." Then came his final words to me before my expulsion from Detroit's Cody High. Looking directly across his desk, his eyes peering over his glasses, he said, "You are our worst student in a school of 4,000 students, a hoodlum, and you are never to return. Goodbye, Jim."

But my fate wasn't sealed that day in the principal's office, and decades later I was still among the living, not imprisoned and, in fact, had even seen a little success.

In 2010, I boarded a plane headed to Amman, Jordan, to launch a project with thirty Palestinian youth called Shooting Back From Palestine. Completing the project, I travelled to Hong Kong to consult with the Ho Family Foundation about youth projects they were planning. There had been a one-week interval between the two destinations, so I planned for my wife, Lynn, and our daughter, Sofie, to meet me in Italy before boarding a flight to Hong Kong.

After arriving at our hotel in China I collapsed onto a soft chair and looked out the floor to ceiling windows from the 25th floor of a hotel, onto a panoramic view of the Hong Kong harbor, thinking it a far cry from prison. The view from Wan Chai looked east, toward mainland China, in front of which hundreds of small and weathered fishing boats shared the harbor with large shipping vessels.

They looked like children's toys, bobbing and passing in different directions. Cruise ships from around the world floated in and out, and the legendary Star Ferry carried passengers back and forth from Wan Chai to Kowloon every five minutes, while helicopters hovered around to land on a pad near the hotel.

The boats appeared to have directionless, uncontrolled paths, but none collided, and they reminded me of my life, which seemed to have gone without direction, tossing and crisscrossing to unknown destinations, often on a collision course with unknown forces. "How did I get here?"

I reflected on how far I had come, from a tiny brick house in working-class Detroit to a city in China with a lifetime of adventures around the world in between.

Memories swirled in front of me, floating by without any particular logic, though they seemed synchronized rhythmically with the boats' movements on the water. Contrasted to the condemnation of my high school principal, I thought of what Oprah had once said when she featured me on her show. Smiling, looking into the camera she said, "Shooting Back is one of the most interesting projects that caught my attention, and a very special effort in our nation's capitol. Way to go, Jim Hubbard." Without meaning to or even knowing how, I became a "media darling, a mini-celebrity, a man with a great idea."

By the time I reached my late teens, I'd held many boring and labor-intensive jobs. I'd learned that I wanted work to offer meaning, not to end up working in a factory like my dad. Then a powerful memory flashed in my mind, the most tender one I have. When I was a little boy, I knelt every evening at my bedside, my mother next to me, and we prayed for the "sick, needy and afflicted." Then we prayed the classic, 18th century children's bedtime prayer: "Now I lay me down to sleep, pray thee Lord, my soul to keep. If I should die before I wake. I pray thee Lord, my soul to take. Amen." Even then, death frightened me; I sensed its randomness, that it could visit anyone, anytime. Who has control even over their next heart beat?

Until I was thirteen I felt the grace of God in my life, though it hasn't always been easy. Now I have no doubt, and any idea denying God's existence seems bereft of joy and imagination—the terror of a meaningless void. Happiness could only be achieved by being thankful to something higher than the self. "To whom or what do nonbelievers say thank you for their being alive and being fed? Do they believe they are gods? But what about their next heart beat?"

As a younger man, I had been an angry, juvenile delinquent who acted out. In those troubled years I robbed and assaulted people, committed felonies, and struggled from years of alcohol and drug misuse. Can a person change—mind, heart, and will? Can we rewire ourselves? Does anything go the way you think it will, or hope it might?

For some, the plans we make for our lives reveal themselves in a moment of sudden insight. For others, life unfolds gradually. This gradual unfolding may be the highest form of guidance; you take one small step, then another; with a kernel of faith and trust that all will work out, this slow process puts adventure into your life. My life unfolded this way, and each small step was another adventure.

In this rare moment of solitude, sitting comfortably in a Hong Kong hotel room, I could bring to the surface anything to which my mind had returned to again and again over the years, all the sore points of my life. I resolved to be totally honest and spare no buried fear, pain or guilt. Like everyone, I've collected many.

A corpse in a casket in the dress she'd worn on Christmas day, and the blinding darkness that had followed. The sense that I could have, should have done more. The judgments held over others that festered like sores, and the sudden, terrible disappearance of my brother decades ago. Broken promises and families, and the regret of having given in to the temporary relief of flesh knowing full well it was a hollow act.

I needed a new perspective, and sought higher ground. I took to the top floor of the hotel, thirty above my room. The boats on the harbor looked much tinier.

I thought about personal pain versus the enormous pain of others. As a photojournalist, I had witnessed events that had made humans suffer through horror and darkness, as well as the heights of human glory and joy. I'd seen the richest and poorest equally good and evil, only ever human beings.

For the fortunate few, travel offers relief from everyday routines, and a trip abroad grants an escape from working so hard to earn the ability to make that very trip. When many Americans are afforded a vacation to a foreign land, they opt for sheltered resorts, places seemingly distant from sorrow and suffering, though happiness and tragedy are only two sides of the same coin. Tragedy is not something I wanted to see either, but I did, and on a much grander scale than I ever imagined possible. Death and life are sewn together, akin.

When I was a little boy perusing *Life Magazine* and the *Detroit News*, studying the photographs that depicted war, famine and natural disasters, I was captivated. Like most people looking at photos in publications, I saw them from a safe distance. They merely symbolized an event, horrible or grand. The photo never truly captures the scents of flesh and death, the sounds of cries and screams, the frantic motion of people rushing toward or fleeing from one another. When I became a photojournalist such scenes became vivid for me. I saw bodies burned, cadavers laying in water for days. People butchered by knives, guns and bombs. Some choosing to end it all in suicide.

The Munich Olympics were one such event of human accomplishment and horror. For all the fellowship of those games, evil surfaced after only a few days, and before dawn, leaving over a dozen dead. For nearly fifteen hours we took pictures, and after over forty years the strangeness of it has never left me.

Is there a God, or is it all meaningless? How are we supposed to find any answers, especially after having taken photos of not only the victims but the monsters who had murdered or raped innocents, leaving haunting images as indelibly affixed in my mind as the layer of silver salts on the film in my cameras. These are permanent memories, not the kind I could repress.

What better place than the seminary, where I eventually landed, to ponder meaning and sift through the paradoxes of good and evil, to wonder why good existed in the same seeds of human nature as evil?

I returned to my room, thinking about Aldous Huxley and Jean Paul Sartre. Huxley did not want the world to have meaning and assumed that it had none; he found reasons for his assumptions. Sartre simply proclaimed there is no creator. But life absent meaning—and God—is an assumption without appeal.

When the consultations had concluded, we flew back to Los Angeles, but the memories weren't nearly through—from my youth, my struggles with work and faith, the time spent abroad and at home with every kind of person—it all kept rushing together as one surprising story.

PART I

"Remember not the sins of my youth, nor my transgressions: according to thy mercy remember thou me for thy goodness' sake, O Lord."
— Psalms 25:7

EVICTION NOTICES

A writer for the *Washington* Post called one day and said he'd like to write a story about my work with the poor and homeless. "It'll be a long story, seven to ten pages, including some of your photographs. It might run on the November cover. I'd like to spend a few days with you, meet your family, accompany you when you're on the streets taking pictures."

"You want my whole story from childhood to now?"

"Yes."

"That's a major story, seven to ten pages. Me?"

"I read some other stories about you and thought you'd led an interesting life. Besides, my editor thinks we should check you out. You've done something quite unusual, Jim."

"What's that?"

There was a pause. "You left one of the cushiest jobs in your field to attend a seminary and work with the homeless. Some photographers at the *Post* told me about you. From what I heard, you seem like a guy who wracks his conscience with questions that most adults stopped asking themselves years ago, if ever."

"Look, I'm flattered, but a little nervous. It's a bit scary. People in DC, you know how they are. Everything is about power and image. I don't know if it's what you're looking for. But if you have the time to listen, I'll tell the story."

I invited the writer, Peter Carlson, to accompany me on a project that documented people evicted from their homes. I warned him that evictions are very sad, charged situations, and that the newly homeless are often emotionally explosive. It's one of the worst days of their lives, and homicides and suicides are not uncommon. Undeterred, Peter agreed to come along.

I picked Peter up early one morning, and we drove to the US Marshal's office for a list of the day's evictions. I explained to him that there are over twenty per day, totaling thousands per year in a small city like DC. The federal marshals deliver the court documents to those about to be ordered to vacate, and the armed officers remain at the scene until movers finish carting off possessions, leaving them and the family who owns them on the street.

On our drive to the first address in my battered Volvo, Peter asked, "Is this the way you always drive, Jim?"

"What do you mean?"

"Well, you're an aggressive driver but you seem very relaxed. You have your left leg stretched out so you can prop your left foot on the dashboard, while your upper body is stretched so far you're nearly leaning over on top of me. One hand on the wheel."

"Peter, it's known as the 'Detroit Lean,' a habit from growing up there. I think it was adopted by Motown guys who thought it made them look tough and cool."

We arrived at the first eviction address, where movers had already carried some large furniture to the curb in front of the apartment. The scene was high drama. A young mother with several children was crying and screaming. The marshals stood by idly. I approached the woman and asked whether she minded that I took pictures. She was outraged and became verbally abusive.

I attempted to tell her that I'd be trying to show the world her plight. She softened and stopped yelling, saying, "Okay, maybe it'll help someone else in this situation. It's unfair. Who wants the pictures?" I explained that a group called Congressional Families for the Homeless did, and wanted to put on a photo exhibit for the Corcoran Gallery of Art across from the White House. I explained that the photographs were what had made the organizers want to have a show at the Corcoran. I also made sure to tell her she would need to sign a release form, indicating her permission to take photographs.

A few minutes later one of the woman's relatives arrived and started putting tossed items in her car. "Come on Peter, we've got places to go," I yelled, and we set off to the next address on the list. "Scary stuff, Jim," Peter said in a soft voice, "And there are nearly five thousand evictions every year? Talk about the under belly of the nation's capitol."

Peter was astonished by the first eviction. "That woman running from her apartment was berserk, pulling her hair, her face twisted and screaming. What a scary thing for her children to see, no wonder they were all sobbing."

"She reacted like many do during the evictions. When I arrive with the cameras, everyone hates me at first. No one wants to be photographed, not the federal marshals, not those being evicted, not even the movers."

"Well, it's painful to watch, that's for sure. It's another one of DC's dirty little secrets."

Like many writers I had worked with, Peter was cerebral and quiet. In short, he struck me as a nerd. I learned later that I was wrong in thinking him shy or self-conscious. I had worked with dozens of writers and generally they seemed stuck in their own heads. Unlike writers, photographers only have the events unfolding in front of them—they can't reconstruct events after the fact, but only react to the circumstances best they can. It always seemed to me that writers who are covering an event are already constructing the story inside their head, and a lack of either patience or skill prevents them from simply observing. I often used to tell reporters, "Don't trip over your brain."

During the extensive time we spent together, Peter wanted to know about my sixteen-year career with United Press International (UPI), especially while at Reagan's White House. He wanted to know why I quit a job that he thought most photojournalists would covet, and details about why I had enrolled in a seminary. He wanted to learn about my drug and alcohol use and what recovery was like. He asked about the people who'd been lost over the years. We talked.

I couldn't help but feel at times that our conversations were like therapy sessions with a shrink, and I wanted feedback and to learn more about him. I was curious about his motivations, but I did most of the talking and he revealed almost nothing. I hoped he wouldn't turn out like the actual psychiatrists I'd encountered.

One meeting was over lunch at Ben's Chili Bowl, and it promised to be a long one, because he wanted to know my religious beliefs and seminary life. His first question caught me off guard, though: "Jim, are you a do-gooder?"

"Don't insult me," I quickly reacted. He looked surprised.

"Why would that insult you?"

Without hesitating I responded, "I try and do good but being labeled a 'do-gooder' has a connotation that I'm not comfortable with. The label's derisory. The perception of a 'do-gooder,' religious or secular, is that they're naïve. I don't consider myself naïve—I know what comprises our world and it's far from being all good. Do-gooders tend to look at the world through rose-tinted glasses, and quite often their actions leave unintended consequences.

"Do-gooders share the blame for the plight of the homeless. In fact, they might be the single worst culprits. It was their idea to tear down the flophouses and empty the loony bins without an understanding of the city and how its society works." Peter leaned in, reflecting. I continued:

"Remember when people on skid row had a roof over their heads and could afford shelter in the flophouses? When those areas were bulldozed, the people were dumped onto the streets. Mentally ill people, too, were de-institutionalized in the name of protecting their rights, and because of inadequate care. The institutions were closed without a well-conceived plan or an adequate safety net, and those people wound up on the streets."

Before taking a large bite from his chili dog, Peter asked, "What about your life at Wesley Theological Seminary? Tell me a bit about your specific focus for ministry when you graduate." Peter had revealed his interest in religion before, and it was obvious he knew something of it. He had placed his pocketsize tape recorder on the table and held a pen over a stenographer's notebook.

I named classes and attempted to vaguely describe my focus: "I'd have to say it is to serve the poor and needy in some fashion." I told him that my concern for the poor stemmed from scripture, that there are about 2,000 verses in the Bible concerning their struggles—more verses than on any other subject. I explained that God's grace is a gift offered through our faith, not just by our works. More liberal churches often emphasize and practice works, while the more conservative orthodox churches focus and emphasize faith.

Peter interrupted, "Can you describe how faith and works have been part of your life?"

"Let me try... if I can find the right words. Faith has to ultimately transcend into good works. It isn't enough to simply say 'I believe,' and do nothing. When the body is apart from the spirit, the spirit is dead, and also faith apart from works is dead."

"How does this translate into life?"

"I've tried to be disciplined about work. I haven't been as disciplined about faith. For that I've floundered. Your creed is your deed, the thing you believe in enough to put into practice. Christianity is not something you merely believe, but something believed in enough to act upon."

Peter smiled and said, "What about what you think about Christianity, about Jesus?"

"I've been a half-hearted Christian. I've put God in the passenger seat too often, while I drive the car, sometimes recklessly."

"Sounds like you're still learning. That sounds reasonable. Were you always involved in a church?"

"That was kind of on-again and off-again for many years. I attended AA meetings for twenty years, but got tired of the tales of woe, and started to miss church. In hundreds of meetings I attended, I couldn't help but notice that many people in recovery are wedded to being unhappy. If someone is constantly singing the old Negro spiritual 'Nobody Knows the Trouble I've Seen,' people start to notice. There has to be a payoff in preventing the possibility for joy and happiness. It might be as simple as having others feel sorry for you. Some people have a taste for sickly sweet pity. A joyous, happy person doesn't want pity."

I told Peter more about my views. The Christian path engaged my imagination, letting it be taken captive and reshaped. "Remember Peter, I covered President Reagan and many of his news conferences. He taught me something. Just because a reporter asks a specific question doesn't mean that's the one that has to be responded to."

"If humans are the most evolved in the animal kingdom, it seems like there's little hope for humanity. Why not, then, explore and accept the possibility of the existence of a greater mind, a creator, a deity and God? Our problems today in the human family are the same existential questions and problems faced by people thousands of years ago. We're not more enlightened now in our so-called postmodern world." Peter squirmed, but I added, "We're both journalists, and I suspect you, like me, have seen a lot. It's not all pretty or even fair. But the world is mysterious, and beautiful, and humans are strange and wonderful creations. But we're good *and* evil. I don't know about you, but I have little confidence humans will ever much reform the world. I don't see any historical evidence it's possible."

I started to laugh, "Peter, the world is a beautiful place, except for the people."

Peter was good at his job. When he thought I wasn't answering a question he had an arsenal of follow-ups. He sometimes asked one that might prompt me to answer what he really wanted answered.

I tried to explain that Jesus is arguably one of the two most profound figures to ever exist, the other being Buddha. That I felt the Bible, in its entirety, could be summarized in the declaration found in John 3:16: "For God so loved the world that He gave his only begotten son, that whosoever believeth in Him should not perish but have everlasting life." That is the redemption story.

Finally, Peter announced that his deadline was approaching, and he asked, "Are you trying to return to the faith of your childhood after wandering the world?" I stared out the window for a few minutes. "Until my early teens, my faith in the church was a huge part of my life, and even the music gave me chills. Not to mention some of the sermons. 'Just A Closer Walk With Thee,' 'How Great Thou Art', 'Amazing Grace,' and other songs moved me like nothing else. There was warmth there."

"Now I'm in my mid-forties. I still have a sense of comfort when I go to church and hear the old hymns. I'm thankful for having been in the Baptist tradition at an early age. But if you think that I believe now exactly what I did when I was ten, then I wouldn't have lived, or I'd have denied life."

Peter interrupted, "I wasn't implying that, I'm only trying to understand how you came to this point today. You've told me about some things that might lead one to think you've struggled."

Peter's insights were painfully correct. "I'd been a waffler for a long time and betrayed my beliefs. Baptists refer to people like me as 'backsliders,' Experience can change even people who are committed to a life of faith. The gospel hasn't changed for a couple thousand years, but many people do.

"My understanding now feels deeper, broader, but fundamentally, the gospel is unchanged for me. Life has been a little like a ship tossing on rough seas, tipping my balance. I needed an anchor. When some people learned I had enrolled in seminary, I sometimes felt defensive when they challenged my beliefs. They were pointless discussions, and we weren't going to resolve them."

Peter announced the tape in his recorder was full. "That makes sense. I can relate to a lot of it." He fumbled with the cassettes. I told him, "You've become a friend, Peter, maybe a best friend. You listen to all my crap, scribble on your pad, record my words. You don't pressure me and we've talked about a lot. You've been patient. Let me know when the story's on the stands."

He smiled, "It's been good for me too. I've learned a lot. I think it'll be a strong story and hope you like it."

Finally, I said to Peter, "You mentioned there were one or two things you wanted to know more about."

"Yep, a little more about your early years and teen challenges"

"You mean when I was little and what my family was like?"

"Yes, the formative years."

"I'm still forming."

Molly, a seasoned photo editor at the *Post*, looked through the stack of photographs I had delivered to her and carefully selected ten images for their story. She asked me about a white family I'd photographed during their eviction from an apartment building in Alexandria, Virginia. She'd noticed that all of the other photos were of African American families, and I explained that in DC's suburbs, evictions were more likely be of white families, given different demographics.

She held up a powerful photo of a mother, Angela Fitzgerald, with her four young children, sitting on their pile of belongings that had been dumped, with them, on the street. She said, "This is a strong photo. Except for the TV, it reminds me of the photographs from the Depression. Your images aren't subtle, but they're undeniably strong.

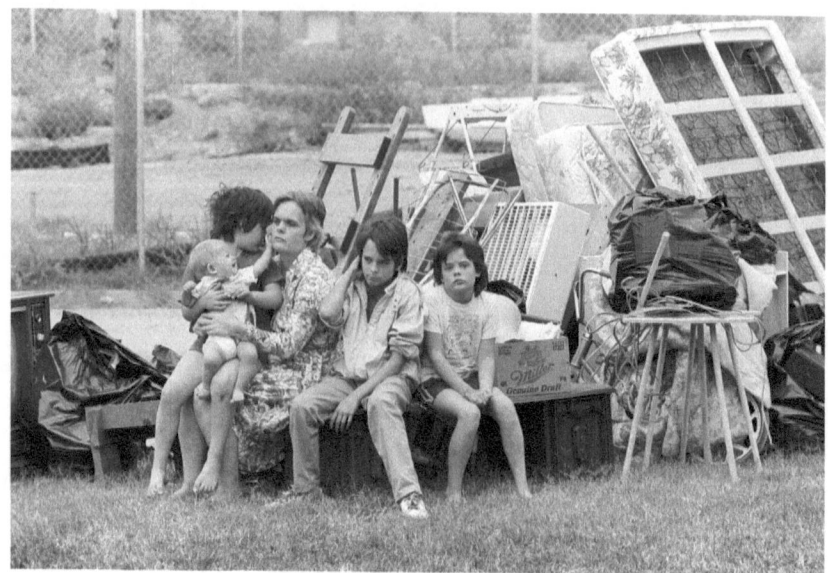

Fitzgerald eviction 1987

Molly picked up another disturbing image of six-year old Amanda Fitzgerald who went ballistic, screaming in terror, as a large animal control employee carried cages with the families two pet cats to a truck. The pets were taken to an animal shelter.

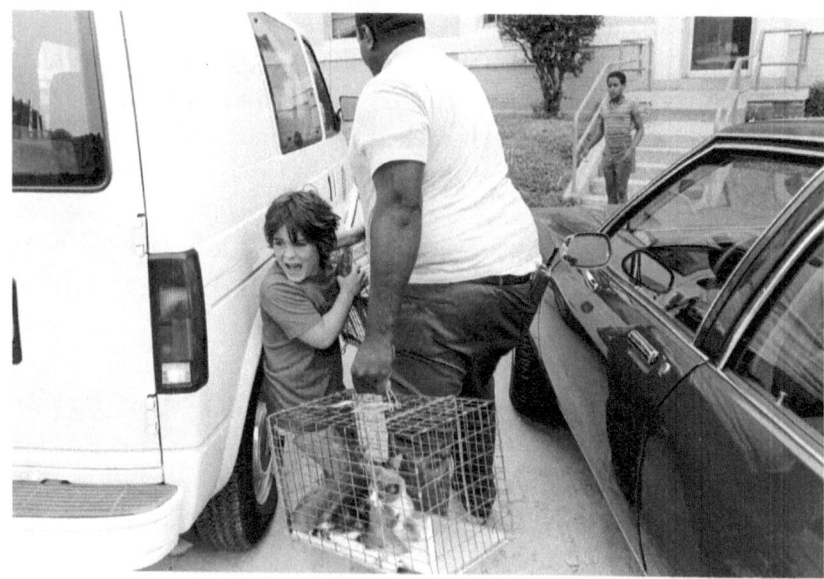

Fitzgerald pets taken to animal shelter 1987

Molly asked, "What was it like to take the Fitzgerald's photos?" "What really struck me was that Angela's son, Dennis Fitzgerald, who was about twelve or thirteen, was very sullen, maybe depressed. He wouldn't make eye contact and I think he was embarrassed about being photographed when his life was coming unhinged. He was angry.

"I've been visiting with the Fitzgerald's since their eviction and taking additional photos. They went to a shelter for a few days and then moved into Section 8 housing. We meet for lunch and sometimes to have an ice cream cone together, but Dennis never showed, only Angela and her three daughters. I'd love to see Dennis again. He seemed like a bright kid. His mom said he'd tested like a genius on an IQ test. She's quite forthright and told me about some horrible things they've had to face. Her husband went berserk and murdered her mother, stabbing her sixteen times. Angela hid Dennis, who was two at the time, in an upstairs room. Her husband was sentenced to eighteen years for it."

Molly told me they'd run a photo of the Fitzgerald's. Peter called me a few week's later to say that early copies of the magazine would be delivered to his office—I raced over and a secretary handed me one. When I was outside and a block away from the *Post*'s offices, I leaned against a utility pole and flipped through the pages, my heart pounding and my palms sweaty. It's bizarre and stressful to be the subject of a story, somewhere in print. I felt like I was going on stage to perform. My legs started to quiver when I saw a portrait of myself across almost two pages. It showed me kneeling in an alley with cameras slung around my neck.

The story was titled "Shooting From the Heart: Hubbard gave up the cushy life of a White House photographer to walk mean streets, to capture the faces of the people who live there, to try and save the world with pictures, in his quest to serve God and man."

By the River, on Skid Row

My dad was a factory worker with a sixth grade education, born and raised on a farm in cotton country, southeastern Missouri, along the edge of the Mississippi Delta in Dunklin County. Most commonly known as Missouri's Boot Heel, the area once had a reputation for lawlessness, and is exactly like any other rural area in the Deep South, from the way food tastes to the accents you hear. Its relatively large black population made it distinct from the rest of rural Missouri, and its culture was uniquely reflected in its music and churches. My mother was raised on a farm a few miles from my dad; she grew up in a large, devout family.

My dad, on the other hand, was the son of a dirt-poor sharecropper with seven kids, right around the time of the country's descent into the Great Depression. His stern father had de-emphasized education—he preferred to have his five sons stay home and help with the farm. That obviously resonated with my dad—he couldn't have done more to stress attendance and good grades to me and my two brothers.

Like millions of other white and black folks living in the rural south in the 1930s and 40s, my parents moved to the industrial north in The Great Migration, the largest migratory movement in US history in search of a promised land of money and jobs. They settled in Detroit's inner city, started having kids and found a Baptist church to attend. By the time they bore three sons, Paul, Michael and me, they had settled on a church and my dad had steady work in a factory, where he repaired enormous machines that manufactured truck axles. Smoke, grime and grease were a daily part of my dad's work at Timken-Detroit Axle. Though he was only about 5'8", he had a husky build and was strong as an ox. He worked long hours and was deferred from military service during the early years of World War II because Timken Axle was, like most factories in Detroit, converted from producing cars and trucks to producing tanks and planes.

When I turned seven in 1949 we moved from our inner-city flat to the far west side, into a newly constructed brick home, where the streets had not yet been paved and the city was stretching its borders with thousands of new homes for working-class Detroiters. The homes were all small and had similar design. The move was incredibly exciting for our family, and my parent's dream come true. They took out a $10,000 loan to pay for the house.

Rouge Park stretched for miles behind our house, with Rouge River running through the park. The river was deep and muddy and a strategic waterway for industry, and the park was a virtual jungle camouflaged with thousands of trees and shrubs. We knew we could hide in that park for months if need be—Rouge is more than 40% larger than New York's Central Park. It became the favorite play area for the new neighborhood's hundreds of children, especially the boys. My brother Mike and I spent

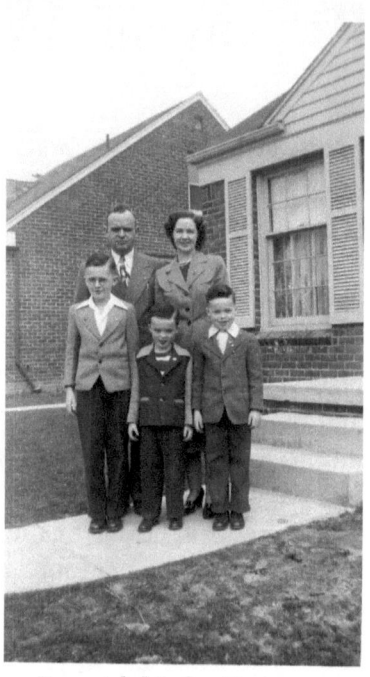

Jim with his family at new Detroit home 1949

hundreds of hours playing cops and robbers and cowboys and Indians with toy guns there.

My older brother Paul, on the other hand, was a bookworm. He always stayed home when he wasn't in school, or in the basement with his chemistry set, mixing chemicals that sometimes set off small explosions. His goal was to become a nuclear physicist.

In the park, Mike and I organized boxing matches in a roped off ring, and a gang of us played tackle football without gear. We loved to go to the edge of the muddy river winding through the jungle, as we called it. We each pretended to be a soldier, carrying a toy rifle or stick, and the terrain was eerily similar to the pictures I had seen of far away places. Mike and many of our buddies, unbeknownst to them, could have viewed our activities in the Rouge Park jungle as training for when they shipped off to Vietnam, as far away as the Mekong Delta. My brother Mike became a Green Beret, serving three tours in southeast Asia.

My dad stockpiled a small arsenal of real guns in our home. We often went hunting with him, traipsing through the woods, hearing the sounds of the crinkly, crunching leaves underfoot, smelling the fresh fall air, and generally delighting in the colors of the vibrant leaves that were stunning—an array of red, yellow and bluish green—a natural high. I loved to hunt pheasants, squirrels and rabbits, and our beagles, David and Tippy, often lead the hunting expeditions, scaring the pheasants airborne and running and yelping behind them. "God sure made a beautiful world," I thought. Finally, we would shatter the quiet of the woods with blasts from our shotguns, sometimes causing a beautiful, fluttering pheasant to crash to earth.

When we returned home we plucked the pheasant and my mother cooked it. One dinner, my dad noticed I was picking at the meat. He may have been concerned I might grow up to be a serial killer, since it was rumored that serial killers liked to carve up dogs and cats when they were young. Who could be sure? He asked, "What's wrong Jimmy." I looked at him and responded, "I just ate some small round things that were hard as steel. I think I chipped a tooth." He fired back using an expression he rarely used, "Dadgumit that's just buck shot from the shotgun shells. Just eat your food Jimmy. There are people starving in China."

By the time I was twelve, I became aware of the dark side of humanity just within a block of my home. My dad's mood swings had shown me how a person can swiftly explode out of a seeming calm, but my first encounter with evil was when a Boy Scout I knew, only two years older than myself, used his hunting knife and hatchet to mutilate his mother and sister. He stuffed their bloody bodies into a closet inside his small, white, wooden-framed house. It sat vacant for years.

A year after that tragedy, we were having Sunday dinner when a strong explosion shook our house. My brother Mike and I jumped up from the table and dashed down the block to find our neighbor Mr. Fisher lying upright on his sofa—on the street outside his home. His small house had been leveled. Mr. Fisher was alive, bruised and bloody. A heating and furnace specialist, he had turned the gas on his kitchen stove to high, laid on the couch in the living room and when a few minutes had passed he lit the match. The couch had flown fifty feet with Fisher on it, landed upright, and thoroughly aborted his suicide. He sustained only minor injuries and was sent to a psychiatric facility.

It was discomforting, to say the least. It was also unsettling to become aware that evil spans the globe. One day, on several acres of the park, the US Army started digging up the earth and mysteriously began working underground for several months. When their work ended we would sometimes see a sleek, white Nike missile lift from launchers aimed at the sky. If we were attacked by a foreign enemy, the missile base would aim, fire and destroy the attackers. At school, we would be herded to the school's dark, ominous basement during air raid drills.

Our dad often took us down by the riverside, which as the years passed took on an increasingly surreal aspect. We saw a few dead bodies after storms caused the water to swell over the banks. Police divers and rescuers dredged the bottom to pull a drowning victim from the swollen waters. One victim was a child, who had slid into the river while stepping too far on the slick embankment. A dead body, especially one soaking for hours or days, no longer resembles anything human.

Three fundamentals guided our family: church, work and education. We were members of Berean Baptist Church, which was quite comfortable compared to other Baptist churches we visited. The old Baptist hymns stirred my soul and made me want to sing and shout—I felt the spirit moving inside in joyous, spirited celebration. I also liked the simplicity of the service and the decorum: long, old, wooden pews, and a picture of Jesus on the cross hanging up at the front. Lastly, the preaching style of many Baptist ministers always appealed to me.

I sometimes peeked inside the Catholic Church in our neighborhood, which some of my pals attended. My dad made it perfectly clear he did not like us associating with Catholics, but of course we did anyway. The interior was ornate; candles burned and people dipped their hands in large, colorful ceramic bowls. The stained glass windows were majestic while also disturbing. I knew that my Catholic pals relied on mediators, priests, to reach God. Baptists could go straight to God, like my mother and I had for years, kneeling at the side of my bed. Another bonus offered by the Baptist tradition was that a person seeking forgiveness could confess in solitude. "Dear Father, please forgive my sins and shortcomings," was my prayer. In my view, Jesus was a working class man wearing sandals. I imagined him being more comfortable in a Baptist church than a Catholic one, which looked to me like an art museum.

Church was integral in determining our social lives. We would be with friends every Sunday's morning and evening services, and Wednesday evenings we gathered for prayer meetings. In our weekly Sunday School classes, I memorized Bible verses and sang lyrics like "Jesus Loves the Little Children."

That song became gospel for me in the lines, "Jesus loves the little children, all the children of the world, red and yellow black and white they are precious in His sight." Even as times grew more turbulent in Detroit, especially around racial issues, I had always believed in that song. It seemed incongruent that my Dad's decision to move our home had been racially motivated—he wasn't comfortable with the arrival of black people in our old neighborhood and at school.

My mother was the peaceful force in our lives. I can't recall her ever screaming or yelling, cussing or demeaning any other person. Her prayers always ended with the words, "Bless the needy, sick and afflicted." I don't recall my dad being much involved with our spiritual practices. For work's hard hours he was early to bed and early to rise.

My mom had a few unusual habits. While everyone else was sleeping she read her Bible. She said that she journeyed into the celestial realm, and it was a touching scene to see her on the sofa, with her big leather Bible open on her lap. But she would also go down to the basement to wash clothes, staying down there into the wee hours of the morning. I suppose she felt solitude and comfort there. Years later, she was asked by a reporter, "What was it like with three sons, Lois?" She laughed but then turned deadly serious and said, "Three sons, oh you don't know what that was like. Boy, that was something, you just don't know." When I asked her if it was hard, she responded, "Oh boy, you just don't know."

I was baptized by submersion at the age of understanding—in

our church parlance, "born again"—in a tank behind the pulpit, before the whole witnessing congregation. Ephesians summarized the fundamentals of salvation: "For by grace you have been saved through faith; and that not of yourselves, it is the gift of God. Not by works lest any man should boast."

I did not completely understand the fundamentals of being "saved." But it was a requirement for acceptance, in both the church and my home. We were told all about the wrath of God, but it was wrath on earth, from church members and my dad, that convinced me to follow the script. Being "saved" and accepting Jesus insured that we'd go to heaven after death, and skip that whole trip to hell for an eternity of pain and fire. Avoiding burns was a powerful motivator for a twelve-year-old. The paradox of a loving and punishing God became my first existential dilemma—or maybe the second, right after my dad's nature love and punishment.

As children we were told over and over how Jesus loves little children, everywhere in the world. But what did I know about following God for all my remaining days? There would be so many other humans and things to follow in all those days ahead. Life happens. I would adhere to some principles and disregard others. Becoming born again would take discipline and the commitment could burst forth in a second or span a lifetime.

The congregants were mostly blue-collar families like our own. The heads of the households were factory workers, and, like my dad, mostly skilled and worked with machines as big as three story buildings, and were often large, mean-looking men.

One of these intimidating congregants often sat in one of the back pews. He was a Detroit Police detective and a member of the feared police teams called the Big Four. His hand was the size of a boxing glove. The Big Four, or Tac Squad, roamed the streets searching for bars to raid and prostitutes to arrest. Three detectives and a uniformed driver cruised in big black Chryslers or Buicks, and most of us knew that in the trunks were a weapons-shop worth of firearms, including shotguns and machine guns. If you were ever pulled over, your responses to their questions had better include a "sir" at the end of every response, or you were about to have a very bad day. They were known to be zealous when interacting with black folk, but they would never hesitate to beat the crap out of a white punk, either.

Not everyone entering our church came with a tough demeanor—most were gentle worshippers. Our denomination was rooted in the southern tradition and forbade drinking, dancing, gambling and swearing. Smoking was not restricted; every man I knew smoked. My dad was vehemently opposed to alcohol and preached against it. He often used the rod, by way of belt, when his words no longer kept his sons away from wine and beer in our early teens. No alcohol had ever been brought into our home that I was aware of, except for vanilla extract.

Until my brothers and I weren't too old, we would all fit in the back seat of our black 48 Chevrolet and head downtown to watch freight trains pass at Boulevard Docks, wiling away the Saturday by watching brakemen jump on and off the boxcars.

After visiting the train yard we headed to skid row near Tiger Stadium, pulled up to the curb along Michigan Ave and relaxed for an hour or two watching the fallen. It was one of the country's largest skid rows, and only a few blocks from gigantic factories spewing noise and grease. We watched men lying on the streets tilting whiskey bottles, and others who got in fistfights until the police arrived in paddy wagons to cart them off. My dad would turn around from the driver's seat and sternly tell his three little sons, "If you drink and don't work hard, this is what will happen to you." Terrified, I promised myself I'd never drink.

Sometimes while driving home my dad would stop the car abruptly on a busy street and get out. He stopped once, got out, and when he returned he announced, "This pair of pliers was lying in the road." He already had a garage and basement full of every tool created since the invention of the hammer. He was a journeyman machine repairman in the factory, meaning tools were precious to him.

Returning home, my mom and I would kneel and pray together. "Dear Heavenly Father, please bless the sick, the needy and the afflicted, in Jesus name, Amen." She continued to sow the seeds of compassion for fallen humans, even if their suffering was self-inflicted.

While the cool waters of baptism were chilling me, my first crush, on a girl named Marilyn, was warming. It was that first innocent interaction of a boy and girl holding hands, sitting in a pew. Our legs leaned against each other. We were in a spiritual place and I felt what might have been akin to spiritual feelings. After church, we snuck to the basement to hug and kiss—my first brush with lust. The feelings were overwhelming when we sat side by side again on the wooden pew. Alarmed, I sat up, erect.

I had one other crush on a tall and slender woman with blond hair that ran down to the middle of her back. When I was near her, her fragrance enveloped me, and she looked like women from Sweden or Norway I had seen in magazines. She was my art teacher. She ignited my interest in art and beauty—mostly hers, of course—and left me with warm mysterious feelings.

I loved when guest evangelists visited and preached during revivals, not unlike the outdoor tent revivals that were popular in the south. Their voice's cadence and flamboyant movements were mesmerizing, flailing their arms and waving the Bible. Sauntering across the stage, they would carry the pulpit, voices blasting from a bass to a high tenor, all fire and brimstone.

Every eye in the congregation was glued to them. After church, I would go home and grab a Bible. I poised to preach in front of my mom's mahogany dresser, which had a large mirror attached. I imagined the small bedroom magically was a huge church, with hundreds of adoring congregants enraptured by every word. I was sure I wanted to be a preacher.

I had one other vision, too: I wanted to be a big band leader, in the tradition of Jimmy and Tommy Dorsey. I used to draw pictures of my band, and each bandstand I sketched prominently displayed the initials JH on the front. But despite lessons, I never mastered the trumpet, and disliked the metal pressed against my lips. The vision faded.

Mike would sometimes open the door to sneak a peek at his brother preaching and he'd sit on the side of my parents' bed and chuckle. He always wanted me to come outside and ride bikes while he, acting like a cop, would chase me, pull me over and write me up in his little ticket book. It amused our parents that my mom's father, Papa Bohannon, had been both a minister and his small town's lawman.

During some evening services, missionaries from faraway places visited. They showed us slides from an old, battered Kodak projector on a torn and ripped screen. They told stories about their missions in India or Africa, and they were usually quite soft-spoken. They wore simple, conservative clothing, and were often a husband and wife team.

But despite their quiet demeanors, the pictures they brought from Africa were fascinating. They seemed to fit all my pre-conceived ideas about life in a deep and dark jungle: the people looked primitive, that their reality was one of subsistence. Though our congregation was working-class, we were comparatively rich. The images were not unlike the magazines I had studied as a child, and though I didn't know it at the time, some new vision started to take shape for my future.

GOING DOWN HOME

Every summer our family went down home to the Boot Heel of southern Missouri. It was the place we considered our real home, where my parents' had their heart and soul planted. Their feelings for their birthplace were as deep and strong as the roots of a giant magnolia tree, and my brothers and I loved going there. I'd always considered my heritage rooted in the south, and that I'd simply lucked into the added bonus of being an urban kid who lived in a diverse sociological laboratory. My dad didn't always make the trip, but when he did we used to drive the 800 miles, rather than take the train.

I remember meeting my dad's father only once; his mother had died much earlier. We sometimes visited his sister Ruby, who worked in a beauty parlor in Blytheville, Arkansas, and occasionally we visited my dad's brothers, George and Ezra, who owned a gas station in St. Louis. His other siblings, Mabel and Henry, lived in Detroit, and we never met his youngest brother, Calvin, who we learned had severed ties with our dad after a fistfight. It didn't seem right that brothers would cut ties so completely, but we never learned much more than that.

The drive was tedious. Dad, despite our pleas, never stopped at a restaurant. He was an impatient man, but still believed in feeding his kids. "Okay, we'll get some food, let's pull over," he would announce at some small-town grocery store. He stopped long enough to run into the store and return with a loaf of Wonder Bread and a pound of bologna.

My mom had thirteen siblings, seven of whom died young. She was the only one in her family to leave the south, yet she and her siblings had a profound love for one another. My dad's side of the family was less pleasant to visit, so we rarely did.

My mother's sister and brother-in-law, Lola and Gene, farmed

800 acres of vast, fertile fields, growing cotton, corn and soybeans. Near their house were the barn, pigpens, cows and a henhouse for the chickens. I loved this place almost as much as I did my uncle and aunt, who were kind and had no children of their own. I suspected my mother harbored some resentment toward my dad for transplanting her to Detroit, and that he may have had a more sinister plan than simply to look for work in the city. He might have wanted her far away from her siblings, who had always given her a strong system of support and love. It would have been more difficult for my dad to attempt to control and dominate her near her family.

When we drove down home we would go through Memphis, only seventy miles from our final destination. At the gas stations, the drinking fountains had hand-written signs instructing Negro and White usage, racial distinctions which I hadn't seen in Detroit. We sometimes ventured a few miles past Memphis into the state of Mississippi where we saw shameful poverty.

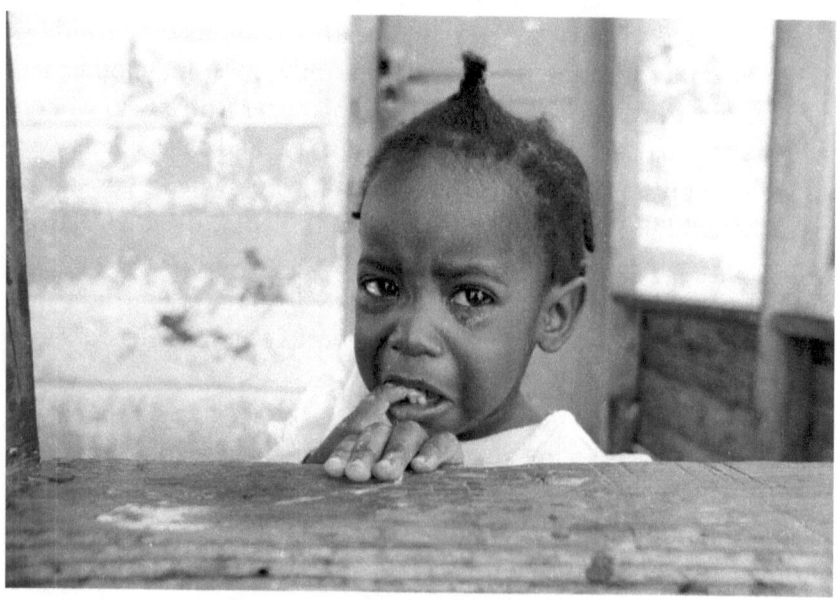

Rural down home Mississippi girl

Our early trips preceded the mechanization of farming. When we arrived at my uncle's, there were dozens of African Americans working in my uncle's cotton fields. The women brought their small children along, and they played in the dirt next to their mothers, who used hoes to chop away at the weeds growing near each stalk of cotton. The temperatures would soar to 100-plus degrees with high humidity. Some of the pickers would walk over to the farmhouse where Aunt Lola pumped water from the well to serve them cold water. I knew the workers were dirt poor and overworked, and it was clear that there was no special kinship between them and my relatives. No one ever said much about farmhands, but I felt sorry for them.

Across the state border a few miles away in Leachville, Arkansas, lived another sister, Mary, with her husband Joe and their two daughters Judy and Joan. They were also favorites, and we would spend weeks with them at a time. Uncle Joe owned a hardware store, had one of the first propane distributorships in the south, and was also a deputy town marshal. Mike and Paul were fond of Leachville and had little interest in the farm life Uncle Gene offered.

During our visits, the Bohannon family usually gathered from near and far for a family reunion. Over a hundred cousins, second cousins, aunts, uncles and grandkids descended for the feast. It was a real clambake without the clams. There was, though, an abundance of catfish, deep-fried in a huge, black, kettle over an outdoor fire. Also on the menu were southern-fried chicken, black-eyed peas, corn-on-the-cob, cornbread and watermelon. We gorged. We thought of it as gourmet food to be washed down by iced tea or a bottle of Dr. Pepper, topped off with pecan pie.

Papa Bohannon was the star of these reunions. He wore many hats; sometimes he worked in the Senath cotton gin as the regional expert on the quality of cotton. He would hold a boll of fresh picked cotton in his hand and roll it between his fingers while an anxious farmer waited for him to determine the value of the whole trailer-load. He taught and tuned pianos, and composed Christian hymns that inspired all his children to take up music. He had also been a town marshal, though he liked to say that he'd never been forced to fire his shotgun.

Papa was patient during incidents that would upset most people, especially my temperamental dad. Once, when Mike and I were playing gas station with Papa's 1949 black Chevy coupe we got the garden hose and filled his gas tank with water. My dad was furious but Papa took it in stride. Fortunately, my dad could fix most anything mechanical—he was a journeyman mechanic, after all. He crawled under the car, removed the tank, and emptied the water. He wasn't happy about losing a couple hours on a hot summer day, but it blew over thanks to Papa. If ever there were a saint he would be Saint Papa. I imagined him as a southern Jesus, the Prince of Peace with his dress shirt stained by tobacco juice from his corncob pipe.

Papa would take me to the henhouse behind his old white, wooden home to gather eggs for breakfast. "Jimmy," he'd say, "I have names for the chickens," and he'd touch their feathery bodies with one of his large, elegant hands, while ruffling the hair on my head with his other. "That's Trutro, over there is Bulah, and that's Honey," pointing to a dark brown chicken staring back at him. He handed me eggs, which were warm and had feathers stuck to them, and I put them in the basket, thinking how strange, when you pull them out of the refrigerator they're cold.

By the time Papa was in his eighties he had an unusual habit of going to bed at night wearing his wrinkled dress shirt and tie; he explained it was so he didn't have to put the tie and shirt on the next morning. His white shirts started to show brown tobacco stains from where he drooled. He died peacefully in his home at eighty-seven from natural causes, and we were devastated. His corpse was placed on his bed for the initial viewing. A few days later he was placed in a coffin in his living room, next to his piano, and relatives and friends filled the house.

Between the tears, the lyrics from a song he wrote in 1954, "Glory of the Soul," were sung by our cousins, who were professionals in a gospel group called "The Harmony Boy."

"When the toils of life are over and we cross the stream of death,
Oh what sorrow it will bring to those who stand around our bed,
But just over on the other side is sunshine, love and smiles,
For Christ the Lord will meet us there and lift us to the skies."

The sweetest memories I would carry with me throughout my life came from our visits to the Boot Heel, down home.

When we returned to Detroit, we resumed our daily lives with school, work and church. We sometimes visited my dad's sister Mabel, who lived with her family in a rundown neighborhood in the inner city. They were devout Pentecostals and Mabel's husband was a part-time Pentecostal minister named Jim. We once attended their church when Jim was preaching. People spoke in tongues and literally rolled in the aisles, which left me perfectly terrified. "No wonder people called them, "Holy Rollers."

Jim was the sort of man who acted like he was possessed by a demon. They had several kids, some with serious problems. Our cousin JT, one of the older sons, was in and out of prison. We sensed that dark things went on in their family, so we did not see them often. My cousin Artie May's lifestyle prompted questions about her safety, and her younger sister Caroline was also headed for trouble. I learned of her recklessness years later, while working on a story about vice cops for the *Detroit News*.

My brothers and I were working by age ten, and were never without a job growing up. There were three major papers in Detroit in the 1950s, and my older brother Paul was a newspaper boy for the *Detroit News*, while I had a route with the *Detroit Times*. Paul's route consisted of about two hundred homes; mine was significantly smaller, so I had a lawn-cutting business on the side with my younger brother Mike. Around this time, too, I joined the Cub Scouts and won my first Brownie Instamatic camera through cookie sales. I would take pictures of family events and my pet rabbits and dogs. It was almost just a little brown toy, but it stuck with me.

When Paul entered high school he handed over his larger route to Mike and me. I dumped my route at the *Times*. We delivered papers after school and on Sundays when the paper was twice the size of the weekday papers. We had to be awake by 5:00AM to travel about two miles to get the papers from a centralized distribution location. It was the dawn of a new era, out of the south and growing up in the city.

DETROIT DAZE

The newspaper boys gathered each morning to meet with Mr. Rawleigh, the man who controlled distribution and collected the money from our deliveries. This very large man made it clear that the money we gave him had better be exact, to the penny. To really hammer the menace home, these transactions took place in a wooden, one-car garage in an alley, near a row of Polish businesses and behind small frame houses of first and second-generation immigrants.

Mr. Rawleigh often arrived late. He was a huge man and his car simply gigantic, an all white, four-door Chrysler. He always arrived in a suit and tie, and always with two other men, both bigger than him. When he walked into the garage he would take a seat at a long table surrounded by hundreds of stacks of bundled papers awaiting delivery. In the act of sitting, he'd take his suit-coat off, roll up his sleeves and pull out the Colt 45 tucked in the front of his trousers to place on the table. He'd pull out a wad of bills ranging from hundreds to ones. We estimated that this wad totaled thousands. The two men accompanying Rawleigh stood one by him, one by the door, and they both distinctly resembled the mob goons from a James Cagney film we'd all seen on TV.

We nervously paid him and collected our papers for the day's delivery. Rawleigh, we learned, was involved in all aspects of distribution of newspapers in the Detroit metro area, including the trucks that would bring the papers to the small garage. Teamsters controlled trucking, and the teamsters were in bed with organized crime; they had associations with none other than Al Capone years earlier. Without Rawleigh, I would never have made it to where I am today.

Suffice to say, the teamsters were powerful. They could shut down not only the newspaper, but all the vital products delivered by truck to the city. Jimmy Hoffa, their president, lived a few miles from our house on the west side. My dad drove us by Hoffa's house many times, and his lack of pretention and that his house looked just like ours made us feel a kinship with him. He disappeared in 1975 and his body was never found.

On weekends and during the summer months I also helped with Bob the milkman's Twin Pines Farm Dairy truck in our neighborhood. At 3:00AM each morning I'd crawl out of bed so Bob could pick me up, and we'd go to the dairy where the bottles were filled with fresh milk stored in huge tanks that filled hundreds of white and chocolate milk bottles for delivery. While Bob drove, I'd place glass milk bottles in the metal carrier, and from house to house I'd jump out of the truck and dash to the resident's milk chute, pull the empties and replace them with fresh ones, then dash back, hop on and proceed to the next house. I loved the mini-chases.

In the 50s, Milky the Twin Pines Clown was my hero—an icon, a screen giant, the king of the Saturday kid shows. Helping Bob deliver Twin Pines milk was helping sponsor Milky the Clown's television show. Milky was an imposing figure, head to toe in white, his face painted like a mime's with a wide, gap-toothed, scarlet-rimmed grin and diamond eyes. His crisp, mesmerizing voice was unforgettable. We watched him do magic tricks every Saturday on our black and white TV—not that we had much choice, with only three channels.

Each Saturday, Milky always had a child appear on the show to help with the magic tricks. The kid was the winner of the weekly Smile of Sunshine contest, and families from all over the city submitted a snapshot of one of their children, smiling, of course. I fantasized about winning, obviously, and my mom shot the requisite picture. A wide smile on my face and glass of milk in my hand. A few weeks later a letter arrived from NBC informing me that I was the week's winner.

Appearing on the set with Milky impaired my sense of reality and popped that balloon of fun. The studio set was tiny but through my young eyes watching the show on our TV set created an illusion of enormity

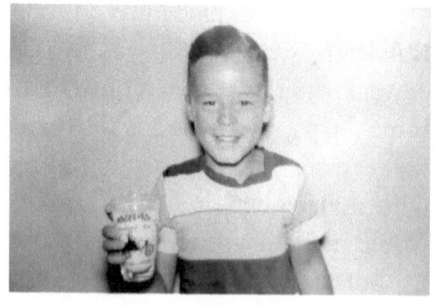

Jim in his Smile of Sunshine photo for Milky the Clown

and, secondly, he smoked after his magic tricks and whenever the producers flipped back to the movies. Regardless, I won and was on the show with the magic clown. I was a happy kid wearing a sunshine smile.

Mr. Wells was a neighbor down the street who I delivered newspapers to over the years. He had a warmth and gentleness belying the fact that he worked as the top manager for a very large construction company; he managed several major project sites, several hundred construction workers, and was responsible for building highways, expressways, bridges and deep underground water and sewage projects throughout Michigan. He also had a cute daughter.

When I was mad at my dad for one reason or another I'd go visit him, sometimes helping him do yard work. He became a positive, non-threatening male role model for me. He told me all about the construction industry and the hard work he expected from his employees and said, "Maybe you can work for me when you are a bit older." I liked this idea.

• • •

At thirteen, life changed with all the urges the teen years ignite. That first puff on a cigarette instantly made me light-headed. All the families of Detroit underwent enormous social change during the 1950s and into the early 1960s. Urban renewal and freeway construction demolished Detroit's black ghettos; formerly segregated white neighborhoods, including those not far from my school, Cody High, were rapidly integrating. The national media started to refer to Detroit as a model city.

While the suburbs were growing, there were still great developments within the city limits. In 1959, Berry Gordy turned his little New Center-area home into a recording studio, developing the "Motown sound." Domino's Pizza added delivery to the pizza business when they opened their first store in Detroit in 1960. Our church, too, was undergoing change. Pastor Dickerson retired and excitement over a new preacher cut into the sadness of our old one's departure. Dr. Hugh Horner, a Canadian, delivered his first sermon—we were impressed before he said anything, though, simply by the "Dr" before his name (almost no one in the church had ever attended college).

His doctorate of divinity was so mysterious that someone looked into what it meant exactly, and what seminary had granted him such a prestigious degree. Turned out he only ever spent a few bucks and received it from a mail order house.

My dad hated folks who thought too highly of themselves. He often told us, "No one is any better than you." I believed him, but suspected he might also have felt inferior to others. Regardless, his message was constant and sunk into our lives. Dad also set himself firmly against whatever he considered wrongdoing. He'd challenge anyone, regardless of power or status, and some of this rubbed off on Mike and me. But dad would take it up with his bosses in the factories, and sometimes with the police. Here he was a man with a sixth grade education challenging the credentials of someone claiming the highest degree of an academic institution. My dad couldn't take it. How dare the preacher claim something he had not earned? My dad acted like it were a personal affront—perhaps it made him feel smaller than he already felt.

When word leaked of the fraud, at least half the parishioners were outraged just short of wanting to lynch the man. They demanded his immediate dismissal. The others were not so bothered by a phony doctorate. The pastor refused to step down. Meetings were held. Even the young people attended, and we saw pious Christians demeaning each other with language and the near violence rarely seen in most bar rooms. Shockingly, my dad was one of the most vocal and abusive. For reasons unknown, he could not let go of this deception—he was obsessed with ensuring the deceiver's fall. He seemed on the edge of a nervous breakdown. All that mattered was his rage for the fraudulent pastor and leading the insurrection against him.

Half the congregation remained in the church and the other half left. My dad never again attended church and for my mother years passed before she started visiting new churches hoping to find one for her sons. Leaving the Baptist church set in motion a downward spiral for my family. Each of us felt a betrayal in our hearts and minds, though not all due to the new pastor's phony degree. There was a hole in us that our spiritual life in the church had filled. Years passed before I seriously looked for another church. The best I could do at the time was sometimes go with my best friend and his mother to the

Church of Christ in our neighborhood. Absent that anchor, I drifted to another course.

My mom harbored resentments toward my father over those venomous rages, and she was humiliated in front of her closest friends. Being only thirteen, I was angry without much knowing why. I lost my connection to Marilyn, the girl who held my hand every Sunday. I was relieved, though, that I would no longer have to put on a suit and tie on Sundays or wear freshly polished Buster Brown shoes. My dad started to give everything to work. When he wasn't spending long hours in the factories he brought machines to the garage, rebuilding them to sell. When he was laid off from time to time, he would drive a taxi. His workday often stretched beyond twelve hours.

I loved my dad but was afraid of his anger. It lay just below the surface and was horrible when it burst. I did all the little things that a teenager can do to escape. My buddies and I hung out in Rouge Park, where we smoked and roughhoused, and began to devote more and more time to thinking about the opposite sex.

Our dad had his flaws but he taught my brothers and me a valuable lesson: if he suspected significant wrongdoing by another, toward another, you should go after them with full force. He cared not about political correctness but in direct confrontation in challenging wrongdoing. It was a wonderful lesson and I am grateful to him for passing it on to me.

• • •

I entered my first history class as a freshman at Cody and the teacher, Mr. Goodman, a short, bespectacled man, had each of us introduce ourselves. When I announced my name Mr. Goodman paused before turning to the next student. He asked, "Are you Paul Hubbard's brother?" to which I responded affirmatively, feeling apprehensive. Mr. Goodman was a dead ringer for the star of a television show called Mr. Peepers, a nerdy science teacher played by Wally Cox. My brother looked and acted a bit like Mr. Peepers, too. Goodman just smiled and said, "We'll expect great things from you."

I sat back down at my desk and knew the "great things" Mr. Goodman expected would never happen. I mostly recall C's on those report cards, never an A. By the time I was a sophomore my grades had slipped to D's and lower. I often skipped classes and had disputes with teachers, in which I'd said some pretty nasty things, the result of which, of course, being a trip to the principal's office. Once a student fell behind at a large public school, officials were too busy and ill equipped to mentor students individually, especially the clearly problematic ones. The only class I liked was English and the kind teacher, Mr. Bothwell.

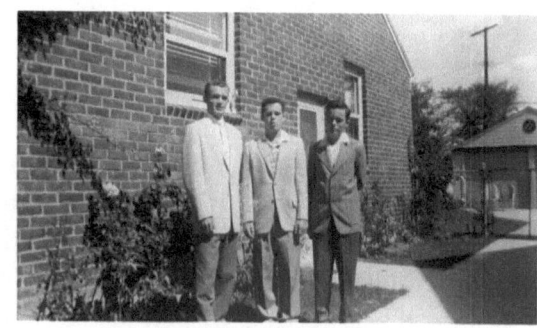

Jim with two brothers, Paul (L) and Mike(R) 1957

It wasn't long before my buddies and I started sampling wine and beer in Rouge Park. The first time I drank a couple beers, we were taking a few swigs each from a bottle of 69-cent wine called Thunderbird. We'd like to go back and forth, "What's the word?" "Thunderbird." My head started spinning and, feeling nauseous, I threw up. Immediately I felt better and drank some more. A sure sign of an alcoholic in the making. My gang's favorite lament was "Let's drink and be somebody." Drinking to get high became part of my life for decades to come. I denied I had a problem, but there's a reason twelve-step programs refer to alcoholism as the "disease of denial."

Some of my buddies started getting cars or borrowing a parent's, and we subsequently enlarged our boundaries. I eventually purchased a junker and removed the muffler and front fenders to make it look and sound more like a hot rod. We'd pile in and cruise the neighborhood, parks and drive-in restaurants usually with two of us in the front and two in the back seat. Each evening our first mission would be to find an older acquaintance to buy beer and wine for us. We always ordered a case of beer that would sit between the two guys in the back seat, each armed with church keys as bottle openers and other, larger metal items that we loosely called weapons, needed later in the evening for frequent altercations with other young toughs around the city.

On weekend evenings we would gather outside Santia's Pizzeria on Warren Ave,. three blocks from my house, the first pizzeria in the neighborhood. It was opened by Italian immigrants and headed by their matriarch, Mama Santia, a short, stout woman who spoke broken English. Santia's was nestled next to a grocery store that sold beer and wine on one side and a beauty salon on the other. It was very small, with a few tables inside and four booths covered in Naugahyde artificial leather, and a brightly lit jukebox. Every weekend there were thirty or forty young men from the neighborhood sitting in their cars or standing on the corner, and we called our loosely knit coalition Santia's. Mike and I were among the found-ing members, and an-other gang kept their own turf a few miles east on Warren Ave., the Warrendale gang.

My gang focused on partying, chasing girls and fighting outside our turf. Unlike gangs as they're known today, we didn't traffic drugs or weapons, but many of our unofficial members carried guns and some

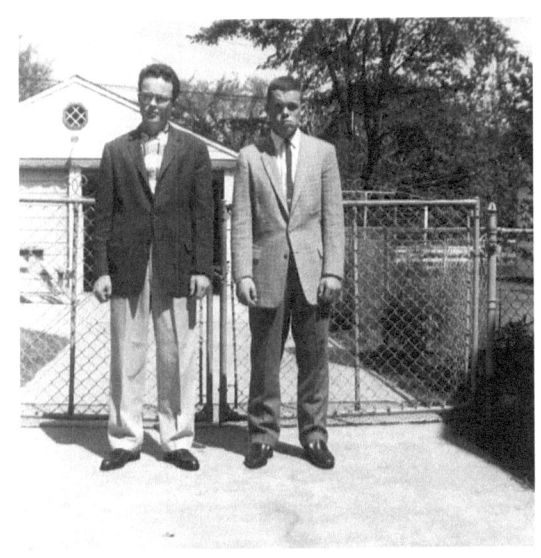

Mike(L) and Jim 1959

dabbled in drugs. Most of us held steady jobs. Our code was simple: you earn respect by being tough and covering each other's backs.

Mama and our crew kept a mutual respect; we never trashed her place as we'd done to other restaurants before running out on the tab. She liked our business and sold hundreds of pizzas to us over the years—she was a tough old Italian woman who fascinated us. We were her problematic children. Mama Santia was often annoyed with us, though, and sometimes came out of her restaurant swinging a broom like we were stray cats, which never worked out quite like she hoped. She had more success when she called the Detroit Police. Warren Ave. ran east to west across four lanes, and the center yellow line demarked one side as Detroit city limits and the other Dearborn Heights, which had its own police force. When the police were called to deal with us on the Detroit side of the street we just strolled over to the other side, where they had no jurisdiction.

We cruised through our neighborhoods, through our favorite drive-ins, among them Rose's. We would sit in our cars and order burgers and fries to go with our beer. Kids drove round to see who else was around and to be seen by those already parked. We went for cars full of girls. When they pulled into a stall to order we'd walk over and start flirting. But a few of us came across as too tough for their own good—even among the ten regulars I ran with, a few were dangerous.

The brothers Holland, Jughead and Jerry, were two of them. They'd recently moved to Detroit from the Deep South, and lived with their mother above her beauty salon next to Santia's Pizzeria. They didn't always hang out with us, but when a fight with rivals was imminent they'd never fail to participate. They were both small, wiry and experts in the art of French foot fighting; they could kick, then tackle anyone twice their size. They drank as much as any of us and were feared as street fighters. We were friends, though Jughead and Jerry could be aloof. Jerry had a pilot's license and they spent time renting single engine planes for a flight. Unfortunately they met their demise one foggy evening when they got loaded, went to a nearby airport, and stole a single engine Cessna. The fog was thick, visibility low, and shortly after take off the plane crashed.

Often on Friday and Saturday evenings, we would meet several buddies at Rose's and get involved in disputes with the two security guards who worked at the drive-in. One night a verbal exchange between one of the guards and I lead to a fistfight. My brother Mike was in another car with his crew; when he saw me tumble to the asphalt with the guard on top of me, he ran over. The uniformed guard had his wooden baton pressed against my throat. Mike slugged him, letting me roll from under and standup. By this point the police arrived and joined the fracas. I kept punching at men in uniforms, though they were now the real and much meaner cops. Mike and I along with a few buddies continued brawling for the next minute or so. One cop punched Mike in the mouth, leaving him with a few less teeth and the rest covered in blood. The police, perhaps feeling triumphant, decided not to arrest us for assault—they only sent us on our way with the ultimatum never to return to Rose's.

Some evenings after a night of drinking we'd head to Hastings St., in the ghetto only a few blocks from downtown. Six to eight of us drove in two cars, our common sense dulled by alcohol and not caring about any risks. The street bustled late at night with hundreds of young black prostitutes, standing in alleys or along sidewalks in front of dilapidated apartment buildings and stores and only in their panties and bras.

We cruised back and forth along the lively street until we parked the car to talk to the hookers and their managers. Slick-haired pimps roamed the street adorned in sharkskin suits that changed color from gray to purple in the fading sunlight and shifting streetlights and shadow. Hustlers clad in bellbottoms and with jangling spurs on their shoes went from car to car, ransacking them while the unwary owners satisfied themselves in the brothels or in the dive bars along Hastings St. Revelers sporting gold pants and black silk shirts danced to the endless Motown, which blared from the neighborhood jukeboxes along the sidewalk.

One pimp, standing next to his shiny, four door Cadillac, talked with three hookers. Dressed in a white and leopard skin faux fur coat, red top hat, yellow trousers over shiny black shoes, the reflections off his clothing illuminated the street. He couldn't have been brighter wrapped with Christmas tree lights. As we walked past he said, "You guys want to buy some reefer?" My buddy Willy responded, "Not now, but maybe if you can get us some girls we will later." He smiled and said, "Take a look, fool, what do you think I've got here? Take your pick." The young hookers smiled. After my buddies negotiated a fee, some of my friends were lead to a dingy, dilapidated, cockroach infested apartment.

The young hooker would first take the john to a small living room, where several other young women gathered with a group of male friends, relatives or pimps, all smoking dope. Then they would proceed to a smaller room with a single mattress on the floor or resting on a metal frame. Two of us would stay in the street to guard our cars, and I was always one of those two. I feared contracting a venereal disease, and unsurprisingly, rumors were rife about the risk for clap, syphilis and crabs.

Twice, when our friends returned to the car, somebody discovered the money he had hidden in his socks or pants had been stolen, which made everybody vengeful. We usually had a beer case in one of our cars, loaded with twenty-four empty bottles, so on our last visit to Hastings, we threw all twenty-four at the apartment windows, breaking glass everywhere and speeding away.

In the early sixties the Hastings area was bulldozed for the I-75 freeway, and many of the residents moved into the Brewster Housing project, new vertical ghettos, where poverty and crime remained high and the transplants included the soon-to-be-famous Supremes, along with Smokey Robinson and Lily Tomlin.

Many of the small businesses along Hastings, legal or illegal, later relocated a few miles away to Twelfth St, and replicated the colorful scene there. A large number of shops were Jewish owned, and in a few years the area would become infamous around the world. In a few years I would spend a week on Twelfth St., when it became an inferno.

When I had been carousing with my friends, as often happened, my dad would sometimes wait for me to get home. Decades later I was always amused at how stupid I was during this troubled time; I actually believed I could sneak into a tiny brick home, no more than 800 sq. ft., and drunkenly climb a few stairs without my dad noticing. I was too old to spank but he would slap me or even punch me, threatening with further repercussions for continued drinking. Drinking was his capital crime, but by this point my fear of my dad had dissolved into anger. I did not yet physically fight back but was getting closer to it.

Sometimes I lay quietly in bed, in total darkness, and pondered the path my feet had taken. Once I thought about the allure of visiting rough and colorful parts of my city, like Hastings. I was acquainted with the stories of prostitutes in the Bible, and that God forbade involvement with them. In Proverbs 5: "for the lips of an immoral woman drip honey, and her mouth is smoother than oil; But in the end she is bitter as wormwood, Sharp as a two-edged sword. Her feet go down to death, Her steps lay hold of hell." Jesus had consorted with prostitutes, though, as in Luke, when Jesus said to Simon, "Do you see this woman? Therefore I say to you, her sins, which are many, are forgiven, for she loved much." Then he said to the woman, "Your faith has saved you. Go in peace." Jesus determined the woman's faith was rock solid. Mine had been built on sand. Some of the young Detroit prostitutes had perhaps a better than average chance being forgiven their sins if they repented and Jesus promise to all, "your faith has saved you."

My life had drifted down a dark alley. By now I had experienced a few broken hands and concussions from brawling either in our sandlot football games or street fights. I still managed to hold several jobs, from a clothing sales clerk to working in an A&W root beer drive-in; to the grease of small tool shops to a large factory, where I rolled recoil steel onto giant thimbles, each weighing about two tons, which I then drove on a forklift to stack on top of each other. I spent my days aching under steel-tipped boots, coveralls, a helmet and goggles, and promptly spent my nights beating on people with my bare hands or getting beat in turn.

The root beer job arose when Bob the milkman bought an A&W franchise and hired me to be a fast food cook, making burgers, ice cream floats and hot fudge sundaes. I only worked there evenings and some weekends, and quickly got tired of ice cream and root beer. I quit, and eventually the business bellied up. Some time later, Bob committed suicide.

Paul was away at the University of Michigan in Ann Arbor, having made my dad proud and riding on a full scholarship, and by this point my dad was showing signs of giving up on me, in turn; he had reason, given my low grades and poor attendance. But I knew I wouldn't end up in a factory like him.

The first time my principal told me that I was a retard—but before expulsion—he sent me to a class under the stewardship of a Mr. Weaver. We were called Weaver's Rangers. My academic life had devolved dramatically junior year, and besides skipping classes I was creating havoc inside and outside the school's walls.

Weaver's Rangers were not a distinguished group. The teacher, Mr. Weaver, seemed mentally challenged. Students in the special class were physically and mentally impaired, and the so-called normal students often laughed and made fun of them when they clustered together, marching down the hall on their way to lunch. I was humiliated. They always walked in a group, and some of the Ranger's wore helmets, others had crutches, and some had uncontrolled body movements. Within the group were slow learners, troublemakers and thugs, too, a category that I felt was somewhere in between.

After sporadically attending Mr. Weaver's classes for a week, I quit school altogether—even though my parents still thought I went every morning. Instead, I joined my buddies in local hangouts for a day of drinking, chasing girls and assaulting students on or near Cody's campus. We'd shake them down for beer money. School officials called it strong-armed robbery.

One of my acquaintances, Crazy Charlie, regularly cruised near Cody in his souped up '52 Chevy, which had louvers on the hood and chrome pipe running down the lower sides. He was not a Cody student and a bit older. He was, per the nickname, crazy. He operated as some sort of Lone Ranger-type, but in his lucid moments spent a little time with me. His hair was cut close to the scalp, in brush-cut fashion, and he had scars on his athletic body, and his eyes suggested a mind that was far, far away from wherever you stood at the moment. One day, across the street from Cody, someone angered Crazy Charlie—he picked up a cinder block and smashed it on the offender's skull. Charlie was sent to prison for homicide and the long stretch. He wouldn't have flinched from using the cinder block on me if I had upset him in some way. In him I saw that some underlying evil can metastasize in people, and that it's all a matter of degree and triggers.

Another new friend I sometimes hung and drank with was Johnny, a large guy who lived with his family across the street from Cody. Johnny played varsity football for Cody but we liked to have him around for a completely different reason: his dad was one of five senior commanders within the police department and slated to become commissioner. Johnny might get us a free pass in a sticky situation.

On a number of occasions, I'd wake up in the morning after an evening of heavy drinking and not remember a thing from the night before. Most often I'd be unable to recall how I got home, and I'd sink into a sweating terror for fear that I'd been in an accident or killed someone. These episodes are called, "Black outs," never experienced by social drinkers. "I'd race downstairs to inspect the car for damage.

Not all my friends were as crazy as Charlie. Some did well in school and planned on going to various colleges. As much as I didn't want to admit it, they made me feel intellectually inadequate. They talked about things I was unfamiliar with, and we were only connected by our love for drinking and partying.

Although I'd had a few brushes with the law, I was not prepared for felony charges. A friend of my brother's, Dave Meachem, shared a fondness for guns with Mike and picked me up one evening so we could get some beer and wine for our crew. We drove over to a large grocery on Southfield Rd.; he went to the front and I walked to the rear to steal a couple bottles of wine. When I got back to the front door for a quick exit, Dave was already outside. We jumped in his Dodge and sped away.

Dave dropped me near Santia's with the booze and drove away. I drank for an hour or so with another friend, until a buddy named Spook walked up. Spook was a bit ghostly in appearance, with pale blue-green eyes, and he worshiped our delinquent lifestyle, feared us a bit, and did just about anything we asked. I'm sure he thought that his nickname was more menacing than his given moniker (Henry Fegley). Spook née Fegley told us that the cops were scouring the neighborhood for the thieves, and just then I saw three or four police cars driving slowly along Warren Ave. I jumped out of the car and headed down the alleys towards home, hiding behind garbage cans when I caught sight of any police car. I thought all this was for stealing wine. I made it to a friend's house two blocks from my home and called my dad.

He sounded concerned, if irate. He told me to get home, and that the police had just come to the house looking for me. I told him I was wanted for the armed robbery of a grocery store, but he said they just wanted to question me. He picked me up near another hangout, Stromboli's Pizza, and we drove to the 16th precinct.

With my dad seated next to me in the small interrogation room, the detectives started asking questions. They threatened and intimidated me, and I couldn't help but remember my high school principal who had prophesized my future in jail. I told them what I had done. After going over the story several times they told me my accomplice had pulled a gun on the clerk and emptied the cash register. My heart racing, I just stuck to the truth: that I had only stolen wine and was unaware of the gun or cashier robbery.

By about 4AM the interrogation ended. They had developed a sense of me; more importantly, they sensed that my dad was as tough as any cop and that his punishment might be swifter (and perhaps more immediately painful). Fortunately, Dave, the armed thief, collaborated with my story most likely out of fear of what my brother might do to him if he didn't come clean.

Summer arrived and I had not graduated, but the school offered me the chance to take a few summer school classes and receive a high school diploma—no doubt for the administration's eagerness to close the book on me. I took three classes and earned a diploma, but a friend picked it up for me because I couldn't bear to go to the ceremony.

I also needed a job. For a few months I worked unloading semi-trailer trucks in a freight warehouse for UPS, and decidedly the best thing about that miserable, exhausting job was heading with my coworkers to a dive called Mary's Bar, where we'd down schooners of the beer on tap and put a quarter in the juke for some Elvis, the Coasters, and Fats Domino.

I couldn't stand indoor jobs. My old neighborhood friend Mr. Wells hired me to be a laborer at one of the construction sites he supervised, and I joined the crew to construct the Southfield Freeway. The other laborers were mostly big black men with biceps about the size of healthy elm trunks. My arms were more like the branches of a much less impressive tree. But I was in good enough shape, and confident I could pour concrete and operate a jackhammer, too. I liked the physical work. Most of my coworkers had not finished school; for none of us could this experience be called intellectually stimulating.

When fall approached some friends headed off to college and the rest of us headed only to whatever corner we were partying on that night. We were standing at a bridge going exactly nowhere, and I stood with them at its tollbooth of no return, conflicted. I knew I shouldn't pay that price, and that I had to find another bridge to cross.

The close call with prison was a necessary jolt. It etched another principle deep within me: avoiding being confined in small, controlled spaces, whether the innocent classrooms at Cody or the far more terrible walls of a prison cell.

But my many careless indiscretions continued, including an encounter with a girl who left me unable to walk or even stand for two days. I had contracted gonorrhea, treated with penicillin and had a reaction, which is what caused my feet to swell. I thought this was God's punishment for my sins. Lying in bed I picked up a Bible that was on a dresser nearby, and started reading chapters from Psalms. The words stuck, and I read the verse several times. Psalms 25:7: "Remember not the sins of my youth, nor my transgressions: according to thy mercy remember thou me for thy goodness' sake, O Lord."

COTTON FIELDS

I had always loved my Uncle Gene's cotton farm in the Arkansas Delta, and he had once invited me to come and work with them during cotton-picking time. With my parents' help, we contacted Uncle Gene and Aunt Lola and asked if I could come in the fall. My parents told them it would be a much needed lifestyle change. My aunt and uncle, who believed that the big city only caused a life to spiral downward, and they knew I loved their farm. "Come on down," they beckoned.

When I arrived in early September the heat and humidity overwhelmed me. Naturally, I wanted the delicious, novel flavor of the south: an ice-cold Dr. Pepper. The country's sweet smells assured me that this was down home. My whole second day I wandered around the farm and helped feed the chickens, hogs and piglets, while the five or six cats also wandered about chasing mice (or they simply slept wherever they fell). There were always a couple of dogs—whenever a car rolled by, which wasn't often, they'd race toward it, chasing the spinning wheels and barking.

I loved the fresh, pungent country smells near the barn, where the cows, a couple quarter horses and many muddy and wet pigs crowded within the wooden fence. There was also at least one gigantic sow, which had recently given birth to seven or more baby pigs, all nursing on the mother's teats while she sprawled in the mud. Strangely enough, I loved the smell of the manure, too, which popped in your nose and instantly woke you up to all the fragrances of the farm.

I spent an afternoon walking through the growing cotton, corn and soybean fields, and the fertile dark earth softly cushioned each step. I leaned over the cotton stalks and opened the blossoms, revealing the soft fluffy bolls nearly ready for picking. Bending down I picked up handfuls of soft, rich dirt, which slipped through my fingers almost magically. I walked over to a creek outside the field and stepped slowly down the slippery bed, as the frogs and turtles scurry away as quickly as they could.

My aunt and uncle always impressed me, and the tensions of my own home vanished in their country. They never had their own children so I felt like a son to them, and they felt similarly. They knew life in Detroit was tough, and Uncle Gene had said more than once that my dad could be hard on his sons.

By my first Sunday morning I hadn't been out drinking with my buddies for two consecutive weekend nights; this shift in routine offered promising benefits. We dressed in our finest and drove to the First Baptist Church on Main St. in Senath, Missouri. Aunt Lola sang in the church choir and played piano, and she always told me I had a nice voice and urged me to consider joining the choir. I did love the Baptist hymns, and by the third Sunday I was looking into the eyes of the congregation as I sang with my aunt, perched high on the choir loft.

It was comforting for me to be back in a church after several years, especially one magnifying old Baptist hymns and a preacher with the style I had cherished in my childhood. I would be a regular attendee for the next three months, and I marveled at how much I had missed the warmth and security of our old church. There was a mysterious sadness I felt knowing that my life may have been different had the church of my boyhood not been riven as it was.

When the first rays of light shone across my bedroom through softly filtered cracks in the darkened curtains, I felt a calm descend on me. Dishes and pans rattled in the kitchen while Aunt Lola prepared her three thousand calorie breakfast that she made every day. I wasn't at all worried about gaining weight, since I'd work off most of the calories by day's end. Uncle Gene knocked on my door and said, "Jimmy, you ready to work?"

The menu: homemade fluffy buttermilk biscuits and dark gravy, prepared in the remaining grease from the red pepper, spicy sausage. Uncle Gene and I devoured it in under ten minutes. He put on his overalls and we walked off to the barn to feed the livestock, after which we headed off in his green pickup truck to Senath to meet Gene's farmer friends at a gas station. The conversation there usually focused on the current harvest, a daily ritual. There would be ten to twelve soft-spoken gentlemen sitting on the station's benches, ten feet from the gas pumps, like a scene from a Norman Rockwell painting: each man held a cup of black coffee in his hand; old and new stories were told; a few vehicles passed by, most tractors and pickup trucks.

Back at Uncle Gene's, before 7AM, we drove around the fields and stopped occasionally to assess the germinating cotton, corn and soybeans. We then drove further along to look for rotting or fallen fence posts, which we would need to replace, or sagging barbed wire that needed tightening.

Long gone were the black cotton pickers hunched and scattered throughout the cotton fields in the late '40s. The age of mechanization had arrived; my uncle now owned a red one-row picker. He would be the first to start the day's picking, maneuvering the large machine along the rows of cotton. He only worked a few hours, as he suffered from back problems, and had to wear a brace and lie on the living room floor several times each day for relief.

A farmhand named Herb sometimes helped; he lived half mile down the road from my uncle, in a dilapidated one-room house built from unpainted, weathered planks. The little shack was reminiscent of the sharecroppers' houses scattered throughout the south, and memorialized in some of the famous Depression-era FSA photos taken by legendary photographers like Dorthea Lange and Walker Evans. Herb was a sharecropper who farmed a few acres of his own when not working for my uncle. The few teeth he had left needed major, never-to-arrive dental work. Herb and his wife had four little children who could often be seen playing on the sagging, rotting wooden front porch. When I once visited him inside his home, rays of light shone across the tiny living room area through spaces in the plank walls, and some of their only furnishings were a wood-burning stove and a small icebox that never had enough dry ice. The family looked identical to rural, southern, Depression-era subjects described in James Agee's book *Let Us Now Praise Famous Men*.

My uncle briefed me on the fundamentals of the giant cotton picker. He warned me that sometimes the spindle prongs, which removed bolls from their plant sockets, would jam, and that I needed to shut the machine off before attempting to clear weeds and other debris. He said if that I didn't, I might lose a hand or arm—he then lifted his own arm, graphically illustrating how he had lost his right hand in a picker years earlier.

We climbed three vertical steps to the driver's platform, ten feet above ground, and Uncle Gene took the seat and told me to stand just behind him for instructions. He started the engine and maneuvered it to a row of cotton, then moved a lever to make the metal spindles pluck the fluffy cotton from the stalks and shoot them into the large caged basket directly behind us. The large rear tires were now in the front, and the smaller tires for controlling the turns of the tractor were at the rear. The driver needed to make inverted turns on the steering wheel—turning the wheel to the right would send us left and vice versa. We moved along several rows and finally filled the basket with cotton, at which point we drove to a large meshed trailer at the end of the field and dumped the cotton. Now it was my turn. My initial anxiety dispelled by the time I turned onto the second row I could aim the picker straight down a single row.

Over the next several weeks my life would be in the fields, operating this large, fascinating machine for about 12-hours a day. I felt surges of power. My days operating the picker would start just after lunch and end around midnight. When darkness fell, a single headlight illuminated the row in front of me, just enough light to guide me along. It was at times lonely, but the work offered solitude and even exhilaration under the perfectly clear stars and bright moon. The fresh country air revived me with every breath—at least until the dust and dirt clogged my nostrils and caked my face with a layer of earth. It didn't take long, however, for monotony to set in.

Desperately needing a diversion, I noticed a red Cadillac convertible slowly moving along the road past the cotton field, driven by a lovely young woman with three female passengers, all with eyes on me, a new boy in the fields. Word had spread that there was a big city boy working on his uncle's farm. The car passed three times. Later on, I asked my aunt who drove the convertible. She told me it belonged to Diamond Jim Manley, a man who lived on the gravel road adjoining their property on a big farm; he was a wealthy landowner and businessman. She added that the girl driving was one of his two daughters, either Ethel or Marilyn. Soon enough, I bumped into Ethel in the grocery store and we started dating. She was gorgeous and had a warm, welcoming smile.

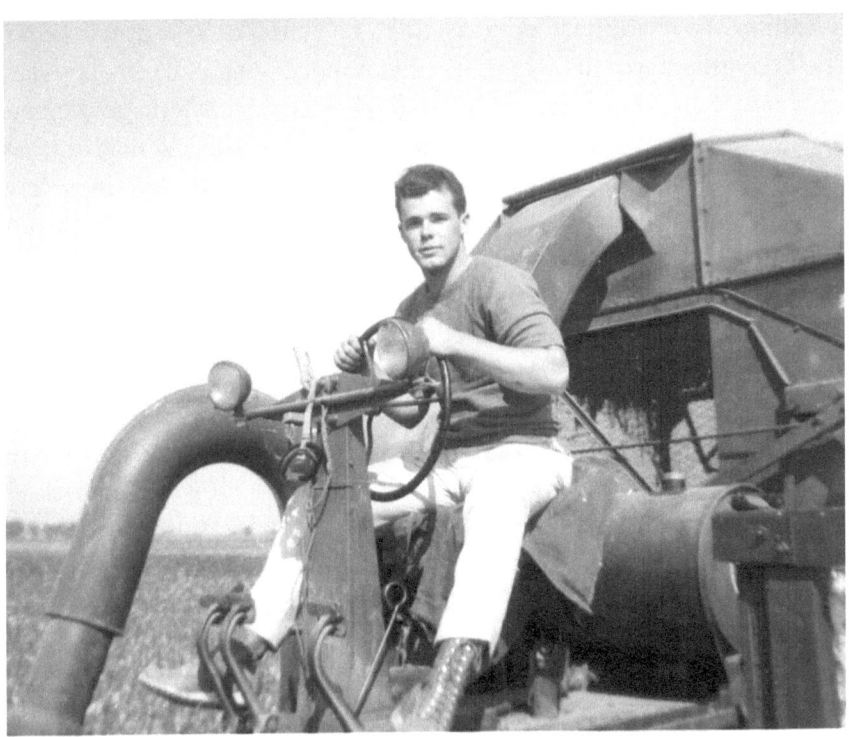

Jim driving cotton picker on uncle's farm in Bootheel

I tried to be on my best behavior with Ethel—I suspected Diamond Jim had his own connections and in some ways was much like a rural, southern mobster, if such a thing ever existed. After all, he owned both a large four door Cadillac as well as the red convertible, and he had the nickname 'Diamond' affixed to his first name. Secondly, the alcohol that had defined my earlier folly wasn't part of the equation on dates with Ethel.

One day it rained so hard the fields became too wet and muddy to work for a few days, so I called Ethel and suggested we grab a late lunch. We drove to a drive-in restaurant in Kennett and afterwards we drove down a black top country road, watching the raindrops dance on the windshield. We talked until I edged closer to her, wrapping my arms around her, laying her down on the leather seat, which sufficed well enough for a bed as far as I was concerned.

On the way to her home, she told me she had a half sister living at home, the illegitimate daughter of Diamond Jim. Fragments of more information illustrated that the Manley family considered themselves socialites—not ordinary country folk. The parents held dreams that their daughters would meet upwardly mobile young bankers, lawyers or doctors in Memphis, or other upper-class Southern gentlemen attending the prestigious crown jewel of the south, Vanderbilt, in Nashville. She said she would be leaving for Vanderbilt in a few weeks. The message was there would be no room in her life for an urban-bred farmhand from a working class family in the north.

Once she got a sense of me, Ethel realized the mysterious, attractive out-of-towner hid some rough edges. He did not have the promising future she had been groomed for. A plan to go to a drive-in would be our last encounter.

During my last Sunday on the farm we went to church, where Aunt Lola and I sang two of my favorite old hymns. Tears welled up in my eyes as we sang "Just a Closer Walk With Thee" and "Trust and Obey." The minister's sermon was about redemption and renewal. It was uplifting. The next day I went home with a renewed sense of self. I was proud of my ability to navigate both urban and rural environments and commiserate with both country and city folk. This social flexibility would be a valuable asset in the years that lie ahead.

THE WRECKAGE ON JOY ROAD

On Thanksgiving Day 1942 my mom gave birth to me—my dad loved to say, "Instead of a turkey we had Jim." The Thanksgiving after my time down home, Mike was about to graduate from Cody and Paul had just graduated from University of Michigan; he managed a machine shop while considering graduate school. He was dating a ticket agent working in downtown Detroit for the British airline, BOAC, and rumor had it they would soon marry. Mike and I caught up on news about our buddies; he had been working at the clothing store that had employed us both before. The manager hired me, too, for the Christmas season, and both Mike and I were to be selling men's clothing at Richman Brothers beginning Black Friday, the busiest day of the year.

Though I loved the holiday feast, my mother's cooking technique with vegetables left a lot to be desired, frankly. She put the veggies in a pot over fire and left them for a couple hours, thus defining vegetables in my memory as a soggy and tasteless horror. I still gag at the thought of vegetables, but have since discovered that other people can in fact make them not only edible but also fresh and even delicious. I had a lot of surprises coming.

Working full-time in the clothing store with Mike left little time for anything else. Our shifts varied and sometimes we would meet after nine at Rose's to sip beer, meet new girls and commiserate with old friends. Mike still ran with his group. Christmas approaching, our family planned to drive the eight hundred miles down home for a reunion.

On the evening of December 23, 1961, I left work and headed for Rose's in my dad's red, Chevy—the plan was to drive south on Christmas Eve. At Rose's I saw Mike and hooked up with an old buddy Bob Peltz. We drank only a beer or two and decided to take a joy ride; I yelled to Mike that I would see him later. We turned out of Rose's and made a left onto Joy Road, which runs parallel to Warren Avenue, both four-lane thoroughfares separated near Rose's by hundreds of parkland acres. It was a cold, dark evening and a light snow started to fall. We had not gone more than a mile when the engine sputtered and stalled in the right hand lane, along a darkened stretch of the road that wound through the edge of the park. We were less than a hundred yards from the bridge where the road crosses Rouge River.

I looked under the hood while Bob attempted to restart the engine, to no avail. Just then a dark, old Ford pulled up slowly behind us. I walked back and recognized only the driver, a man named Bill Young. His younger brother Jerry sat in the passenger seat and there were two young girls giggling in the back seat. He offered to push my car to a nearby service station, and when he nudged his car forward his front bumper slid up over my rear bumper and locked. Anything further and my dad's car would've been damaged badly on the rear.

After trying to disentangle the bumpers by jumping on them, I sat on the right side of the hood of Bill's car and Bob took a seat on the left fender, our legs propped on the locked chrome bumpers. The sound of a roaring engine from a fast approaching car caught my attention, and I turned my head and saw a car speeding towards us, about to plow into the rear of the car I was seated on. Instinctively I fell backward with my torso on the hood and and head against the windshield.

The explosive sound of metal crushing metal instantly freed the bumpers in the destruction. My dad's car went rolling down the road. I was launched airborne like a shot from a cannon. The flight seemed to last forever—until I landed hard on the pavement and slid alongside my dad's moving, two ton car, my head inches from the rolling right front tire. Terrified and barely thinking, I quickly rolled to my right to get away. I had hit the road cushioned by my buttocks, but my back and shoulder were in brutal pain. Each of us came close to mortality that night. As happens so often when a drunk driver snuffs or nearly snuffs out lives in auto accidents, the inebriated driver who hit us at over sixty miles per hour was not injured.

When my slide across the road ended I watched as my dad's car kept moving forward. Shrill screams prompted me to my feet. I looked back at Bill's car engulfed in flames—the fuel tank exploded. I could see two people lying on the ground a safe distance from the inferno but saw another crawl from the car, clothes on fire, and start running across the park. I ran to her and pulled her to the ground, got to my knees and patted out flames on her winter coat while also tearing it off her. Only by frantically patting and pressing with other clothes could we snuff the flames burning her.

Diane, only thirteen-years-old, was in enormous pain and horribly burned. The emergency vehicles started to arrive and I suddenly remembered the severe pain in my right shoulder, which was drooping low. The fire department medics laid me on a stretcher for the ride to the hospital. I felt the terror of the moment and feared my dad's wrath when he learned what had happened.

On the way to the emergency room, I noticed a pay phone on the wall. I waited for the doctors to leave, at which point I got up from the stretcher and called my dad. He said he would come immediately and I was instantly relieved that he seemed more concerned about my condition rather than the fate of his car. The relief was apparently too much for me: I then lost consciousness and crumpled to the floor. It turned out in the end that dad's car had rolled into the park, came to a stop in a ravine at the edge of Rouge River, and was only slightly damaged; the other car had absorbed the brunt of impact.

The doctors told me I had been in shock and had a few back injuries and a broken shoulder. I'd be in the hospital for a week or so. I asked about Diane and they reported she had been badly burned and was in serious condition, but would probably survive. Within a few days of lying on my back in a hospital bed I requested a visit with Diane. A nurse, Annie, wheeled me to her room and she smiled at me and thanked me for putting the fire out on her body. Feeling uncomfortable, I said that it was the only thing to do and I was happy she was alive.

The nurse wheeled me back to my room and stayed with me longer than probably required. We were both flirtatious, she a bit older than me, and quite cute. She visited me both in the line of duty and out, and made the hospital stay much more pleasant. Time passed more quickly with her around, and it was hardly an unpleasant way to spend Christmas, despite the situation. When I was discharged we arranged to meet and dated several times for a little over a month.

The charm of our initial attraction probably had something to do with my having been a captive audience at the hospital, but things cooled off as I became less attentive released from the bed. But Nurse Annie had risen above the call of duty, becoming an angel.

• • •

It took more than a month for my shoulder to heal. During the hours of idle time convalescing, I often flashed back to the night of accident, when I felt my life spinning out of control. As happens when death hurtles into your life, my perspective shifted—but I was still a young man. About six months afterwards, I sat in court watching the driver on trial for drunken negligence, which had nearly claimed six lives. I was awarded $2,000 from his insurance company and spent every dime on a candy-apple red 1962 Chevrolet Corvair—a turbo-charged Monza Spyder convertible.

The clothing store retained me in a part-time job for a few more months, but after the holidays, sales plummeted, leaving a sales clerk with inordinate time. Folding clothes, taking inventory and replenishing stock was all extremely boring; I only had my wandering mind to escape into. I had a nagging, yearning feeling for new challenges. Higher education was not an option, I thought, but I also wanted to change that. I had horrible grades on my high school transcript. I hadn't even gotten through multiplication, never mind anything like science. What college would accept me?

On a off day I drove to a new community college to meet with a school counselor. Henry Ford Community College (HFCC), in neighboring Dearborn, Michigan, was situated next to the University of Michigan-Dearborn. As you might expect from the school's name, the place was hardwired with Michigan history: Henry Ford built his first car in a shed on 1,300 hundred acres named Fair Lane, which UM Dearborn later owned. I felt a twinge of jealousy for my brother Paul, who had been recruited for U of M's main, Ann Arbor campus on a four-year free ride. I wanted to earn my acceptance at U of M, though I had insured that wouldn't happen.

The counselor described what they wanted in a student, and instructed me to send her a high school transcript. I sent a report card from my junior year and followed up with a call. On the phone she said I would not be accepted. I begged, "Is there any possible way?" She hesitated for a moment, then said that I could try taking classes in a business or trade school.

In the yellow pages I found a business school and made an appointment. The admissions office staffer seemed pleasant and not noticeably bothered by the realization that this school had not been my first choice. Being a business school, like most businesses, they would probably take my money for classes. After finishing two courses, one in accounting and the other business principles, at the business school, scoring B's in both, I was eager to share my success with the folks at the community college, and showed the same counselor my grades. A day later officials accepted me on a trial basis. They had obviously done a background check on me; they warned: "Don't cause any problems." I promised that I would not be a problem. Leaving her office, I felt elated, like I had beaten the odds, created by me, against me. I would begin by taking no more than three classes in the fall of '63, juggling school with full-time work.

My first major problem in the fall, one I delighted in, was deciding what classes to sign up for. Three classes seemed like an energetic beginning, so I signed on for English, introductory psychology, and sociology— two classes about individual and group behavior.

Construction work continued into the late fall, before the first freeze enabled me to save enough money to coast for three or four months and have more time for school. My first semester grades were enough to continue at HFCC, but I only made a few friends and didn't spend much time there. The next spring, I registered for courses I knew little about but had been drawn to the challenges and mystery they might provide. One was journalism, another public speaking, and the third a required science course. By semester's end I earned a C in science, B in journalism and A in public speaking. The A was an almost magically new experience. Journalism also fit with my first collegiate activity, writing a few short articles for our small school paper.

• • •

The speech class was spellbinding. First, I liked to speak, even if I was shy in front of the class for the first minute or two. Second, my teacher took a special interest in me, and I liked her soft manner of offering advice. There was something old in my new passion, that little boy preaching in front of his parent's bedroom mirror after church, re-enacting fire and brimstone evangelists.

After one such speech about my Baptist upbringing, Mrs. Wright, my teacher, suggested that I consider applying to Bob Jones University in Greeneville, South Carolina where they train preachers and missionaries, telling me that many of them had become quite well known. I was impressed by her plan, and flattered that she thought I had potential. I did not understand the real meaning of her pitch, nor know anything about Bob Jones University.

I had never planned my life's course before, and my decisions tended to be impulsive. Making it this far at HFCC was the best I'd ever done. But now a plan was suggested from someone who liked me. I heeded her advice and wrote Bob Jones for their catalog and application; Mrs. Wright offered a letter of recommendation.

In the fall I boarded a train from Detroit for Greenville, nestled in the Deep South. I instantly didn't like either my dorm or dorm mates. The countryside was to my liking, but once I understood the student handbook and rules for entering students, I panicked about the choice I had made, and signed up for classes with trepidation. I learned that the famous preacher Billy Graham had attended Bob Jones but hadn't lasted, and left without very positive feelings about the school. If Billy Graham couldn't make it, how would I?

Bob Jones' campus extends over pristine, beautiful land, but the university had many high walls, both real and imagined. My devout aversion to control and confinement fast turned the grounds into my worst nightmare. I wrote a letter to my parents after a few weeks. The strict rules limited the possibilities of exploration of the community, dictating when one could venture off the campus grounds, and where one could and could not go. I mailed the letter.

> *Dear Mom and Dad,*
>
> *This is the hardest situation I have ever had to adjust to, and probably never will. The rules are unbelievably stiff. I haven't had a cigarette since arriving and can't as long as I'm here. You have to be careful what you wear and what you say. You can't*

listen to 'questionable' music on the radio. I have to be in at 10:30pm and can't leave campus except in the daytime, with written permission. I am ready to catch the train home. I saw the dean of men and promised I would try another week. Some of the things I have to do here just don't jibe with me. I mean, I can see religion and going to church, but they just carry it too far around here. There are a lot of girls around but you can't walk with them, can't hardly talk to them. Because of the rules. As a freshman you can date three times a week. Now this is the funny part:. You can only take them to the dating parlor for two hours three times per week and sit there and talk, while staff watch. This is a campus?

Love, Jim

I was beginning to believe that my speech instructor hadn't recommended Bob Jones to nurture my talent. Once again my life's subtext to be a preacher, or better yet, a smooth, silver-tongued evangelist, was put on hold. I persevered at Bob Jones for another week after the letter, then left for the train station with my first semester unfinished. Back home, I reenrolled at HFCC and accumulated almost two years of credits.

STEALING SOUTHERN COMFORT

I heard about a job opening at a higher-end men's clothing store, applied and started working fulltime. At Hughes & Hatcher I was told to sell ties, shirts, sweaters, etc., and the store manager, Sid Schusterman started me off with a pep talk about security: "Watch the schvartzes"—schvartze being a Yiddish slur toward black people. Loosely constructed from Sid's other comments, our job was to insure that African Americans, who he believed were inclined to shoplift, were to be made aware that they were being closely monitored.

Sid handled suit sales and could sell a suit to a man retiring to a nudist colony. But it was uncomfortable to stand too close to Sid himself, as the man's body odor seeped out through his pores and food stains discolored his dress shirt and coat.

While working at Hughes & Hatcher, I applied and was accepted to Wayne State University (WSU). Juggling work, I could only manage two or three classes per semester. Once again, except for the required courses, most of the classes I took focused on psychology and sociology, like Personality Development, Socialization of the Child and Deviant Psychology. My fascination with human behavior in academe coincided with my religious interests, in that both were concerned with the human condition and the quest for perfection—or, putting it another way, the push of good against evil. Often feeling inadequate when talking to my college educated friends or my brother Paul, I continued honing my speaking skills with two more speech classes and political science and a course in English.

Sid liked the way I was doing my job, and appointed me manager for the men's furnishings. Another young fellow, named Steve, was also promoted manager of the men's department and we formed an instant connection. Steve and I had similar tastes: not wanting to wait until after work, we started planting bottles of liquor inside shirt boxes for store hour consumption in the stock room. He would say, "Men's Hathaway oxford dress shirt, button down, size neck 16, sleeves 32," which designated the exact box containing a bottle of Southern Comfort or Jack Daniels. To avoid getting caught, we moved the bottle each time and announced the new location. By day's end, usually 9PM, we were well on our way to being hammered and the boring job became fun.

We raised the stakes. We started carrying merchandise home with us, at first an item or two, but the level of theft escalated rapidly. When my mother cleaned my bedroom she would often say, "Jimmy, where are you getting all these nice clothes from?" I'd answer, "We get really good discounts at Hughes & Hatcher, cause they want their sales staff to be well-dressed."

One day during a severe blizzard, I dug my car out of the snow and got to work late. It didn't matter, though, as the only other people who showed up were Sid and Steve. Sid was in his back office on the phone; he announced that the store would be closed for the day. With Sid busy on the phone, Steve and I immediately started making trips to our cars carrying new clothing items we could wear later.

Inventory would not be taken for another month, meaning the loss would be attributed to shoplifters. Like criminals who never stop at one bank, our thefts quickly becoming a spree. We were out of control. There was also some easy cash to be had when a customer, usually in a hurry, would lay down the exact sum for an item—instead of ringing up the sale, we'd pocket the money. And it all continued for several months, petty theft escalating into grand theft.

• • •

One day a customer walked in the store in a distinctive suit, and there was a split second of recognition between us. He strolled around, looking at suits and when he finished he stopped by the counter and asked, "Remember me?' I didn't recall the name, but told him he looked familiar. He said, "I'm Mr. Rawleigh. You and your brothers used to deliver papers for me." I laughed but he still sent chills through me, even though he looked quite a bit older and less menacing. We talked briefly and he said if I ever needed a job to give him a call; he might be able to help at the *Detroit News*. I didn't ask if he meant to being a newspaper boy again, but jotted down his phone number and thanked him.

The week following Mr. Rawleigh's visit, a man and woman stepped to the counter and handed me an exact amount of cash for a shirt and tie. They were in a hurry, and as soon as they grabbed their bag they quickly exited the store. I had the cash in my pocket before the door had closed. It was a beautiful spring morning, and with extra money in my pocket I went to a restaurant next door rather than eat the soggy tuna sandwich my mother had given me in a brown bag. When I returned, Sid wanted to see me in his office. I knocked on the door and once inside I met Sid and an unknown man in a suit, and the two hurried shoppers who had paid for my lunch.

They had me in spades, and the questioning began. The man and woman worked for Hughes & Hatcher—they went from store to store to nail thieving employees. The well-dressed man headed security for national. Sid had instructed us to watch schvartzes, but most thefts were by store employees, who were mostly white in the early 1960s. Everyone in the room, except for me, had been through this drill before. They hammered away to determine exactly how much I had cost the store. For over an hour I tried to convince them that this was one of the first times I had taken from them and confessed to lifting an item or two. They were neither impressed nor convinced, telling me I would probably be charged with grand larceny and face prison time.

I was humiliated and angry at myself for letting my greed get so out of control, not to mention just embarrassed for getting caught. After about two hours of going back and forth we agreed on a few hundred dollars in thefts and stealing merchandise. They followed up the inevitable "You're fired" with a vow to never mention my name as an employee, and a demand that I never mention my time with their store. I walked out with a strange feeling of relief, incredulous that I had narrowly escaped, for a second time, a felony charge. Had they been watching me closely for longer, they would have realized the sum owed was astronomically higher.

For the next few days I secluded myself in my room; I don't believe my parent's ever learned about the whole thing. I swore to never steal again and prayed for forgiveness. Without a job I needed a new plan, and only my WSU classes provided me some structure. I had gotten stuck in the mud of my own making. As I grew tired of obsessing about my current dilemma, I called Mr. Rawleigh and reported that I was no longer happy in retail sales. He said he would be glad to help, and told me the *Detroit News* was looking for copyboys, and that he'd put in a good word.

A call from the newspaper's personnel office instructed me to come in for an interview. The following Monday I was to report for work in the newsroom as a copyboy. For all practical purposes, a copyboy's job is to carry copy and run errands like a gofer.

On my first Monday, I was bursting in anticipation to work inside the newspaper I had delivered for years earlier. I had studied the paper religiously, especially when the story was about disease or poverty in India or China, or about the US's wars in foreign lands.

When I entered the huge newsroom, dozens of reporters were huddled over their typewriters, typing furiously to finish before deadline. An old church pew stood against the wall at the room's entrance, on which two fellows about my age or a bit younger were seated. I introduced myself to a woman sitting at a desk across from the bench and told her I was reporting for work. "Boy," a loud voice heard from across the room prompted one of the youngsters, seated on the pew, to leap to his feet and dash to the desk from which the voice was heard.

A man a little older than me walked up behind and began the on-the-spot orientation for copyboys. He pointed at the pew. "That's where you sit. Just watch and learn from the guys who will be sitting with you." I was told I'd be working the night shift, which was a relief, as I could continue taking classes during the day.

For the next several months I sharpened reporters' pencils, fetched coffee, and was sent one block away to the Anchor Bar, an infamous newspaper hangout in the dingy, smoke filled basement of an old brick building. Like hand and glove, there's always a dive bar near most big city newspapers. The only thing separating the bar from the newspaper was a parking garage, owned by the *Detroit News*, where a fleet of company cars waited for reporters and photographers. My weekly pay was only $55 a week, but I loved being a part of the exciting newspaper world, handling and actually seeing stories and photos before they appeared next day.

When the yell "Boy!" was shouted, I jumped. I was always happy when the reporter wanted a cheeseburger from the Anchor, a request that gave me time to have a cold beer while waiting. I felt especially important when Anthony Ripley, formerly a national correspondent for the *New York Times*, and a prized catch for the stature he brought to the newsroom, yelled "Boy." Whether sharpening his pencils or carrying copy to the city desk, Anthony was warm and friendly to the copyboys, and an errand ordered by him carried special status.

Each evening, staff photographers would drift in and out carrying several photos they had taken on an earlier assignment. Homicides, fires, labor disputes and professional sports photos were among the images. The colorful corps of photographers would often have lengthy chats with the night-editors, exchanges that often included raised voices. I suspected the photographers had had one too many at the Anchor. The photographers would lobby for one photo to be used over another, but the editor was the final arbiter. It reflected a deeply ingrained tension between word-people and picture-people, each believing the other knew less.

I think of this era in journalism as pre-professional. Few reporters had college degrees, and photographers were lucky if they had finished high school. Learning to be a newspaperman was usually done on the job, and often begun as a copyboy. Long before police had yellow tape to seal off crime scenes, they usually invited reporters and photographers in to have a look at urban horrors. I became a regular at the Anchor Bar, in and out, picking up food for the reporters. Journalists, in those years, were legendary drinkers. By 10PM every night, other assorted characters crowded the bar, wanting to commiserate with the reporters. It wasn't unusual to see cops and politicians and some mobsters.

The manager, Leo Derderian, was always eager to talk, and he had enough stories to keep a hardened Detroit newspaper reporter riveted for hours. Leo always wore a short sleeve, faded, flowery Hawaiian shirt, and his nose looked like it had been broken numerous times, squashed against his face. Leo had a deep affection for people on the suspect side of life: drunks, felons, pimps, whores and dopers—as well as certain types of cops, politicians, bankers and reporters. It was also an after hours drinking joint, like others, known as a "blind pig," which meant it was unlikely to ever be busted, given its clientele of high-ranking police and politicos. Leo took care of us in many ways: loan sharking, providing whores, booking our bets, carrying our tabs and even cashing our checks on payday.

After work, around midnight, I would head to the bar to drink and listen to the stories of the rich, often dark history of the industrial capital of the world. I listened to their stories while getting sloshed and it became evident, from observing them, that to practice their crafts successfully, they had to be extraordinarily street-smart. I realized I had the training for their field.

. . .

I was still living with my parents and continuing studies at WSU. In addition to his factory job, my dad was trying to start his own business rebuilding machinery. He rented a small machine shop not too far from the Ford Rouge plant, and Paul helped with the business end. Dad wanted his sons to be part of his business scheme and had cards, invoices and stationary printed that were titled Hubbard & Sons Machines. Paul was in it for only the short term, and I didn't want to work with machines, nor for my dad. Mike was in the Vietnam jungle with the Green Berets.

Dad worked extremely long hours, and around that time he was always deprived of sleep and on the verge of a meltdown. One night, coming home late, I went to my room and heard him screaming vulgar and threatening words at my mother. He was ballistic for reasons unknown, and those days he could be provoked by the slightest things. Because he was more out of control than usual, I went downstairs and confronted him.

He hit me, pushed me against the wall, and I grabbed him and we scuffled, briefly. He stepped back and started threatening me. I told him that if he hurt my mother in any way I would kill him, and I meant it. He went to bed and I didn't see him the next morning. I knew I needed to move to my own place, but also feared for my mom's safety. I believed myself her protector. My mom, in her quiet and passive way, said little but was deeply hurt. She was starting to be afraid of what would happen if our dad didn't get help.

She asked, "You know your dad didn't mean it, don't you, Jimmy?" We cried together while my dad worked on machines in the garage out back.

It wasn't difficult to find an affordable apartment, especially in some of the dicey inner-city neighborhoods near WSU and the newspaper. I stayed in close communication with my mom to monitor my dad's ongoing physical, but more importantly, mental deterioration. He had been verbally abusive for a long time, but we were afraid that he could escalate to physical abuse. A friend living a few houses from me was also looking for an apartment. Willy and I had spent a lot of time together, drinking and going on many double dates. He liked pot, wrote poetry, and loved to listen to Billie Holliday. He fancied himself a beatnik and intellectual. His drinking and smoking weed seemed to hamper any ambition, although he had studied for a couple years at Vanderbilt University. He would be my new roommate.

THE CARNIVAL ON CASS CORRIDOR

We found a hole in the wall at Second and Canfield, a few blocks from WSU, in a six-story, cockroach-infested apartment building, which housed mostly students and assorted deadbeats. The neighborhood was known as Cass Corridor, and just north of downtown Detroit. Some streets along the corridor were as out of control as any in the country, in no short supply of sex, drugs and crime. The skid row on Michigan Ave had already been demolished for urban improvement, so many of its former tenants, along with a slew of other desperate people, found their niches along Cass Corridor. The residents were a mix of Asian, African Americans and white southerners who many simply called hillbillies.

Lining both sides of Cass were Chinese restaurants, bars and barbecue joints, outside of which prostitutes and drug pushers patrolled, guarding their turf around the clock. There were also two or three bars where southern-born white folks sipped drinks and blasted country songs from the jukebox. Young southern girls, some the relatives of the patrons, hung around these joints, too, selling their bodies from the bar stools. More than a few of those prostitutes were murdered after leaving the bar with a john. For a student like me, however, the bars were a panoramic view of human desperation and depravity, both enlightening and entertaining. They reminded me that these troubled people were just plain folk who wanted to experience some momentary happiness, to escape their lonely, monotonous lives on the greasy side of town.

Willy was a great roommate—he kept to his own world and we never had any real disputes. We respected each other, in a strange way; he admired my chutzpah, and occasionally careless demeanor, and I admired his cultural and artistic ideas. There was something to be said for listening to Billie Holliday while reading poetry for hours.

Though our apartment was never as clean or orderly as my parent's home, it was a new adventure; between school and work, at any rate, I wouldn't be in the place but to sleep at night. I came to know quite a few of the photographers at the paper, and one in particular took me under his wing: the smooth-talking and self-assured Rollie Ransom. He often stopped to chat with me and, having a dapper predilection for finely tailored suits, he complimented me on my constantly changing wardrobe of new slacks and colorful, expensive sweaters, nearly every day—clothes I had pilfered from my last job.

The writers were not nearly as interesting as the photographers who, I could not help but notice, were not chained to desks. They were running out on the streets from one story to the next, chasing the story with their cameras on the front lines. When one of the photography department's copyboys left for college, Rollie offered me a shot at the open position. Having become a bit bored by the newsroom, I readily accepted the new challenge.

Rollie had told me that if I liked it, it would be the perfect situation for me to learn every aspect of news photography. I was still an errand boy who had to fetch coffee and food, but the job gave me a chance to learn the skills I'd need later, like darkroom chemistry. I got to see the field, too, when they'd let me lug the equipment on assignments, and an encouraging photographer would even hand me an extra camera.

There were thirty staff photographers and another five technical staffers who developed film, made prints and shot product and people portraits in the house studio. Once, a darkroom staffer showed me how to put a negative in an enlarger, the special projector that creates photographic prints. We exposed the light to paper and saw the picture slowly develop in the tray, the shadows' contours emerging and giving image and life where there had been only blankness before. It's as pure a magic as I'd ever seen.

A man with a camera in the news business could roam the streets, chase historic events, and meet people of every stratum. If a plane crashed, a multiple homicide occurred, a fire, explosion or a baseball game needed covering, you could find your photographers at the Anchor Bar. Drinking was commonplace on the clock and off. Over the coming years I would be anchored there for far too many beers. We'd go for round after round before heading to the garage next door to drive a company car off to a breaking story.

I learned under the tutelage of thirty colorful photographers working for *The Detroit News.* Among them were some sober, intelligent and creative men; others were less sober, many hardened by the streets, and a few carried pistols in their camera bags. On the street, the excitement of a violent story—the kind that occurred all to often in the Motor City—was sprinkled with constant threats from police or citizens who didn't want a photographer meddling around the scene.

On my off days I hung around United Press International's (UPI) news pictures bureau, which was housed in a small office behind the photo department. Art Chernecki, the bureau chief, sensed that I was eager to break into the business. I would stand for hours pulling the long roll of facsimile paper on its spools, looking at the endless photos from UPI bureaus around the world, I wanted to be part of this. I wanted to be dispatched to exotic destinations, photographing unfamiliar people and their unpredictable, unfolding lives. I wanted to see my work published.

My brother Paul, recently married to the airline ticket agent, was about to travel to Japan, a place where high-end Nikon cameras were bountiful and cheap. Upon his return he gave me one, along with two additional lenses, and I wrote him a check for the things which I cherished dearly.

THE BEATLES, THE SIKH

I started stringing, the business's word for freelancing, at UPI, though I still worked as a copyboy for the *News*. I'd cover an event and sell the photo for $10 per print, to bolster my low pay and start building a reputation. I'd heard that a popular music group from England was going to perform at Olympia Stadium on September 6, 1964, and Art said they hadn't planned to cover the concert. If I wanted to go work the show, they might use a shot. I'd seen the longhaired foursome on the Ed Sullivan show and liked their music, but Elvis was still the king.

I was not prepared. There were 30,000 young, mostly female audience members, waiting to see the British sensations. When the band emerged from their limousine, the crowd went berserk. It was unlike anything I'd ever seen. I suddenly understood the word "thronged." People reached out and crushed together in a mix of joy and desperation to be closer, like it were a religious pilgrimage. I shot several photos of the crowd attempting to touch or be touched.

Inside the stadium flashbulbs illuminated the darkened arena and startled you every single time, and the effect was eerily suggestive of the firefights in Vietnam that we'd seen on television. The crowd screamed, girls fainted, and when the Beatles started to play one girl jumped from a balcony at the rear of the stage, crashing through Ringo's drums and breaking her leg.

UPI used two of my photos and transmitted them to their international clients. Covering events like this made me want more. I was hooked. The next week I told my boss I would like to become a staff photographer for the paper. He looked at me, smiled, and said I'd have to get experience at a small paper before considering my request.

Art offered me a job as a bureau assistant at UPI and I resigned from the paper for the new position. Being a bureau assistant for UPI's news pictures operation was a step up the ladder from copyboy, and so were all the jobs; I processed film taken by the staffers, took in negatives from around the world, developed the 4x5 film sheets, made prints, and then ran the wet prints across the street to the *Detroit Free Press* and back to deliver the latest photos to the *Detroit News* desk.

In a few short months it became clear the only way I would become a staff photographer would be to work at a small newspaper and learn the everyday grind of a smaller market. Art had a friend who was the photo chief at the *Macomb Daily*, about an hour's drive from Detroit in Mt. Clemens, Michigan. They had an opening and I got the job making slightly more than $55 per week. Toiling away, I was anxious to get back to *The Detroit News*. That would take longer than anticipated. A new challenge and job presented when Art called me from UPI and told me there was a wealthy young man looking for a photographer to open a new department at a suburban chain of newspapers, *The Observer*, to be published bi-weekly. I met with the owner, Phil Power, at his offices in Plymouth, Michigan, and he hired me to launch the photo department.

My brother Paul and I had not had much regular contact since the time I left home, but we talked occasionally on the phone and met a time or two. He told me he had been trying to help get our dad's new business off the ground, but had decided to go back for a master's at U of M. He said things were not working out well with dad, and that his behavior was becoming more unpredictable and more abusive. Dad was extremely angry that Paul was going to bail on him. I sensed Paul's resentment that Mike and I weren't around to deflect some of the brunt of dad's abusiveness. But neither Paul nor I knew what to do. Ending our conversation, we both expressed concerns for our mother's well being.

In late 1966, I was taking two classes at WSU, and had completed two years credit toward a degree in sociology. One psychology class explored mental illness and required a field internship for the term, visiting patients in a locked ward at Herman Kiefer Hospital, which was less than a mile from my apartment. I'd be escorted into the ward through secured, locked doors, and once inside it was as if I had walked into *One Flew Over the Cuckoo's Nest*. Half-dressed men, others naked, roamed the halls. Some stood along the walls, with their hands locked in cuffs that were attached to the leather belt around their waist. One man sat on the floor masturbating. Men pissed wherever they happened to be, leaving the stinging scent of urine everywhere.

I was lead into the activity room where both black, white, young and old men sat alone or tried to play cards, a few drawing pictures under the direction of a young woman perhaps doing her own internship. My task would be to play games and converse (when possible), for several hours, once a week. I played checkers, and while there was much raving and ranting, little conversation. Many of them sat alone, mumbling incoherently. Most of the patients were labeled by the era's one-size-fits-all diagnosis: "paranoid schizophrenic." Shrinks handed out that term to the mentally ill as often as doctors hand out prescriptions, and would almost invariably bestow it upon the patients who were considered criminally insane and awaiting transfer.

On weekends I'd spend more time in my apartment, bumping into my roommate, who spent almost all his time getting stoned. Every night I'd come home from work, turn on the kitchen light and watch the giant cockroaches scramble for cover. Willy claimed he had a job, but I have no idea what he meant by it.

I met three seniors from Wayne State University who shared an apartment down the hall and loved to throw parties where the beer flowed like a fountain from the kegs. There were always several women invited, usually college students, but there was also one quite different young woman, one whom I couldn't help but notice lived in our building. She was the most beautiful, exotic woman I'd ever been in the presence of. She wore wrist bracelets, two thin ankle chains, and was draped from her neck to her toes in a colorful sari. Her name was Brijinder Singh, and she had been born in Lahore, Pakistan into a Sikh family that later relocated to India.

I felt like I had to meet her immediately, but she left the party early. One of the students living in the apartment approached me after Brijinder left. "Beautiful isn't she?" he asked—a clearly rhetorical question. He told me how he and his roommates had all attempted to connect with her but no dice. "Maybe you'll get lucky," he offered, but it came out like consolation.

But I was more fortunate than my friends down the hall, and soon Brijinder and I were hanging out in my apartment late at night. She never seemed eager for us to meet at her place, and I learned why when I once had to retrieve something from her room. She requested that I wait for her in the hallway, but pulled the door not completely closed, leaving a tiny crack to peek inside. Brijin, having always had a maid or two in her India home, had never had to clean. Without such services in her small Detroit apartment, her room was in shambles. It looked as if a tornado had passed through, sucking up, then coughing out every item around the room, with no regard for furniture or a clear floor to walk on. Perhaps she was awaiting a maid, or a man who might earn enough to provide her one. But at this point in our relationship I ignored it all, even though my dad had earlier wisely warned, "Always know what you're getting into."

We drank, ate and talked for hours about India, her life and family there, and our individual and shared aspirations. Brijinder was teaching in Detroit after earning her master's in Special Ed from U of M in Ann Arbor. Her dad was a high-ranking officer in the Indian Army; and she told me that Sikhs are historically known as India's legendary warriors. Her family had servants, and the kind of stature and stability not afforded most Indians. She told me how Indians valued education and held engineers or doctors in special esteem. She had grown up with rigid rules in her religion, Sikhism, as I had from fundamentalist Baptists. For me it was no dancing, drinking or gambling and for Brijin, no drinking, smoking or having one's haircut. Underlying the stated rules was a tacit one fervently believed by both her parents and my own: stay with your own kind. We felt bound together as rebels.

Brijin soon announced she was pregnant, which caused me instant, awful consternation. I was in deep, would have to tell my parents, and didn't really want to marry. Not to mention that all this could interfere with my career. I had tried to introduce her to my parents earlier but that didn't happen when my dad learned she was an Indian. There had been a similar reaction when Mike dated a Catholic girl in high school. Ethnicity and religion would narrow the dating field for Mike and me, if dad had had his way.

One day, riding in the car with my dad, dreading what I needed to reveal, I blurted out that Brijinder was pregnant. Much to my surprise he remained calm. This was the third time when I was sure he'd go nuclear, but instead, he showed genuine concern and support: the near-miss with the armed robbery charge, the car accident on Joy

Rd, and now this. Paradoxically, when crap hit the fan he showed a softer, more caring side. As we sat in the car quietly, he said that I had to decide what I wanted to do, and then said, "You made your bed, you'll have to sleep in it." I had not planned to marry anyone anytime soon. I thought that "sleeping in the bed I made" required the right thing. We would marry.

My Daddy Breaks

In early 1967, Paul called me to share urgent concerns about dad. He had threatened to kill him and made other incoherent, abusive remarks, even claiming he wasn't Paul's father. My mother was also expressing grave concerns about his behavior, and told us that he was even threatening neighbors. Dad called me one day, sounding manic, and said he was going to kill me. Paul had even armed himself. He offered me a handgun for protection and I went by his place and picked up a .22 caliber pistol. I believed my dad might try to kill someone, but was shocked to be included on his list.

Around that time, my dad only slept a few hours each night. He worked a regular shift at a Ford factory but had also purchased a farm on forty acres of land about an hour from Detroit, in Fowlerville. He bought a trailer, had several head of cattle and a few horses he would oversee while driving his John Deere tractor around the property. When his factory shift ended and on weekends, he drove to his farm and worked the land and tended to the livestock. He was working 16 to 18 hour days headed for an early grave. He was a country boy at heart, and asked my mom repeatedly to move out there with him, but she responded every time only with, "Boy, I don't know." She always made a decision by not deciding, and her reluctance enraged him.

There comes a day when children have to make life-changing decision for their parents, but this day came early for my dad. He was only 54-years-old. Paul and I decided dad needed professional help, and we'd have to force it on him. The decision felt a long time coming, and we both tried several times to talk with our mother about the best course of action. But once again, she refused to make a decision, and she passed the burden to her sons. The moment for action came one morning in early spring, when the flowers were beginning to bloom. Mom called Paul at his home in suburban Livonia, and told him dad was in the garage with a gun and going to kill himself. I was in my apartment ten miles from our west side home. She called me next, and then called the police while we rushed to the house.

When I arrived, four or five police cars were out front. I went inside and found three police officers standing over dad, who was seated on a chair in the tiny kitchen, dressed in a sleeveless T-shirt, blue, grease-stained work pants, and had his hands cuffed behind his back. He was quiet. Paul waited outside; he knew his appearance would provoke dad. Dad shouted, "Look at me. Look what they've done to me."

The police showed me the cache of loaded guns placed on the dining room table. Police had found a small arsenal in the garage, after they'd surrounded it and urged dad to step out and surrender. He didn't show anger toward me, and it soon became clear that his rage was directed at mom, Paul and the police. He was either acting, or pretending, that I had nothing to do with his current predicament; he may have even been trying to use me as a needed ally to send and receive information about my mother and brother. He was losing it.

Mom sat in the living room weeping and wondering whether we had made the right decision. The scene unfolding was her worst nightmare, and she was horrified not only about the decision to call police, but also at the prospect of a cell in jail or a mental hospital awaiting dad. Her life had crumbled, on top of which was the humiliation of the public threats and a platoon of cops surrounding her home, guns drawn, in front of her friends and neighbors. I knew she would be worrying and second guessing our decision for the rest of her days.

The police lead my dad to a police car and he asked, "Can you come with me, Jimmy?" I looked at the police sergeant and he told me I could ride downtown in the back seat with my dad. He was quiet during the ten-mile trip to Detroit Receiving Hospital's locked psychiatric unit, which was used for short-term emergency cases. The plan was after an evaluation, the prisoner/patient would be sent elsewhere for longer-term confinement and care.

We pulled into the busy emergency room driveway. It was a four-story yellow brick building across from the police headquarters. The interior was poorly lit and in dire need of a new coat of paint, making the whole effect creaky and creepy. The large, open wards were totally devoid of privacy. The heart of the hospital was the emergency ward, where ambulances continually dropped off new entrants of the mangled, sick and dying.

This was the place you'd want to be rushed to for a bullet, a stabbing or even a heart attack. For a patient experiencing a mental meltdown, like my dad, it was the last destination in the world they'd want to be heading. The beds had straps. The halls were crowded, and it wasn't even noon. People lay on gurneys, awaiting help, and doctors and nurses scanned the hallways for the most needy patients. The medical staff was legendary for their expertise in emergency measures. Most of the attending doctors had attempted innumerable procedures to save a human from feeling their final heartbeats in those rooms. When a cop was shot, this is where their brothers in blue always rushed them.

The police lead my dad to the entrance and told me to find the admissions office and do whatever paperwork was required; they had their own to do. When I returned the cops were gone and dad lay on a gurney, hands cuffed to metal bars on each side of the hospital bed and brown leather straps holding down his chest and legs. He was screaming that he needed to go to the bathroom, and the sheets were already soaking through with urine. My father, whom I had idolized and perceived to be the strongest in the world, was totally helpless. He had been a giant in my life, and was now reduced to a whimpering, angry child throwing a tantrum. It felt like I was sinking inside myself under the bad fluorescent lights, sick and off balance in the yellow-green hallways.

For years I had had a deep desire to never become like my dad. Looking down at this defeated man lying on a gurney, he appeared a stranger. I certainly never wanted to end up like this, but carrying his genes, I thought I might. I didn't have the skills to cope with this awful moment. This deed had needed doing but with the adrenaline wearing off, I started to quiver with heartbreak and terror and the sheer strangeness of it.

Two large men wearing green scrubs approached and wheeled dad away. A day or two passed and I received word he had been transferred to Herman Kiefer Hospital's locked psych ward, where he would spend several weeks among some of the patients I'd met during my internship. He was put on a diet of Thorazine and other drugs to subdue inappropriate outbursts. He clashed from time to time with the orderlies, and he hated his shrink because he could not understand the doctor's broken, Indian-accented English. In my view, no shrink would ever be able to access my dad's inner mental processes. Not unlike Jack Nicholson' character in *One Flew Over the Cuckoo's Nest*, dad was a clever man, capable of a con. He even went so far as to learn the phone number of the judge who had signed papers ordering his stay in the ward. Dad phoned him with threats, and ended up confined longer than planned. He might have wanted just that.

When dad was released, he seemed a somewhat milder man but possibly because he was under the strong effects of several medications. His only perceptible anger was about the police confiscation of his guns, and about his slim chances of ever getting them back.

Brijinder and I found an apartment about a mile from where we met, still in that dicey neighborhood. The yellow brick, four-story building was at Second and Seward, a few blocks east of the huge General Motors world headquarters. The evening before Brijin and I were to marry before a judge, a friend called and wanted to have a drink. We binged nearly the entire night, and I crawled out from bed the next morning on what promised to be a brutal summer day. We went to the judge and married, and had a small family-only party. Once my dad knew we were married, with a child due soon, we were welcome to visit. He seemed thrilled at the prospect of having a grandchild. He invited us to Sunday dinner at noon on July 23, 1967, which happened to also be a historic, catastrophic day for Detroit.

MOTOWN MADNESS

It was my day off from work at *The Observer*, my cameras in the trunk of my 1962 Chevrolet Impala coupe, white with a black vinyl top. When I stepped outside to fetch my car, I saw dark smoke across the sky, to the west. The plumes rose from several locations, and having covered many big fires I knew that this one had to be widespread. It was about 10:30AM, and even for a Sunday the city seemed eerily still.

Something was not right in my neighborhood. I went back to the apartment and told Brijin that I had to check on a situation nearby, and that if I was gone long to cancel the dinner with my parents. I drove six blocks to 12th street and turned right. Looking carefully as I drove slowly, I saw no one and nothing but plumes of billowing smoke shrouding the street a few blocks ahead.

When I saw a commotion inside a liquor store I hit the brakes. About a hundred people began running out onto the street, over shattered glass on the sidewalk from the store's broken plate glass window, coming within ten feet of me. Each carried several bottles of liquor and ran furiously, like a stampede about to trample me. It was a powerful image and would have made for a stunning photograph, but my cameras were in the trunk. I heard someone shout, "Get whitey!" and after a quick scan of the entire street I realized I was the only whitey within reach. In fact, the only other humans I saw were looting or setting fires. I pressed the accelerator to the floor and sped along 12th St. through thick, black smoke, looting and fires.

Slowing down while approaching the corners of 12th and Clairmont, I saw more than a hundred police officers standing idly in a park, watching people loot stores across the street. I parked, got the cameras from the trunk, and approached them. One of the cops told me that a police command post had been set up in a large parking lot at Herman Keifer, a few blocks away. Astonished, I jumped in my car and raced back to our apartment. I explained the situation to Brijin and pulled the .22 caliber from my dresser drawer and handed it to her. I took pause and thought, about how my wife, carrying my child, had only been in the country for a short time and now had to contend with some sort of urban chaos in our very neighborhood. I explained that I had to go back to the rioting and that if anyone came through the door to pull the trigger. When she asked when I would be back I said "No idea." Having grown up in a military family, she at least knew the basics of aiming and firing a weapon, which gave me some much needed comfort that morning.

I pulled into the hospital parking lot. A large contingent of police and their vehicles nearly filled the lot, but I found a space and threw my press credentials on the dashboard. As I lived only blocks from the rioting, I was one of the first to arrive. I looked up just two floors above where I stood, at the place where my dad had been a patient in the psych ward a few months earlier.

Carrying two Nikon cameras in a bag full of film and lenses, I headed to the park a few blocks away, where the cops huddled idly, watching looters across the street, near the riots' epicenter at Twelfth St and Clairmont. I stood with more than a hundred officers and we watched for over an hour as hundreds of people broke into stores and ran to and fro with their loot. Only a few hours earlier, at about 3AM, the police had raided an after-hours drinking joint—a blind pig—where about sixty patrons were drinking, dancing and gambling. The group was celebrating with some of their friends who had just returned from serving in Vietnam. The police arrested everyone inside the illegal bar, but had to wait for paddy wagons to take the lot to jail. A small crowd began to gather and started taunting the police, and a few people started to throw things at the police and break store windows. Within a few hours approximately 10,000 people were on the street, setting fires and looting. It had become a full-scale riot.

Tensions between Detroit Police and black inner city Detroiter's had been a powder keg, ready to explode for years, and 12th Street had for a long time been a freak magnet, attracting the most sordid cast of characters. It was a volatile place at a tense time, and the friction caused a spark. Police officials ordered their troops to keep their pistols holstered and stand back, believing the furor would run it's course and the lawlessness would end within hours. The intensity of the insurrection escalated as more looters and arsonists arrived. Being a Sunday, the police response was slow. By noon, thousands were on the streets and the mayhem spread to other neighborhoods, both the east and west side.

The city's mayor called Michigan's governor, George Romney, for help and in a few hours state police and truckloads of national guardsmen began arriving. They were little prepared for urban warfare, especially on US soil. Squadrons of police and guardsmen began sweeps of 12th and intersecting streets. Fires raged on, burning hundreds of brick duplexes to the ground, destroying everything owned by hundreds of middle-class black people. Residents screamed in terror, awaiting firemen who never came, and reports even came in of snipers firing at the fire fighters.

I accompanied the national guard's first sweep along 12th, squadrons of Detroit cops trailing behind. Guardsmen had their rifles pointed forward, with bayonets secured to the barrels. It was a frightening drama but my sole purpose was to photograph efforts to restore order in my city, which had suddenly collapsed into almost total anarchy. It was like a war film, each frame moving in slow motion. While we moved ahead, block by block, the police and national guard making arrests and instructing rioters and onlookers to leave the streets. Bottles and bricks sailed toward us, as did racial insults directed at the mostly white guardsmen and cops.

I realized my role was limited to recording the actions and rage of man, an awareness I would be reminded of many times over the years. I could not intervene—which would be unethical from many points of view. We turned a corner and a whole city block of large homes was engulfed in flames. A woman, being restrained by a man, yelled "Mommy, mommy," as she fell to her knees, a man holding her from behind. I focused and pressed the shutter to record the gut-wrenching scene while standing quietly with a contingent of Detroit police watching from across the street.

I found a pay phone and called UPI to see if they needed photos. Indeed, they did. Art Chernecki was vacationing in Canada. The bureau assistant told me they desperately needed photos and we arranged to meet at the police command post, where they would send someone to retrieve my film. I would stay behind to take more pictures. UPI was dispatching photographers from around the country but that would take time. Knowing I had not established myself as a seasoned photographer, I felt timid about my skills.

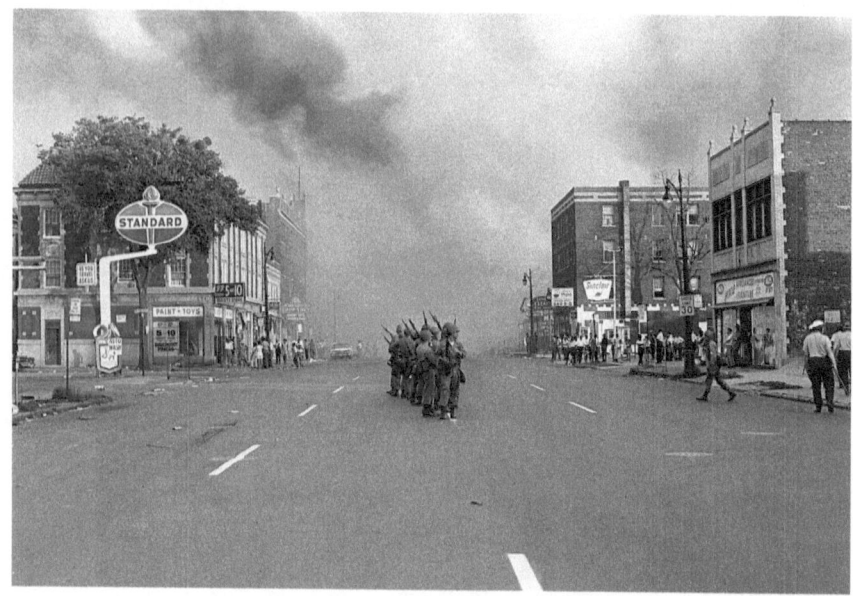

First day Detroit Riot 1967

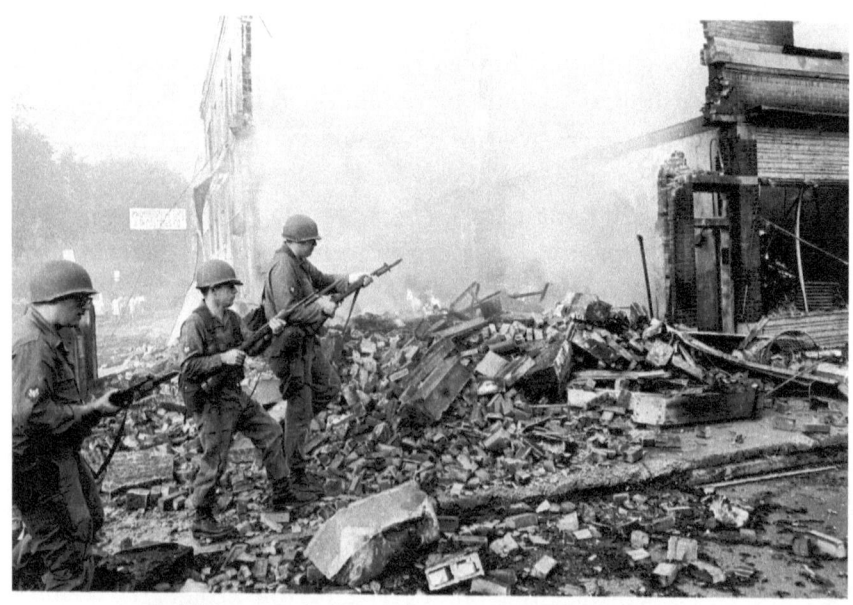

Soldiers march through Detroit during riots 1967

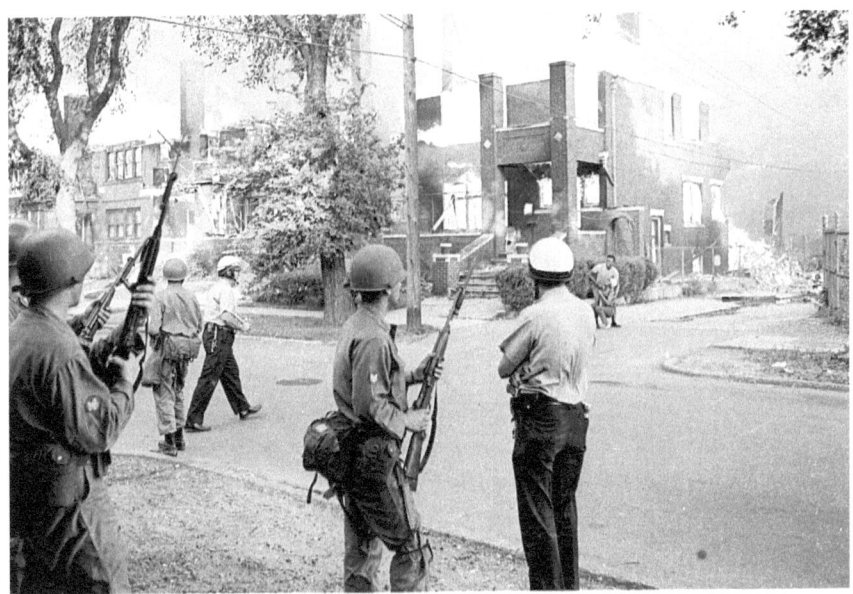

City blocks burn during Detroit rioting 1967

Rejoining police and guardsmen in the late afternoon on 12th street, daylight began to fade. Flames burned from hundreds of buildings; huge plumes of black smoke hung over miles of inner city Detroit. It looked like the whole city was on fire. As the anger and rage spread, I became angry that black people were burning out their neighbors. I understood this was pent-up rage, fermenting for decades. The black community had long complained about mistreatment from the cops and insensitivity of the white power establishment. But it still didn't make sense to me.

By nightfall, 12th Street had been cleared and most of the looters dispersed, although the city was still on fire and rioting had spread. We finished the sweep at 12th and West Grand Boulevard; each police car picked up two additional officers, doubling the cruisers' manpower. One of the cops rolled up and asked me "Want to ride with us?" Maybe he thought a guy with a camera might increase his chances to see his photo in the local paper's next edition. With two guys in the back holding pistols and shotguns and two in front, I climbed in the middle of the front seat, armed with my cameras.

We patrolled the area, awaiting further instructions. Within a few minutes, we saw dozens of looters inside a grocery store grabbing items off the shelves. Thousands of pieces of broken glass sparkled like diamonds on the sidewalk beneath the illumination from streetlights. The driver hit the accelerator and we screeched across the boulevard, but it was too much force, so he hit the brakes. The car skidded and slammed into the low brick wall that anchored the bottom of the shattered window. The driver called for reinforcements on the two-way radio while the rest of us jumped out. The cops raced into the store, weapons drawn and making arrests. I ran into the store behind the police and shot photos of looting to contrast with those in the streets. The police made the thieves line up in front of the store and arrested all but the few who had run. A police van arrived to cart the thieves to booking and jail.

After the incident, I located a pay phone and called UPI. They were grateful for my help and were going to run ten pictures that I had taken in newspapers and magazines around the world. I delivered more film to UPI where I helped process the film and prints. Before dawn on Monday, I returned to the command post and talked with the police and guardsmen about the status of the riot. Unlike past riots in America, this one had produced an army of snipers trying to pick off cops and guardsmen. After only one day of covering these events, I felt like a veteran. Looting and arson continued, and it was obvious that the police and guardsmen had lost control. Rumors surfaced that President Johnson might send federal troops to quell the situation. Detroit was unsafe for all.

The city had an eerie atmosphere as the sun rose, and smoke from hundreds of fires filtered the day's light, casting unusual colors into the air and creating an aura of fear and destruction. I made three phone calls. I dialed Brijin, and thankfully she was fine, if scared. She could hear the gun battles on the streets, some just a block away from our apartment, even though the radio news reported that all was quiet in Detroit. My second call was to my employer, Phil Power, to report that I would not be coming to work at his suburban paper, perhaps not for several days. After describing the events I was covering in my neighborhood he just said, "No problem, maybe we can use some of your pictures in the paper next week."

My final call to UPI let them know that I would be on the streets all day. Exhausted, not having slept for nearly two days, I was also ecstatic that my work had been published.

Shortly before midnight on July 24, President Johnson authorized the use of federal troops by using a law from 1795, which stipulates that the president can call in armed forces whenever there is an insurrection in any state against the government. He gave Detroit the dubious distinction of being the only city to ever be occupied by federal troops.

The battle hardened 82nd Airborne arrived, having recently returned from Vietnam. They were about to engage in urban guerilla warfare with their countrymen. Heavy equipment also came in, including Armored Personnel Carriers (APCs) and tanks, the latter creating a noise never before heard on Detroit's streets, metal halftracks carrying the monster war machines across the concrete. They were prepared to fire on the buildings from where hidden snipers shot their weapons. The tanks had probably been assembled in Detroit factories. On the third night of the riots, the looting and arson slowed. Snipers became the main concern. I hooked up with one of their units and photographed them patrolling city streets in open jeeps, with an array of weapons, and rode in the back seat for a dangerous trip through the inner city in a small convoy of two jeeps comprised of eight soldiers and one news photographer.

Our mission was to cruise the darkened streets in which fires still smoldered in the rubble, and engage any assailants hidden in apartments and houses. Once fired upon, a distress cry would go out on the army's radios and more soldiers, APCs and tanks would come to the rescue. We took fire early, jumped from the jeep and lay on the hard road behind and under the vehicles. A soldier handed me an extra rifle, saying, "Take this. You may need it," and he showed me the safety to unlock the trigger. We sprawled on the concrete, and the soldiers fired a barrage toward the building. Within about three minutes reinforcements arrived followed by one tank. They opened fire on the building but the snipers were never found.

Fierce firefights raged throughout the night, and over a wide area of the inner city. We kept going for another hour, and then they dropped me in front of J.L. Hudson Company, a department store, on Woodward Avenue. There I joined another contingent of federal troops who were guarding Detroit's crown jewel businesses. It was quiet the rest of the evening. However, less than two miles north from where we stood, one block from where Brijin remained scared and hidden, an atrocity was underway inside the Algiers Motel.

A year after the 1967 Detroit riots, noted author John Hersey released a novel titled *The Algiers Motel Incident.* Inside a small motel room three young black men were killed, and two white women and seven other black men brutally beaten, either by Detroit police or members of the national guard, after a report was received that a gunman or group of gunmen had been seen near the motel. The three young men were shot, execution style, lined against the room's wall. No one ever was convicted for the execution.

At the time, I thankfully had no idea of the incident, which would have terrified me. Later that night, I picked up Brijin and drove her to my parents' home. I was dog tired, but felt enormous guilt for leaving her alone and would have to apologize once I was rested. I hadn't slept for three days and it was a long time before I drifted off. I was conflicted over the events that I had witnessed. Did all of this happen out of the cries of the poor, the dispossessed? Conversely, was this the action of opportunists who had sensed a moment to gain from chaos while attacking the white power establishment? Would justice come for all of God's children from the destruction and death that this city had experienced?

The next morning Brijin and I finally had a chance to talk. She asked if we should move out of the neighborhood. It was a reasonable question, and certainly had been extremely dangerous for the past week. I said we should give it a little time, but that we should consider it, especially after our child would be born. But I added, "I don't like the idea of being driven out of my home by thugs. Maybe we should just find a house we can afford and stay in the city. I don't really like the suburbs." She was quiet, and still in shock from the past few days of fear.

Indeed, we might need to relocate. Swaths of the nation's fifth largest city lay in charred, smoking ruins. It would be a long time for Detroit to heal from the insanity it had experienced, and a complete recovery might never occur. Diseased race relations would not resolve themselves in the foreseeable future, and from all appearances they would probably worsen. "White flight," which had already been occurring before 1967, would now dramatically accelerate. It would be a more dangerous city to live and work in for everyone, and especially for a white news photographer.

The unrest, after five days, turned into one of the deadliest and most destructive riots in modern US history, far surpassing the 1943 Detroit riot. At least forty-three were dead, 467 injured, over 7,200 arrests and more than 2,000 buildings burned down. The body count, many believed, was grossly understated.

In my previous semester at Wayne State University, only a few months before the outbreak of the riots in Detroit, I had read two books for a sociology class that addressed the struggles of African Americans in urban America. One was by Claude Brown titled *Manchild in the Promised Land,* and the other was by noted novelist James Baldwin called *The Fire Next Time.* I couldn't get the title of Baldwin's book out of my mind. What about the fires this time?

During the next few days with rioting under control, residents and shopkeepers ventured out to assess their community. Sightseers lined the streets and were bumper to bumper, cruising through the war zone and its devastation. I also cruised through, looking for aftermath images and shots of life returning to normalcy, but also to remember the madness I had seen, and the hundreds of homes and businesses incinerated in just a few days. When I turned around to drive home I looked in my rearview mirror, and saw a striking scene on a street corner. Soldiers were guarding a store and allowing neighborhood kids to hold their rifles. The soldiers and the children were all laughing and smiling. The insurrection was over.

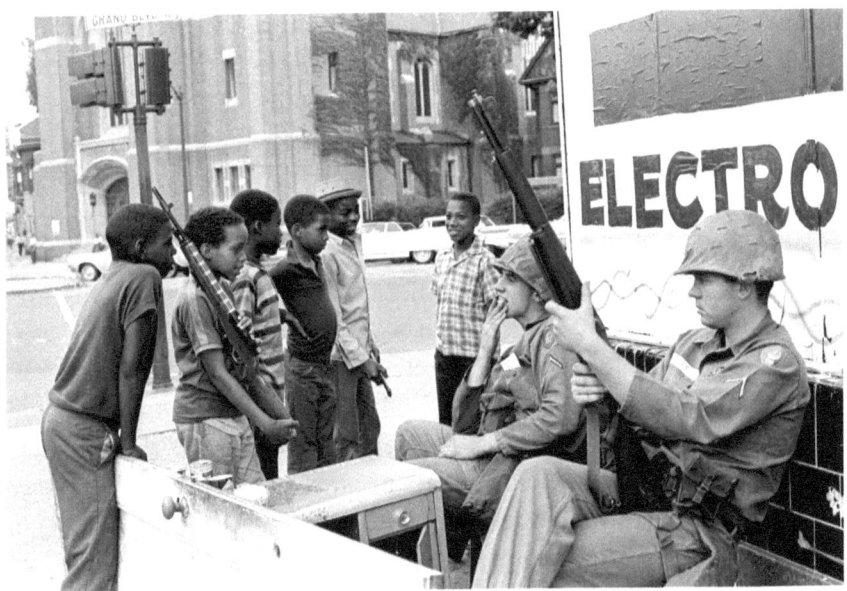

Kids chat with soldiers during Detroit riots 1967

Back in my quiet suburban job a week later, all was calm. Phil was happy to publish my pictures. We both knew that my days with him were numbered, as I had tasted a photographer's life covering a major event that the burbs could never provide. Weeks after the riots I became aware of lingering anger, sadness and loss. I had witnessed two meltdowns: my dad and then my city. I had neither the ability nor the wisdom necessary to work through these feelings. I wanted to understand the ancient Greek aphorism to "know thyself" but was twenty-five years old and sought comfort and wisdom in alcohol and Valium. Not exactly the path to self-discovery.

One day, though, I did think to pull an old Bible from my bookshelf and flip randomly, thinking I might luck into a passage that could provide wisdom. On my second pick, in the Old Testament, I found in the book of Job, 28:20, "Whence then cometh wisdom? And where is the place of understanding?" I continued reading and found Job 28:28, "And unto man He said, Behold, the fear of the Lord, that is wisdom; and to depart from evil is understanding."

Brijin and I were both concerned about our safety. We were living in an increasingly volatile inner city where humans were contemptuous of one another based on skin color. Shortly before the birth of our child, Brijin and I relocated to an apartment in suburban Westland, three miles from my parents. We had decided it prudent not to continue living in the riot's epicenter and joined thousands of other's fleeing the Motor City. On November 1, 1967 our daughter was born. It changed my perspective forever and provided an attachment to life not possible before. She had an olive complexion, with black hair and beautiful dark eyes. She was robust, happy and charged with boundless energy. She brought such joy to my life that when I took the time to be with her, it felt like never enough. She became a central focus of my life. Her name was Brijin Marie, Brijjie.

I kept juggling my various selves: student and photographer, husband and father. Completing college would take years; I could only ever manage two classes per semester due to work demands. But by 1968, two goals and dreams became real: *The Detroit News* hired me as a staff photographer and the University of Michigan accepted me. I started taking classes at their Dearborn campus my junior year.

Brijin's dad, Jugjit Singh, paid us a short visit from India. I had felt nervous about meeting him. He was pleasant but I knew he was unhappy about his daughter's choices in America. Like my own dad who hadn't accepted Brijin's ethnicity, Brijin's dad did not want me in his daughter's life. Perhaps my ethnicity was part of the issue, but what loomed much larger was that I was without adequate credentials. My career wasn't one of science and industry, bettering mankind by saving lives in a hospital or building bridges. When Jagjit Singh learned that I was a photographer, his only image was a man in India walking through neighborhoods, lugging a big camera on the back of a donkey, who would put a child atop the animal and try to sell the parents a shot for posterity. He didn't ask where I kept my donkey, though, before flying back to India. He died a short time later from a heart attack, only fifty.

Over the next year I covered professional and college sports, city politics, antiwar protests, mobsters at the federal courthouse and visits by Washington politicians. Occasionally I was assigned to cover cocktail parties and dinners hosted by the rich and powerful people in Grosse Pointe for stories for on my papers society pages, but I never felt an affinity for the rich and powerful. It was probably a sentiment rooted in my blue collar, working-class roots. Some of the homes I was sent to were heirs to Henry Ford's empire, Henry Ford II and Edsel Ford and the Dodge family, along with international philanthropist Max Fisher. My higher power intervened when my boss Artie summoned me to his office to counsel me on appropriate dress. He told me that if I didn't wear a suit or sport coat, with dress shirt and tie, I could not cover society events. He never saw me dressed appropriately again.

One evening I was dispatched to a diner on Woodard Ave, where an attempted robbery occurred. A waitress behind the counter stuck a knife into the chest of a gun-wielding robber when he tried to jump the counter. The would-be bandit lay there dead, a knife handle protruding from his chest. When I arrived the waitress was sitting on a stool at the counter sobbing, and two men from the county morgue were there to pickup the deceased. They were seated at the counter eating hamburgers. Two overweight homicide detectives stood at the entrance scribbling notes. Everyone at the crime scene seemed calm and detached. It was obvious they had seen all of this many times before. I knew it was routine, and that I had to get used to it. But I photographed the blood-spattered scene and left wondering, "This is the life I've chosen?"

On another night, a fire in a small inner city duplex left three children dead and our radio dispatcher sent me racing to the scene. The mother had left her children unattended and when she returned, had discovered the aftermath of the fire and her terrible loss. She was standing in front of the burned out duplex sobbing. I asked her if I could take her picture and she screamed "No." She went into the front room of her home, which had been left undamaged. I noticed her standing in front of a mirror fixing her hair and applying lipstick. I again asked her permission to take her picture. She sat on her worn couch and posed for the photo, which we published in the paper's next edition.

A welcome reprieve came after Brijin Marie's birth, when I could photograph the tender, playful moments between her and her mother. I often thought of how to protect my daughter from the harm I'd seen come to other children. My camera and my daughter brought comfort to me, affirming the tender side of life and balancing internal conflicts I held about humanity's dark side. Watching Brijjie interact with her mother and playmates sensitized me to the wonders and mysteries of children and strengthened my deep connection to her.

As expected, Detroit's streets became more menacing and dangerous after the riots. Even though I had use of a company car during working hours, I now kept a loaded shotgun, a box of shells, a helmet, gas mask and bullet proof vest in the trunk of my personal car.

On April 4, 1968 Dr. Martin Luther King was assassinated in Memphis, and Detroit fear sprung anew of another riot. Detroit officials declared a curfew to minimize the chances of rioting. A reporter and I were dispatched to report on the areas near 12th St that were most likely to erupt. To keep our identities shielded we used my car, instead of a marked media car, even though our whiteness would give us away and we might end up being mistaken for police. It'd be worse, though, to be caught as journalists.

Gary, the reporter, and I cruised the streets and alleys in the same area that I had photographed a year earlier when it was an inferno teeming with looters and the husks of homes and businesses. We passed many slow moving police cars, with officers heavily armed, the streets abandoned.

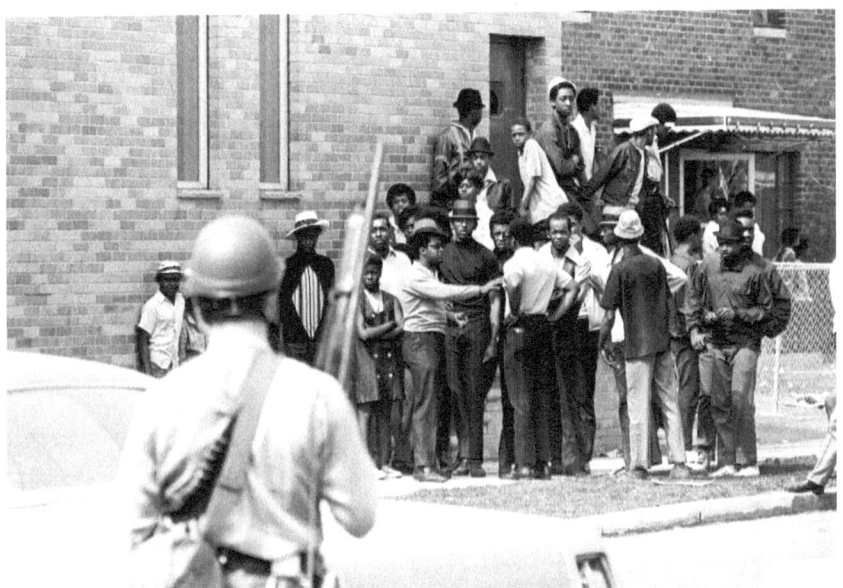

Racial turbulence in Detroit area 1967

We turned into a darkened alley behind some apartment buildings and met head on with three police cars and two others pulling in behind us. The police, carrying rifles and shotguns surrounded my car shouted at us, "get out." They instructed us to stand against a garage with our arms outreached. They commenced searching us, and they put a rifle and shotgun to each of our heads. Other officers ransacked my car and tore the back seat from its moorings.

One cop said they were going to kill us. I was frozen with fear. Looking at the apartment buildings and seeing no one peering from the windows, I knew that they could shoot us without witnesses. I knew they were capable of it, and my mind flashed back to the assassinations inside the Algiers Motel a year earlier. Lined against a wall, just like this, shot in the back. The police continued their verbal assault and kept their weapons pointed at us for a few more minutes calling us scum before finally saying, "Get out of here, you scum, liars. You don't belong here."

Then they got back in their cars and left. Gary and I were speechless while trying to regain composure. We put the seat back in the car and picked up the papers they had thrown on the ground. They had broken one of my cameras with a rifle butt. We drove fast to the pressroom inside police headquarters.

We called the police commissioner's office on a different floor and told an assistant what had happened, but we were unable to provide names or badge numbers. The cops who terrorized us had removed their nametags and badges to prevent identification. Within a few minutes after reporting the incident to the commissioner's office, a deep, authoritarian voice announced over the police radio for all police on the streets to immediately cease harassing reporters covering the tense night in Detroit. The voice was that of John Nichols Sr., top cop and commissioner of the Detroit Police—and the father of my old friend John Jr. at Cody High.

• • •

A few weeks later the paper arranged for me to ride along with the vice squad, a team of four plain clothes Detroit police officers assigned to bust prostitutes. We visited several bars in which hookers met their johns, including a "hillbilly bar" near my old place on Cass Corridor.

We sat at a table facing the bar and ordered drinks. The place was crowded with lowlifes, which, from our appearances, anyway, included the cops and me. We sipped our drinks and listened to the blaring country music, scanning the bar as the hookers bargained with johns. I spotted a young woman at the end of the bar and she looked familiar. A young cop told me she was his first bust. I realized that she was my cousin, Caroline, the daughter of my dad's sister Mabel, who we had visited a number of times when I was kid. I walked over to her at the bar and took a seat. She instantly recognized me and we chatted for a few minutes before I asked, "Why are you here?" "I make good money here." I knew that she had a troubled past and family. I told her to be careful. Johns had killed two hookers working out of this bar in a motel room next door. It was disturbing to discover my cousin was a hooker working this seedy bar.

A month after King's assassination, Robert F. Kennedy visited Detroit in his quest to become president. He held a huge rally with thousands of people attending. I spent several hours photographing RFK and his worshippers. Some of his staff introduced themselves to me and asked if they could get copies of some of the pictures. I said I'd make arrangements and later gave them a few to use in flyers and other campaign material.

One of the staffers told me about an exciting campaign swing Bobby would make into Indiana, a few hundred miles from Detroit, and he invited me to join them in Indianapolis. It would be over a weekend, so I hooked up with the motorcade for several days. I was allowed complete and up-close access to RFK. Security was lax, and I had complete access to him as he addressed crowds in ghettoes and affluent suburbs. It was one month before he was assassinated in Los Angeles.

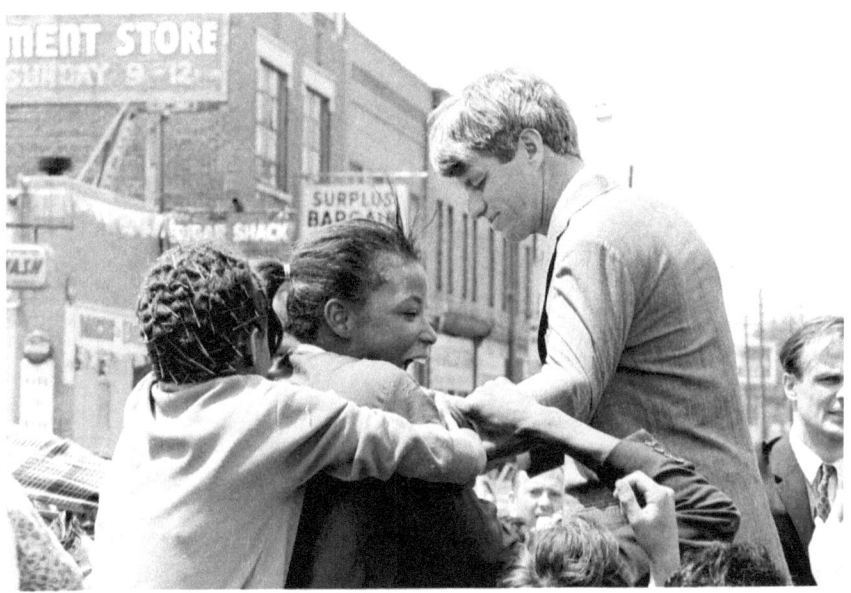

RFK campaigns in Indianapolis 1968

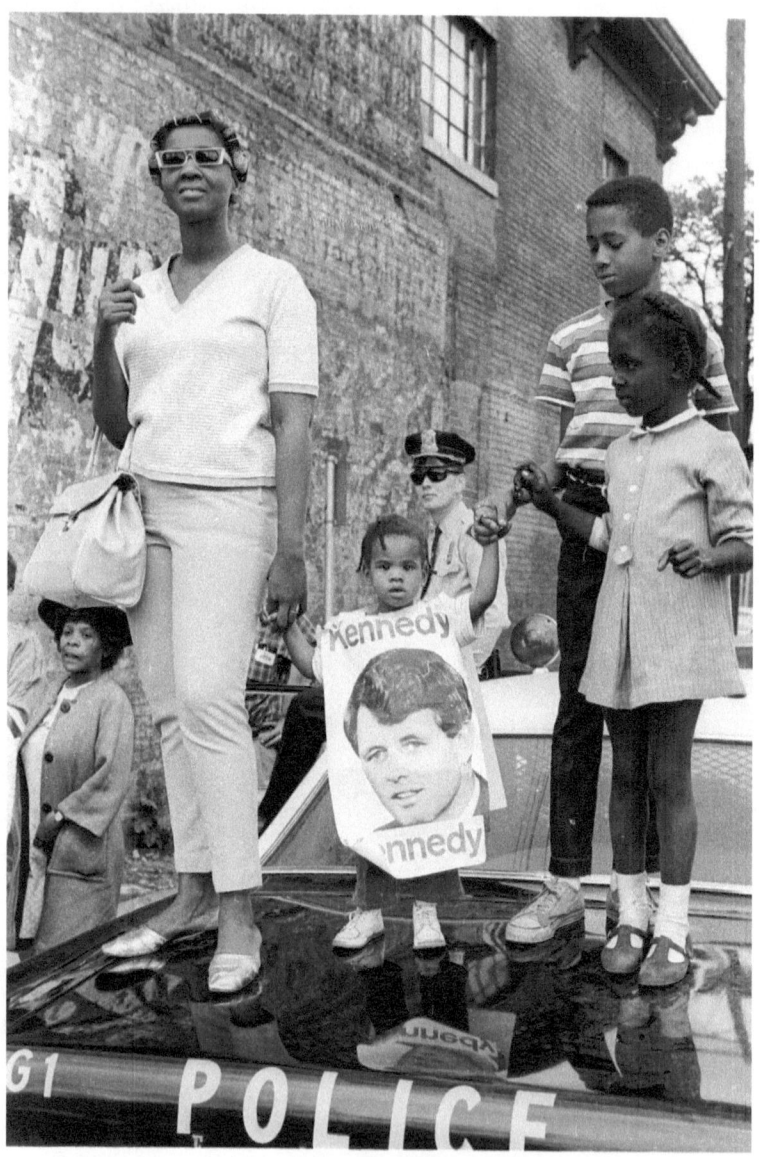

RFK supporters in impoverished Indianapolis hood 1968

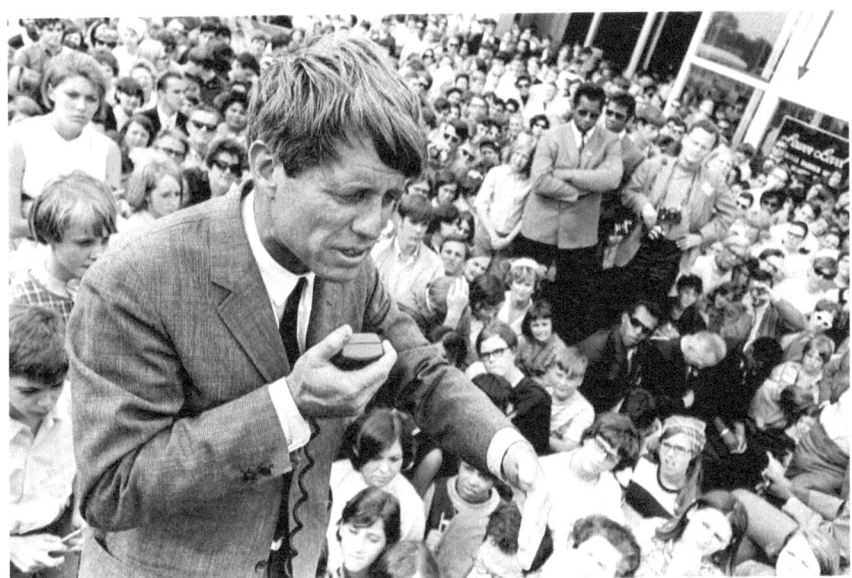

RFK addresses supporters in Indianapolis 1968

Crossing the partisan aisle, I spent a few days covering Richard M. Nixon's campaign in Michigan, but it lacked the energy and enthusiasm surrounding RFK's campaign. Bobby was loved with a similar fervor that music fans had for the Beatles.

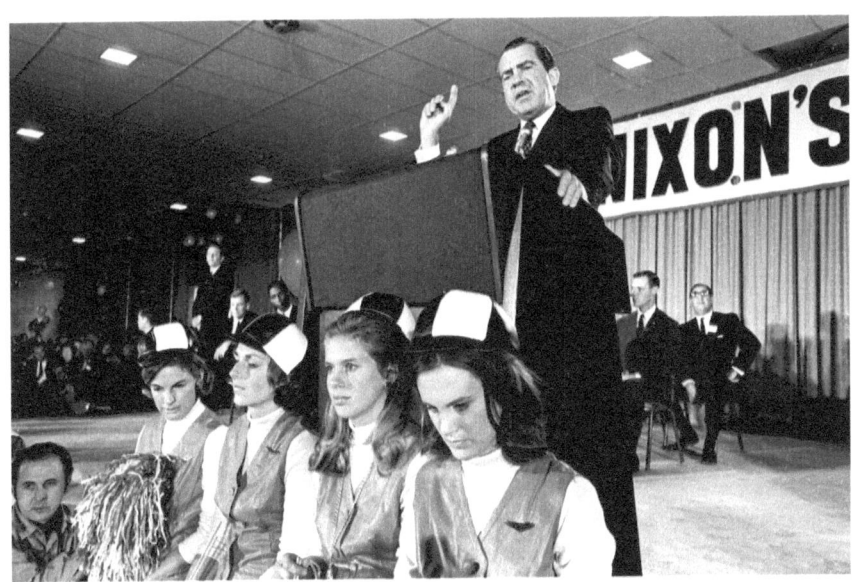

President Nixon campaigns in Michigan 1968

MICHIGAN'S TERROR

Being dispatched to Ann Arbor on a variety of assignments became routine, featuring many University of Michigan football and basketball games. One evening in 1968, I was sent to the police station in Ann Arbor to cover a news conference announcing the gruesome discovery of a body of a murdered college coed. They'd found Joan Schell sexually assaulted and stabbed repeatedly, with her breasts mutilated. Some body parts were missing, like an earlier victim.

As the police described the crime, I remembered hearing about the first victim, also a college student, shortly after the 1967 Detroit riots. Joan had been seen with John Norman Collins, a failing student in Ypsilanti, and a dead ringer for the All American Boy. Joan, from Plymouth, Michigan where I had worked for *The Observer*, had recently moved in across the street from Collins. He was questioned but had an alibi—he had been with his mother miles away. He was released.

The other victim was a woman named Mary Fleszar. Collins had appeared at the funeral home posing as a news photographer and was asked to leave. Leaving the news conference, I was saddened for the parents in their grief, and for their daughter brutalized by a monster. I wondered with a sick feeling how I would cope with the magnitude of such horror and loss if it were my own daughter.

With a serial killer on the loose thirty miles away and still reeling from the '67 riots, the mood in Detroit was rife with terror and frustration. But it briefly gave way to hope and jubilation from an unlikely source: the Detroit Tigers were going to the World Series. The series offered needed mental and emotional relief. On the evening they clenched the Series I was sent to the streets to photograph the city's victory. It was as emotionally charged as what I had witnessed during the riots, but now incredibly positive.

The jubilation was short lived, however, and turmoil continued into 1969. In March, the coed killer dumped two more bodies in the Ann Arbor area, both savagely murdered with the same modus operandi. I raced to photograph the murder scenes and follow up at the news conference.

On one rainy night in June 1969, my reporting comrade Gary and I traveled the thirty miles from Detroit to the morgue in Ann Arbor. The news desk had been alerted that the parent's of the killer's most recent victim, Alice Kalom, a recent U of M graduate, were on their way to claim their daughter's grotesquely mutilated body. We began our stakeout in a long hallway and after an hour passed we heard horrifying screams from a room down the corridor. A door opened slowly and out stepped a silver haired, middle age man, with glasses, wearing a blue dress shirt and khaki slacks. He reminded me of one of my professors.

The man saw us and burst out: "You despicable wretches!" He kept going with other verbal outcries toward the only two men facing him, one with a camera popping flashes in his face, the other with pen and pad. His words were scorching, piercing and sharp; we couldn't help but feel remorse and guilt for being there documenting his shattered life. He looked out of control and started a diatribe, "I don't want her body. I want her alive. I didn't come here for her body," said Mr. Kalom. "I'm not going to claim her body. I'm going to tell them not to go to this university. It's too big. They don't give a crap about anything but money and politics. I'm not going to bury her. Let them bury her on the president's lawn. I've worked too hard to raise her, to send her here. I don't want her dead."

His wife stared down at the floor, sobbing quietly, never lifting her head. He took her arm and they turned, walking somberly toward the exit, along the greenish, yellow, corridor. Later, Mr. Kalom did have his daughter's body retrieved. She was buried in the Mount Ever Rest Memorial Park in Kalamazoo.

While watching them, I remember wondering how do people process the enormity of such a loss, the savage killing of their daughter? A loss greater than any other, with a permanent hole pierced through their hearts? I was the objective newspaper's lens man, their eye in the field. I wasn't supposed to be affected. But I was and would be for decades. I had no idea of the agony felt by people suffering the loss of a child, and what it's like to feel an entire future of possibilities and moments cut off entirely.

On the drive back along the rain slicked freeway neither Gary nor I spoke. Traffic slowed on the I-94 and coming to a standstill. A Michigan State Trooper spotted *The Detroit News* logo on the side of the car and walked up, telling us that there was a fatality on the road ahead. He asked if we wanted to see. I grabbed my camera and walked up to a motorcycle, lying on its side. A blanket covered the dead biker and the cop said, "It's not pretty." I nodded and thought, "Nothing's pretty tonight." He pulled the blanket back revealing a body with no head. The cyclist's head had been run over by two cars, leaving only a strange appearing, dark greasy spot and blood forming a puddle on the asphalt road.

The killer's latest horror was soon discovered. The mutilated body of a thirteen-year-old girl had been found near the Eastern Michigan University campus in Ypsilanti, six miles from Ann Arbor. The serial killer's demons were sending him for new prey and more frequently. I raced to the Ypsilanti area to photograph the fear enveloping the two university towns.

A grad student at U of M was last seen at a party on June 7, 1969 and her body was found raped, stabbed and shot near Ann Arbor. Once again, the paper sent me. More details of the killer's savagery were revealed with each discovery. The police revealed that the killer cut the victims breasts off or bit them, that tree branches and panties were stuffed in their orifices. He was out there, not far from our backyard.

Free Love, Lust, and the Urge to Kill

Ann Arbor, like many college towns, is usually quiet during summer months. Most of the students are away on break, the university goes into hibernation, and a calm descends as residents sit back to enjoy a few months of peace and quiet. The coed murders changed the nature of both classes and summer.

When the U of M's classes were in session during the '60s, it was a hotbed of radical political activity, even eclipsing the radical campus activity at Berkley and Madison. It was the birthplace of the radical faction of Student's for a Democratic Society (SDS) and known as the Weather Underground, co-founded by the student William Ayers in 1969. There were ongoing protests and demonstrations against "the system." The participants had a flair for street theater and guerilla tactics, and although they could be entertaining their actions often ended violently. Squads of tactical police units fired pepper spray at the demonstrators, leaving them and onlookers choking from the gas.

The most prominent organizers of the protest were John and Leni Sinclair, the co- founders of the White Panthers, a far left, anti-racist political collective created in response to a comment by Black Panther co-founder Huey Newton. When asked what white people could do to support the Black Panthers, Newton had said they could form a White Panther Party. Sinclair took the bait, and name, and dedicated his energies to "cultural revolution" with the White Panthers.

One of the protests got out of hand and the sleepy summertime streets were struck by a series of bloody clashes between police and a motley crowd of hippies, radicals and others. The precipitating issue was a pedestrian mall, of all things, a "people's park" on South University Avenue—a four-block shopping district adjacent to the University of Michigan campus that caters to the student clientele.

The *Detroit Free Press* referred to the four nights of conflict in June 1969 as "The Battle of Ann Arbor."

I was assigned to cover it, and driving to Ann Arbor I felt relieved that another body had not been discovered. During that night and the following, I covered police fighting with young people on the streets. The police were aggressive and violent, and were not city police but rather the Washtenaw County Sheriff's department under a tough sheriff named Douglas Harvey. The protesters taunted and threw objects at the police. Large numbers of deputies in riot gear beat protestors and fired tear gas into the crowd. I was among those beaten.

My photos of the rioting were featured on the front page for several days, including a story in the *News* with my account of the sheriff department's overzealousness. I was quoted as saying that it was a police riot, countered by an account of Ann Arbor's mayor saying he was supportive of the police. In an open letter to the university community, he attempted to defuse anger at the police.

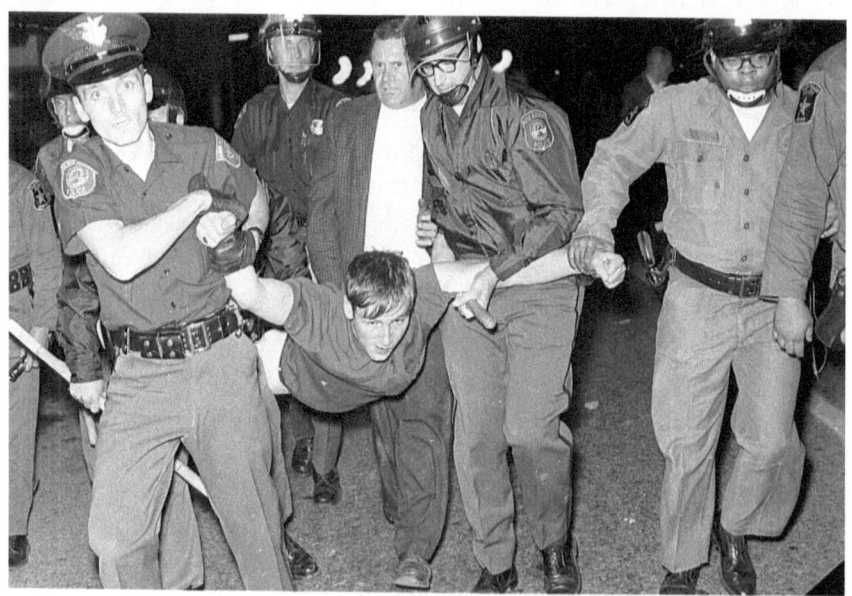

Protestor arrested in Ann Arbor 1969

My paper's page one story read: "News photographer Jim Hubbard disagreed with Mayor Harris's assessment. ... During the final sweep of South University Hubbard saw 15 to 20 cops chasing one man. One knocked the man down and other cops ran up and began clubbing and kicking him." When the paper hit the streets, the *Detroit News* editors received several anonymous calls threatening my life if I returned to Ann Arbor. The editors theorized that the threats were made by police and did not send me back until things had quieted down.

When I was next dispatched, another victim of the serial killer was discovered. On July 23rd, the second anniversary of the riots, the college student Karen Sue Beineman went missing after she left a wig shop and accepted a ride on a motorcycle from a man she did not know. Her body was later discovered in a ravine, strangled. Her face was badly beaten. She had been raped and left nude. The witness from the wig shop could identify the man on the motorcycle.

John Norman Collins was arrested for Beineman's murder after he was connected to the crime through evidence found in the home of his uncle, a Michigan State Trooper—where he committed the murder. Collins had been house sitting for his uncle who was away on vacation. I was sent to photograph him three times in court. He was manacled and escorted by two sheriff's deputies. When he was approaching me he usually had a smirk on his face that could only be described as "menacing evil." Once when he passed by I couldn't help but think, "I should waste this pathetic monster. I certainly have the chance. It wouldn't be hard and I'd be doing the parents of the dead girls a huge favor. The rest of the world to." I thought he symbolized evil incarnate.

• • •

Art Chernecki told me that there would be a position available for a photographer in the Detroit UPI newspictures bureau, and asked if I would be interested. I had long wanted a change to cover national and international stories that would include travel, possibly with UPI, not at a local paper. I resigned from *The Detroit News* started work at UPI two weeks later. UPI's motto stated "A deadline every minute." A wire service photographer had to be a hustler. An old friend from my professional life, Art became a routine figure in my personal life, as well. He had met Brijin a few times and, being a conservative man of Polish descent, was often quite amused by the saris she wore and her ankle bracelets and the toe rings. She was unlike anyone he had ever been exposed to before.

One of my first UPI assignments gave me an unusual opportunity. Several journalists were invited inside the local Black Panthers' inner city headquarters, which was surrounded in a standoff with police and surrounded by the time I arrived. Panther leaders thought it a good idea to invite newsmen into their headquarters, in case the police decided to open fire at the armed militants in the building. It was a volatile situation. I entered a room and photographed a man holding a shotgun at a window and facing police outside. The image showed a silhouetted man framed by a window, holding his weapon at the ready. It was an unusual situation for all kinds of reasons, but the one that most concerned me was that I might be with him during a gun battle with the police. I told the Panther that I had to leave, and as I walked toward the door, he turned to me and pointed his weapon, and gave me my cue to exit: "You're a honky kike." I didn't bother telling him I wasn't Jewish.

My friend John Collier, a *Detroit Free Press* photographer, decided we each deserved a break from our job and family. We decided to spend three carefree, reckless days away at a three-day music festival at Goose Lake near Jackson, Michigan—basically a Woodstock spinoff. There was certain to be public sex, drugs and booze. John and I had a bond that revolved around getting high. We felt like we led double lives, as responsible members of the middle class and as men with less responsible hippie values and lifestyle. Our families were close, too, and our wives had become close friends.

We drank too much during the festival. John's drug of choice was pot, and he was high all weekend. We mixed with the flower children, especially the females, who intrigued me with their sense of independence and commitment to being at the vanguard of the social, and particularly sexual revolution. They did not shave their legs or armpits, a habit that I thought primal and attractive. Humans are related to apes, after all, which are hairy enough—an attraction to unshaven women might not be *that* odd.

Over the free love weekend, many attendees were nude and couples had sex out in the open. The temptations were plentiful. I imagined myself at a dinner party decades later, with Aldous Huxley. I might ask him, "Isn't there a creator? Can we do whatever we want, without inhibitions that would interfere with complete sexual freedom?" Huxley might respond, "A philosopher who finds meaning in the world isn't concerned with a problem in pure metaphysics, he's concerned with why he personally shouldn't do as he wants to do."

"And you know this as truth, based on what?"

"For myself and most of my friends, the philosophy of meaninglessness is an instrument of liberation from a certain morality. We object to morality because it interferes with our sexual freedom."

John and I thought we had a great time at the festival, but the high was short-lived and we certainly did not get much rest. I felt guilty, like I was trying to do good but succumbing to bad instincts. As the apostle Paul had said, "For the good that I would I do not; but the evil which I would not, that I do." Or the other verse echoing in my mind, Romans 8:6-7, "For to be carnally minded is death; but to be spiritually minded is life and peace. Because the carnal mind is enmity against God: for it is not subject to the law of God, neither indeed can be."

Michigan's fall was always beautiful, and it was invariably great to cover a U of M football game. I drove to Ann Arbor to cover the Wolverines play Ohio State. The smell of the leaves on the trees and cooler temperatures lifted my spirits. It was October 1970. A delicious hot dog before the game, played in front of 100,000 fans, guaranteed a delightful day to be alive. Brijin and I had planned to host a party in our apartment after the game. On the drive back, I thought about rumors that had been circulating in our office that while there was a UPI bureau in Omaha, Nebraska with only staff writers and UPI wanted to open a news pictures operation there. I felt ready for a change.

SHOTS FIRED

I turned on the radio just as a report of a cop killing was reported, and suddenly heard a flurry of activity on the police scanner mounted on my dashboard. There was a confrontation between the Black Panthers and Detroit Police near a house at 16th and Myrtle on Detroit's west side.

I exited the expressway to find a payphone and call Brijin, as I had many times before, to say I was on my way to a story and might be there for a while. "You'll miss out on the party," was her response, and all I could say was that "I know and I'm sorry." I made a second call to my boss and told him about the situation; he said check it out—if it became explosive I should stay and cover. I had no idea what was to come.

Upon arrival I walked to where a large contingent of heavily armed police had surrounded the residence housing the Black Panthers. The police were using a bullhorn to demand that everyone inside surrender and step outside. One of the officers explained the situation and told me that if they did not surrender, the police would storm the house and it could get ugly.

As the hours passed the police waited for their brass to make a decision. The cops, having a "brother" murdered by someone inside the home, smelled blood, but they still needed the call for an assault on the premises. I debated whether or not to stay. Brijin would be upset that I wasn't there, and nothing was developing at the standoff. I started off to get another camera and color film, and as I turned the corner I saw fire and smoke billowing from the alley near my parked car.

I walked down the alley just as the fire department arrived. The trucks moved into position to extinguish the four burning police cars that the police had left near the barricaded house. I took a few photos and then decided to grab my color film, at which point Molotov cocktails, rocks, bottles and bricks rained down on the firemen by people hiding in the darkness. I ducked and huddled low to avoid being hit as the trucks made a hasty retreat. Objects sailed past me but at that point I didn't think anyone knew I was hiding in the alley. I was wrong.

When it finally registered that I was the only one in that alley except for the people who would object to my presence there, I knew I needed to get out fast. I was more scared than during the riots. I lifted my camera for a few more shots and suddenly the alley became terrifyingly bright. Two police cars exploded, sending huge fireballs skyward. Gunfire erupted as shells in the cars' trunks exploded. The exploding bullets from the trunks blended in with the shots being fired by hidden snipers shooting at firemen and police. I walked quickly toward my car down the alley. I stopped and turned around to look back and noticed three guys fast approaching me—I was the only guy around and lugging my cameras.

The trio was gaining on me, so when I reached my car I quickly opened the trunk, threw the bag inside and grabbed my loaded shotgun. Just as they emerged from the alley onto the street where I was parked, I fired the shotgun and they ducked back into the alley. I jumped in the car and sped off to circle back near the standoff, where more than a hundred police officers had assembled. I wasn't worried about the blast from my shotgun alarming the cops—it was just more gunfire from bullets exploding all around.

The siege lasted nine hours at the two story structure police identified as a headquarters of the National Committee to Combat Facism (NCCF), an organizing arm of the Black Panther Party in Detroit. I was there until the end, when the Panthers surrendered at about 4AM Sunday, cop killer with them. I photographed him being put in the backseat of a police car. When I arrived home early the next day, I described what had happened and asked Brijin about the party. She reported that everyone had a good time and that after a few drinks no one even noticed my absence. Brijjie was still sleeping and I snuck into her room, kissed her cheek, and crawled into bed exhausted.

I sold two dramatic color photos of the police cars exploding to *The Detroit News Sunday Magazine* that they displayed on the cover page for their story titled "When a Cop Dies," detailing the siege. I was proud that I had spent the entire night, while most people were quietly sleeping, capturing more of the great drama of a seething American city.

VANISHED

Events within a thirty-mile radius of Detroit had left unimaginable pain and suffering in their wake, and my own family was not immune to anguish and hurt. The last time I had seen my older brother Paul with his wife Carol was Christmas Eve at our parents, in 1969. He vanished without a trace after my dad's forced commitment to a psychiatric ward. My brother Mike was invited to have dinner with Paul and Carol in their home, but when he arrived Carol made excuses for Paul, and as they dined, anxiously waiting for Paul, his seat at the table remained empty.

Our mother started calling, worried. She would ask, "Have you heard from Paul?" She reported that Carol no longer knew his whereabouts. We all hoped that an explanation was forthcoming.

I wanted to leave Detroit for other adventures. I told Art that I wanted to go to Vietnam for UPI. He instructed me to talk to the big bosses in New York. I flew to New York and, once at UPI headquarters on 42nd St, asked the head of UPI's news pictures division if they would consider sending me to southeast Asia. They would, but for one glitch. Their policy prohibited sending married staffers with children to a war zone.

In late 1970, UPI offered me a transfer to the UPI bureau in Omaha. Once again, I flew to New York to meet with the head of UPI's photo operations, Bill Lyon. He asked me about the Nebraska post and I asked him in turn, "That's called flyover country, isn't it?" He took it in stride and described the area I would be responsible for; the carrot he dangled was when he said, "In addition to your primary area of responsibility, we would have you travel to breaking stories around the world." I thought I could handle spending a year or two in Omaha for the opportunity to cover the big stories I had dreamed of.

Omaha was more or less what I had anticipated when we arrived there in 1971. Brijin and I agreed we were not going to stay long, at most two years, and that we would make the best of the situation. With a surprise around every corner, I was about to cover some of the most explosive and dramatic stories of the seventies.

But in Nebraska I loved the rolling hills around Omaha and meeting the many wonderful farmers. Cows had long been my favorite animal and there were plenty in Nebraska. My background in rural life in the south as a kid helped ease me into a new comfort zone. I covered a protest in which farmers planned to symbolically dump corn in a river; they were outraged that the prices per bushel had plummeted and had decided to toss the lot rather than sell for less. The farmers, unlike city folk, were quiet and peaceful protesters.

I listened for hours to their tales of government greed as media gathered in anticipation of the act of dumping the corn. I grew impatient and told the farmer in charge that if they wanted to see their photo in the next edition of *The New York Times*, they had better dump the bushels soon, as deadlines were fast approaching. A radio reporter recorded the conversation and ran it on his station and next day my boss in New York called me with a stern reprimand for interfering with a news story with my suggestion they dump their corn in time for East Coast newspaper deadlines.

For the first few months I roamed the countryside, driving along deserted roads, appreciating the farmers in the fields and their livestock grazing. I would often stop to photograph a pastoral scene, some of which were published in newspapers and magazines. Sometimes I brought Brijin and Brijin Marie with me to be human figures in the barren farmland.

Having been a creature of habit at the Anchor Bar, I found an appealing bar in an old market section of Omaha, along its brick streets. It was called Mister Toad and I became a regular, sitting on a bar stool until last call.

PART II

"The house of the wise is in the house of mourning; but the heart of the fools is in the house of mirth." — Ecclesiastes 7:5

A Wedding, a Cyclone and Death

In October, Brijin's brother would marry in New Delhi and we would attend. My old friend John Collier and his wife, Sharon, wanted to visit India with us, so we flew to Detroit, dropped Brijjie with my parents, connected with the Colliers, and were off to India for a few weeks.

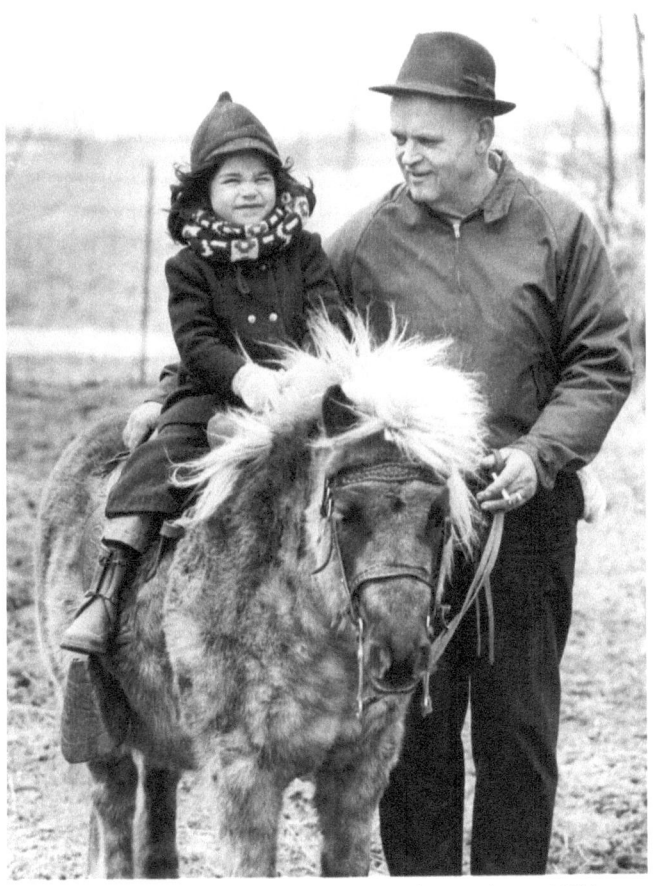

Brijjie with Jim's dad at his Michigan farm 1971

UPI told me that if a major story broke while I was in India they would give me extra time off for any time I spent to provide coverage. Tensions were high between India and East Pakistan, with rumors of war. In case the food was not to my liking during the trip I packed my favorite cuisine, jars of peanut butter and cans of StarKist tuna. Brijin considered the tuna and peanut butter a culturally insensitive act.

We stayed with Brijin's uncle, General Shivdev Singh, Air Marshall of the Indian Air Force, in his spacious New Delhi home. The phone was constantly ringing which had incoming and outgoing calls. One of the calls was for me, from a UPI editor in New York asking if I could cover a story in Bhubaneswar, near Calcutta, where a cyclone had lasted three days and killed upwards of 10,000 people. I consented, and he offered more details and instructions. Finding my way there, though, was my problem.

The wedding was spectacular, with giant kettles of Indian food simmering over outdoor fires; the feast fed over a hundred attendees following the Sikh ceremony. Shivdev, while planning for the wedding feast at his home, was also busy planning air strikes in Pakistan should India engage in conflict. At night, sirens sounded all over the city to warn citizens and prepare them for warfare

John wanted to travel with me, and after nearly a day negotiating with Indian airlines just to purchase tickets, we arrived in Calcutta and secured a driver to transport us the 229 miles to Bhubaneswar. The trip by car took an entire day over crowded, two-lane dirt roads. Once in the vicinity, we rented what could be loosely described as a rickety, weather-beaten boat. The small boat's operator was himself a bit rickety, old and weather-beaten, and he guided the boat along a series of uninhabited islands. There was ample evidence that high velocity winds had roared across the islands, ravaging and shredding most of the vegetation and foliage, even removing the bark from the few remaining trees. Along the way we photographed dozens of bloated, blackened bodies floating in the water or lying on shore decaying several days after the cyclone had passed. The most we could tell of many corpses were whether they were adults or children.

Scattered everywhere were bodies: humans, cows and others. Debris was strewn across the water and land. Entire villages had disappeared, leaving no signs that human life had ever existed in the area, just rubble and wreckage from far away places brought to rest here. The deadly winds swept everything away with a vengeance.

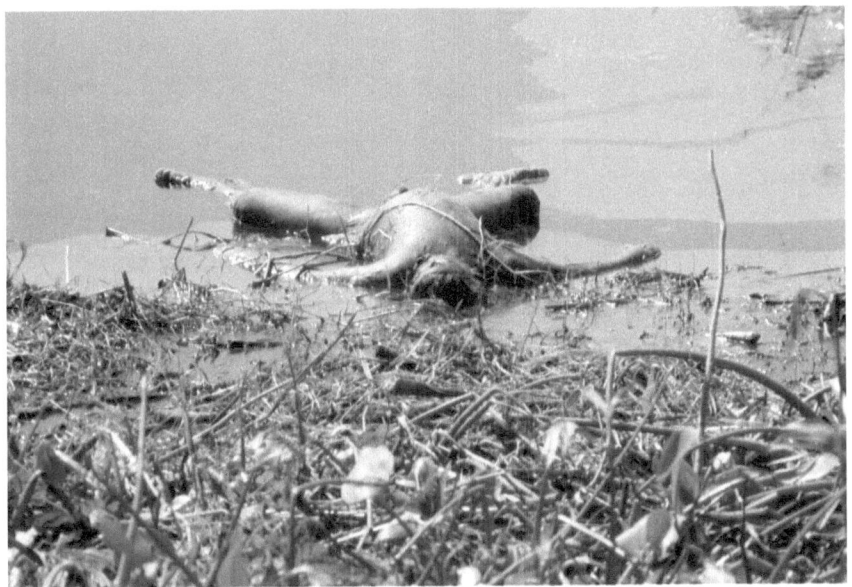

Cyclone victim in India 1971

We passed a few large groups of huddled Indians awaiting rescue, thin, hungry and thirsty. They had lost everything. We took pictures but could offer nothing. We felt helpless. Many of the survivors we saw would not live much longer. Their faces showed their agonizing sadness and utter hopelessness. It was raw desperation. The image and my helplessness haunted me for decades.

After traveling on the boat for several hours, I opened my can of StarKist tuna with a church key that I normally used to pop caps off beer bottles. I shared the contents with John and the boat's operator. There was no other food available anywhere. We had just been photographing survivors who were literally starving and severely dehydrated. I felt sick and disheartened. We could do nothing for them. I could only be grateful for the tuna and peanut butter I had brought.

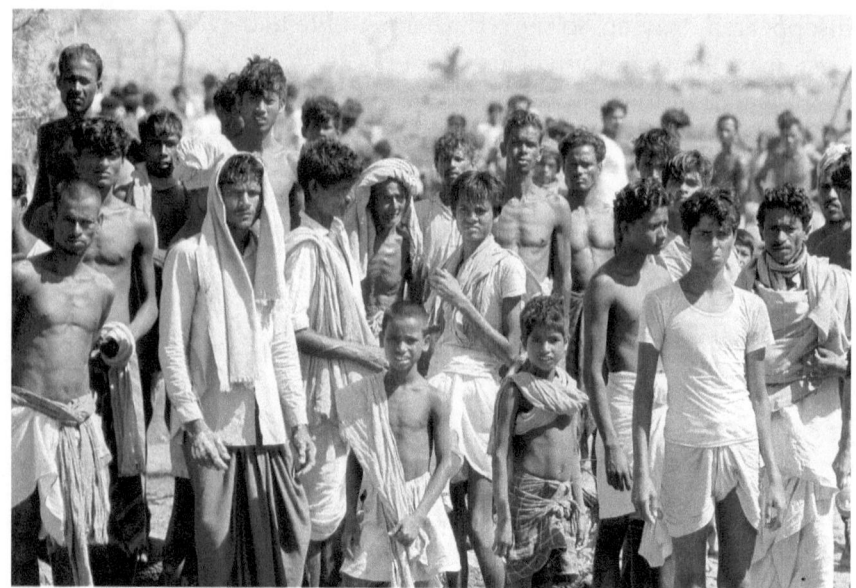

Cyclone survivors in India 1971

John and I made our way back to Calcutta, where I delivered my film to the UPI contact. We checked into a hotel and strolled the streets, our spirits low. Walking through the streets of Calcutta seemed like a journey through the circles of hell. People lying in the streets moaning and crying, many were sick, some dead. We returned to our room, pulled the mosquito nets over our bodies and slept. The next morning I looked out the window at people urinating and defecating in a river below the hotel. Others were cleaning their teeth with small sticks, then rinsing, in the same river. I couldn't help but think that these were some of world's most wretched living in subhuman conditions, the poorest of the poor. I kept thinking of scripture paraphrased, "What you do to the least, you do to me."

We returned to New Delhi and I called UPI from General Singh's home. A war between India and Pakistan appeared imminent and UPI asked if I would cover the conflict, should it ignite, while I was in India. After another week, UPI called and told me that they could not keep me on hold indefinitely and that I should return home.

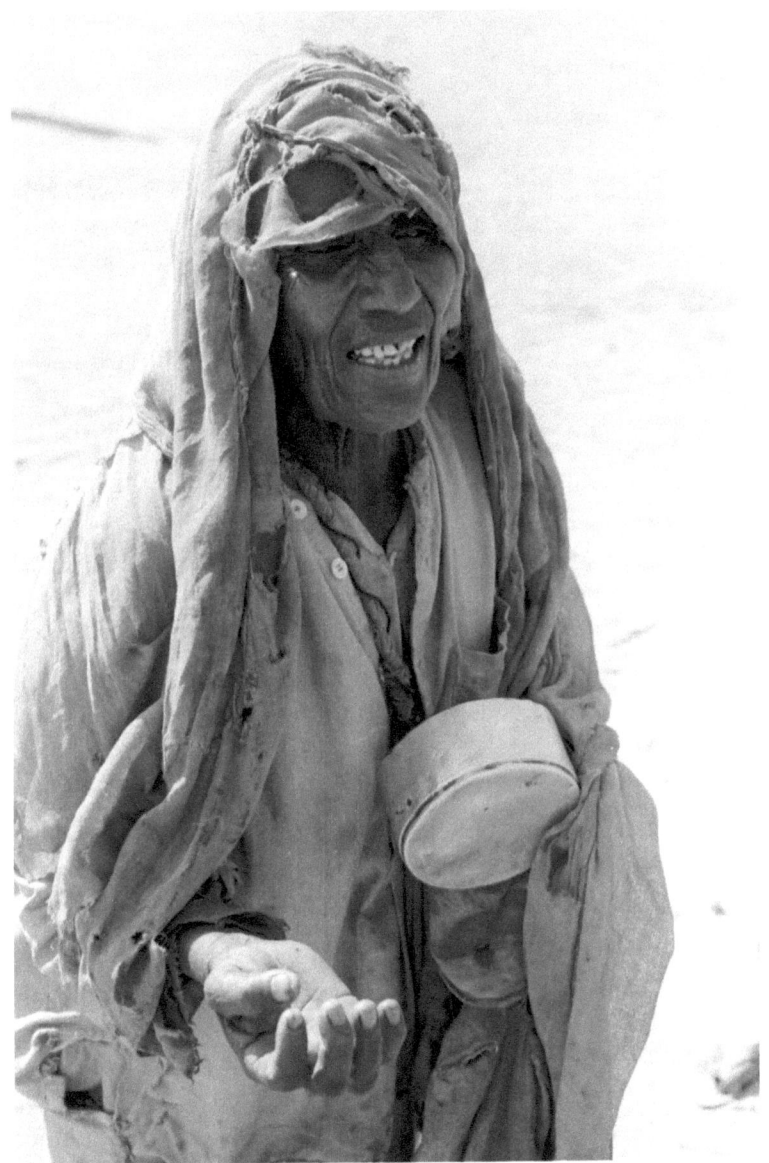

Beggar in Calcutta 1971

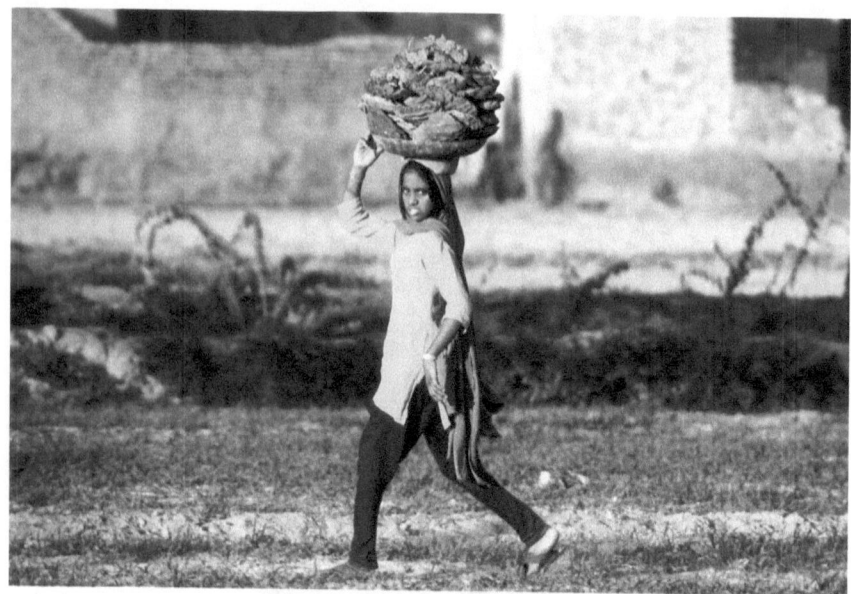

Woman carries cow dung in India 1971

A few weeks after our return to Omaha, the Indo-Pakistan war erupted, with India crushing Pakistan in thirteen days. The Pakistani Air Force had launched preemptive airstrikes on India, and Shivdev masterminded India's entire air operation response. East Pakistan, with a death toll estimated between 200,000 to three million, suddenly became Bangladesh.

In the prairie state, so different from a sprawling megalopolis, I had a moment to think and was caught in terrible confusion. The events I had seen in Detroit and Ann Arbor two years earlier prompted many of my worries about humanity and what a person should do to help others. A larger question surfaced, "What is my role in such a disorderly and unfair world?" Life isn't built for negative achievements, it is made for positive contributions. After witnessing so much death in India, and the scenes of fallen humans on the streets of Calcutta more intense than anything I had ever witnessed, I wondered what I could do, what contribution I could make? I prayed for guidance.

I continued my work creating a functioning photo bureau for UPI. For now, I wasn't eager for a major story—I'd gotten more than I'd bargained for in India, though the wedding was beautiful. Brijin and I were enjoying our life together and Brijin Marie brought continual joy to our lives. We had grown a network of friends, too, and had an active social life of dinners and parties.

One evening we hired a babysitter and attended a party, but shortly after arriving there we received a call. The sitter told us that Brijin Marie seemed ill. We raced home immediately. She appeared to have the flu, or a cold with a fever. We put her in bed with us and were falling asleep when we noticed that her breathing seemed strained. Brijin and I discussed if we should take her to the hospital.

Just after midnight, on a cold and snowy winter morning we drove her to Children's Hospital. I walked to the elevator carrying Brijjie in my arms and she looked up and smiled at me, which just melted me. To me, my daughter was the embodiment and affirmation of God's love. Even though she was sick, she radiated purity. I placed her in Brijin's arms so that she could take her to the room where she would spend the night. I headed to admissions, where it only took a few minutes to fill out the hospital forms. I then raced down the hallway to the elevator and when the elevator doors opened I saw Brijin sitting in a chair sobbing. Without saying a word I pushed the door open and witnessed a horrific scene.

It was like those terrible scenes I'd shot for the papers but this was a feature on my own life. I saw my daughter lying still, lifeless on the bed. Her face had turned into a bizarre, yellow-green color with vomit and saliva dripping from her lips. She had a peculiar pin, with a large opening at the top, piercing through the flesh of her neck and deeper into her throat, to allow air to enter. Several adults dressed in white stood over her handing medical instruments to each other in their frantic attempt to keep her alive. I rushed to the bedside and attempted to touch her. I saw what I thought was a glimpse of life, but I do not know, in all honesty. I panicked. It may have been one of life' mirages. The staff forced me out of the room.

Outside in the hall I hugged Brijin and asked her what happened. Brijin looked up and said, "She stopped breathing." A few minutes later a doctor walked in. It seemed like hours had passed since the doctor had gone to see our daughter, but it had only been minutes when he walked out again.

Without saying a word we watched him walk past us, down the hallway, toward the exit. I ran after him and grabbed his shoulder and screamed, "How is she?" He looked at me for a second, upset by my aggressiveness, and said, "I'm sorry, she expired. We couldn't save her." I turned and walked slowly toward Brijin, who was still seated outside the room in a quiet, dimly lit, extraordinarily lonely hallway. It was January 16, 1972.

I momentarily flashed back to 1969 to the father outside of the Ann Arbor morgue, and remembered his rants, when he saw me after viewing his daughter's murdered, mutilated body, in 1969. I now understood his rage toward anyone in view. I felt it. I was angry at the doctor, who had cavalierly walked past Brijin and me. I felt about to burst.

During the next few days, funeral arrangements were made and family members arrived from around the country. I will never forget the moment when I learned that the funeral home wanted us to send over the clothes we wanted our daughter to wear in the casket. I was catatonic. Brijin and I finally instructed a family member to retrieve the red dress from her closet and take it to them, the one she had worn on Christmas day less than a month earlier.

At the funeral I collapsed, sobbing over the coffin containing my daughter's body. Words cannot describe the grief and despair Brijin and I felt. The world darkened and would not again illuminate for many years. Like the mother and father I had photographed at the morgue in Ann Arbor, no photographer or writer could capture the loss. Why had Brijjie died? I wanted to trade, to have her brought back and me taken. Brijjie had made the world a better place. I thought, "Had Brijjie been destined for only a brief visit into this world? Was she ready to pass? Why am I the one still among the living?"

For the first few weeks after her death I just wanted to curl into a ball in my bed with the pillow over my head. I did not want to be in this world. It was a nightmare. When I could fall asleep it would only be for a few hours. I'd awake and pray, "Dear God, let this all be a bad dream and when I arise from my bed please let Brijjie be here. Oh please, please let this be so. I cannot live with this."

Days, weeks and month's passed with horrific slowness, Brijin and I were both numb, functioning like machines at best. I was void of intelligible feelings. In the evenings I knelt and prayed, like I had as a little boy. A Psalm of David in Psalm 23 prays, "Yea, though I walk through the valley of the shadow of death I will fear no evil: for thou art with me; thy rod and thy staff they comfort me." I was afraid. I believed myself to be evil. I thought, "Why not die now? Am I ready?" In that moment I was. God was not ready for me though, only for Brijjie.

In desperate need of solace and comfort, I pulled my Bible from the bookshelf and began to read from chapters I was familiar with from childhood. I turned to II Samuel, Chapter 22 wherein David's song of deliverance offered comfort and I read from verse 7. It said, "In my distress I called upon the Lord, and cried to my God: and he did hear my voice out of his temple, and my cry did enter into his ears." I continued and took long pause after reading verse 29, "For thou art my lamp, O Lord; and the Lord will lighten my darkness."

Many weeks passed before Brijin and I could enter our daughter's room. I remembered: "The Lord will lighten my darkness." When I finally entered her room I instantly felt a light shining into the darkness. The room gave us graphic reminders of her life and the magnitude of our loss, especially seeing her small clothes hanging in the closet, her toys and stuffed animals on the floor, her bed empty, even her scent. It was terribly sad yet there was also a sweetness that pierced grief.

To this day Brijin sometimes blames me for our daughter's death, for not having taken Brijjie to the hospital earlier. I blame myself for taking her to the hospital at all. No one knows for sure what caused her death.

I went back to the hospital a few months later in search of answers. The autopsy report had arrived in the mail and it said, "Cause of death was, officially, cardio respiratory failure due to a consequence termed anoxia, from an additional consequence labeled acute infection epiglotitis, listed on the death certificate in boxes a, b and c in the autopsy report. The medical staff brought her back to life two or three times before they ruled death." It was then that I realized that when I had walked in the room the morning she died, they had revived her the first or second time.

Those at the hospital who would talk to me didn't have any answers and probably thought we might sue. I wish I had, to punish their incompetence in the language they understood best: money. Adding insult to injury, I noticed that the death certificate listed Brijjie's ethnicity as Hindu, which is not even an ethnicity but a religion. I never showed the document to Brijin.

Brijin was angry and blamed God. I didn't blame God and believed there was no reason to question God. We simply do not know what happened. She could have died from an injection they gave her when she arrived at the hospital. She may not have reached the hospital in time. Regardless, God made the final decision. I was beginning to understand the views of existentialists like Sartre, who believed that there is no creator. He said, "Human beings have no essence before their existence because there is no Creator." He believed that human beings, through their consciousness, create their own values and determine a meaning for their life because, in the beginning, a human being does not possess any inherent identity or value. In my grief I was beginning to believe that life had no value. The loss of life's meaning in my life was born out of death. A belief in human meaninglessness is a form of death, without hope and void of the beauty exuded in a child. As time passed debilitating emotional pain lingered. I wrote my parents a letter after they called requesting pictures of Brijjie.

January 26, 1972

Dear Dad and Mom,

Enclosed are some pictures from Christmas showing Brijjie opening gifts. Included too, are a couple of Paul and Brijjie at the farm on New Year's Day. I wish now I had photographed Brijjie in color on Christmas and had photographed her with the two of you and Brijin and myself. But, as we all know, we didn't know what was ahead for Brijjie. I will probably never make another print, from a negative, of Brijjie. When I look at a picture of her it brings back the living memory of her live and now that she is gone I find it hard to accept her in any other way than living the happy life she has led.

If you do, however, need more pictures of her I will make them if you really want them. Brijin and I are holding our chins up as well as possible and I hope the two of you are also. I hope, Mom, you are feeling better and you should see a doctor as soon as possible for a complete checkup. Dad too, should have a checkup.

As I said, Brijin and I are doing pretty well but that little girl meant so much to me that I get sick to my stomach when I stop to think that she is gone forever. A sad thing is that I didn't even get to say bye to her in the hospital she stopped breathing before I could get back to her room from filling out the admitting forms. She loved her Mimi and Papa very much and I know you are deeply hurt too. But, keep your chins up because Brijjie would get so upset whenever she saw anyone crying or upset in any way. She doesn't want any of us to be sad and we must live up to what she would want.

If for no other reason at all, her death is going to make a better person of me. I am going to make sure of that. I have asked Christ to help me and Brijin and to bring me closer to him. We pray each night that Brijjie is taken care of in Heaven and I know she will be. I will never understand why Brijjie had to be taken, but even though she has, one positive aspect is that she had made me a better person even though her passing has caused so much hurt. Every now and then I become very angry that she was taken but I realize that God controls this world and what ever he wants is the way it has to be.

Brijin and I are trying to readjust our lives and we hope we can have more children as we have discovered that children bring so much joy to life. Once you have had children you discover that life is pretty empty without them.

Love, Jim

It would take many years for me to learn that if they don't kill you, sorrow and grief can make you stronger. Pain, not the joyful times, forces you to look at the world and oneself differently, maybe more compassionately.

Searching scripture again, trying to understand and cope, I came upon Ecclesiastes 7:3-4, "Sorrow is better than laughter: for by the sadness of the countenance the heart is made better," and in the next verse: "The house of the wise is in the house of mourning; but the heart of the fools is in the house of mirth."

I found comfort for my sorrow in the psalms, one hundred fifty chapters of poetic, profound prayers offering a mighty God who promises to be our rock, shield and wings. Brijin and I wanted another child as soon as possible. We felt desperate to replace our loss.

FLASH FLOOD, HAUNTING
AND ELECTRO SHOCK

One day I sat in Brijjie's bedroom and I stared at a colorful miniature carousel my daughter loved. I wound it up and it spun round and round. It reminded me of the world. My life had stopped but not the world. I was alive and needed to step back on. UPI had let me take several weeks off work to emotionally heal. I returned to work and for several months things were calm and routine. There were no breaking, dramatic news stories to chase.

Then one day when I returned home from work and Brijin was at the front door waiting for me. She grabbed and hugged me tightly kissing my cheek and screamed, "I'm pregnant." Stunned, I yelled, "Oh my God." Brijin was impregnated a few weeks after Brijjie's funeral, though I have no memory of psychological or physical efforts on my part required for enabling a pregnancy. I certainly had no interest in sex. In Job 1:21,"And he said, naked I came from my mother's womb, and naked shall I return. The Lord gave, and the Lord has taken away, blessed be the name of the Lord." I was elated though in a quiet melancholy way. But I couldn't wait to see another child in our lives.

Unfortunately, Brijin and I had become isolated in each of our internal sorrows and were losing the ability to ease the other's pain, to soothe or comfort the other. We desperately wanted reasons for this loss. There were none. I was in shock from our daughter's death and in sorrow and any joy had been swept as if pulled away by a strong ocean tide.

In June, five months after Brijiie's death, I received a 2AM call from UPI reporting a flash flood in Rapid City, South Dakota. I had come home late that night, having been at a bar consuming too many drinks, and had just dozed off when the call came. Brijin and I had both increased our drinking, and I mixed my drinks with a dose of Valium that a doctor had prescribed for anxiety.

The UPI editor instructed me to hire a private plane and make my way to Rapid City, pronto. All communications with Rapid City were no longer possible; the water crashing into the city had wiped out power and phone lines. The pilot landed at a small airport in Pierre, South Dakota. Still suffering from too much alcohol a few hours earlier, I had not made plans for how I would reach Rapid City, which was still 191 miles away. As luck would have it, CBS correspondent Bill Plante and his crew had arrived in a small plane from Chicago minutes before, and offered me a ride to Rapid City in one of the two cars they had arranged. Nearly 250 people had been killed instantly, after a heavy rain, a powerful wall of water cascaded down the Black Hills. Houses had washed away and cars were stacked on top of one another some were wrapped like toys around utility poles from the water's powerful force. I photographed the devastation and the survivors searching for loved ones. I had no idea that water could leave a town looking like it had been bombed.

Early in the morning, UPI told me to locate a temporary morgue for pictures of victim's bodies requested by European clients who had an appetite for illustrating death for their readers—a predilection not shared by most American publications. I entered a large garage at a city facility, where they were holding bodies for funeral homes to retrieve once identification was determined and funeral arrangements completed. It was wet inside with incoming bodies hosed down to clean mud and debris from them. In one corner there were bodies of several children covered by plastic yellow sheets. I took several photos of the stack of children with their little feet visible.

Walking outside I started to sob. I started to unravel, haunted by the dead children, flashing back to my daughter lying dead in a hospital room. On the fourth day, not having had a shower because our motel had no running water, I told UPI I needed to go home. UPI knew I had lost my child a few months earlier and let me go with kind words.

Time passes yet doesn't necessarily heal all wounds, at least not perfectly. Staying busy helped but didn't quiet the feelings in bed in a dark room at 3AM. Embracing grief head on, feeling its crippling grip, allowing the tears to rise from deep within and, ultimately, reaching acceptance is, no doubt, the most effective road toward recovery from loss. It's also the most frightening and seemingly difficult road. Indeed, I was busy with my work and traveling for weeks at a time. During the year I would travel for seven months. The stories I covered were often fascinating and challenging, but I was acting mechanically, not allowing for nor savoring any aspect of my life.

My next assignment was to spend two weeks in the Black Hills in Custer, South Dakota. Senator Gerorge McGovern, along with his family and staff, would be vacationing there after having received the Democrat's 1972 nomination for president. There would be ample time to relax and reflect in a gorgeous location. There would be few photo ops. I took only one even remotely interesting image of McGovern riding a horse. There was one newsworthy event. Halfway through the vacation, McGovern's running mate Thomas Eagleton arrived at the cabin and a crowd of journalists waited for several hours while McGovern and the vice presidential hopeful discussed recent disclosures about Eagleton's psychiatric history. He had undergone electroshock therapy while in a psychiatric hospital.

A short time later, the Democratic nominee for veep withdrew his candidacy at McGovern's urging. Eagleton had been besmirched with a damaging label. He was crazy, just like my dad was considered crazy after his stint in a psych ward.

I had been wrong when I thought nothing newsworthy would happen in the region, but not about the city per se. I covered several major national and international stories, none in Omaha. But I'd also seen far more of life than I'd ever seen in a dream or nightmare, while living in that quiet Nebraska town.

BLACK SEPTEMBER AND REVENGE

In early August a call came from my New York boss asking me to join the team covering the 1972 Olympics in Germany. He told me I would be in Munich for a few months covering the games themselves and pre- and post-game activities. My colleagues and I had ample time before the games commenced to bask in Munich's culture, eating savory meat and potatoes and drinking giant mugs of beer in the famous Bavarian Hofbrauhaus, serving suds since 1859 near the central square, Marienplatz.

The games were about as thrilling as you'd expect, and made all the more incredible by my luck at being assigned to all of the swimming competitions. Mark Spitz' events earned seven gold medals that year, setting a world record that would last for thirty-four years. During the second week of the games, at about 4:30 in the morning, three other photographers and I were awakened by a knock on our apartment door. We were told by a messenger to rush to the Olympic's press center and pickup long lenses and ladders for a breaking story. For the next fourteen to sixteen hours I either stood on the top rung of a six-foot aluminum ladder or I perched on a tree limb with a 400mm lens. We were angling for a clear view of the Olympic Village where several Israeli athletes had been murdered and others were held hostage.

In the early morning hours on September 5th, eight tracksuit-clad Palestinians, carrying duffel bags loaded with AKM assault rifles, Tokarev pistols and grenades, scaled a two-meter chain-link fence with the assistance of unsuspecting athletes who were also sneaking into the Olympic Village. Once inside, they used stolen keys to enter two apartments being used by the Israeli team, shot and killed two people and held the others hostage. The world was riveted to the television coverage for nearly twenty hours. The men were from a group called Black September, and the event was the beginning of international terrorism as we know it today.

For nearly fifteen hours I photographed the movements of the German police as they sneaked, crawled and ran to new positions on rooftops and behind bushes for a possible assault on the apartments. The terrorists, hoods covering their faces, frequently stepped out of the apartments onto the balcony and looked toward us; we were only a short distance away, separated by a cyclone fence. About two hundred of us clustered together, not taking our lenses off the scene for even a second, granting the terrorists exactly what they wanted: press.

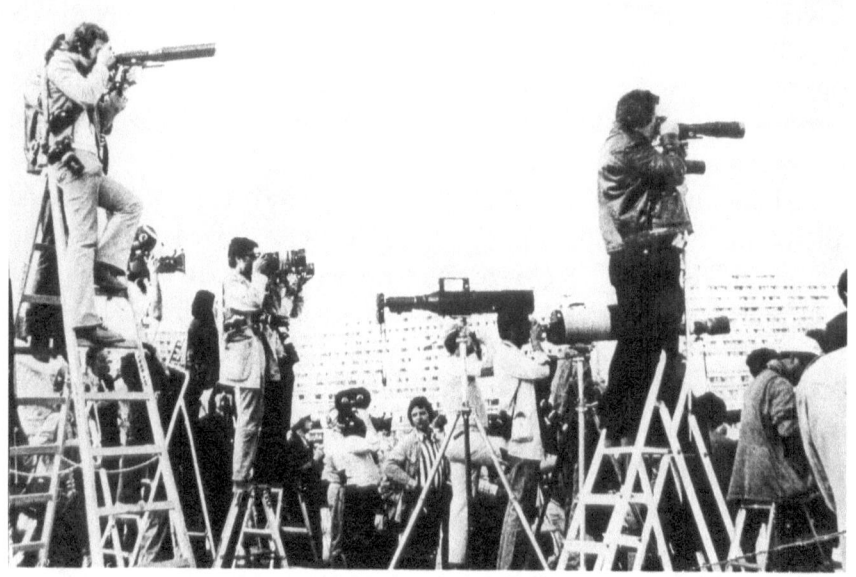

Jim on ladder(R) covering Olympics Munich Massacre 1972

It became known as the Munich Massacre. By the end of the ordeal, the terrorists had killed eleven athletes and coaches and a West German police officer. Five of the eight members of Black September had died. When I returned home I gratefully put away many of my recollections of the Munich Massacre—Brijin and I were anticipating the birth of our second child. We were excited and happy for the first time in far too long.

• • •

On October 30, 1972 Priya Singh Hubbard was born and I would not miss this wonderful event no matter what happened elsewhere in the world. Priya may have been a bit reluctant to enter the world, as she had a breech birth, her butt entering the birth canal first. Unlike Brijjie, she was fair complexioned and red haired, but she had her mother's dark eyes and she was full of life like her sister. I suspected she would be a handful. Brijin and I could not have been happier. She was born at the University of Nebraska Medical Center—there was no way we were ever returning to Children's Hospital.

My travels for UPI contiued and in March 1973 I was dispatched to South Dakota. A heavily armed, radical group of Native Americans, members of the American Indian Movement (AIM), began an occupation of Wounded Knee on the Pine Ridge reservation. They prepared for a fight when the US military and the FBI surrounded Wounded Knee for a seventy-one day standoff.

I spent almost two months covering the conflict between the Native Americans and government. Two Indians were killed and many wounded during the conflict, surrounded as they were by better armed Feds, who had armored personnel carriers (APC's) mounted with fifty caliber machine guns, helicopters and camouflaged snipers all along the hilltops overlooking the historic village. Journalists from around the world descended into Pine Ridge. Without lodging on the reservation, I secured a spot on the concrete floor of a Catholic church's basement in nearby Pine Ridge, where I could spread my sleeping bag, a few miles from Wounded Knee.

Native American lore is incredibly popular in Europe, Japan and other spots in the world, although many Americans don't give it a second thought, finding it easier to keep the existence of Indians—not to mention the high rate of abject poverty on many reservations—out of sight and out of mind. My first objective was to learn the lay of the land in the rugged, desolate Northern Plains. When I entered Wounded Knee I saw rundown shacks and old, weather-beaten trailers. There was a log trading post, more like a grocery store, that stood in the center of the village. It had one gas pump, but the large underground tank for containing the actual gas was bone dry. AIM used the Trading Post as their headquarters and armed young Native Americans, and a few white supporters, wandered in and out.

A white, wooden Catholic church named Sacred Heart was topped with a steeple and had a cemetery nestled behind it—the historic Wounded Knee burial site for victims of the 1890 massacre. During the occupation, bitter cold, and occasionally fierce, blinding blizzards limited visibility to no farther than the front of our car. Travel became impossible. I crashed my rental into a boulder during one of the many storms. The other journalists covering Wounded Knee had all rented cars from Rapid City agencies a hundred miles away, and many of their cars were stolen by the occupying Indians, usually found the next day in ravines, stripped of body and engine parts for the junkers that the thieves drove. After a few weeks, the rental agencies would not rent to anyone admitting they were going to Pine Ridge, as they had already lost over thirty vehicles.

I roamed the roads with young Indians, who kept their fingers on the triggers of their guns, and which were pointed in the direction of anything that moved and sometimes, at me. They remarked incessantly about how they wanted to kill the "White Man," not hesitating to add "even you." They said it so often that the threat lost its effect.

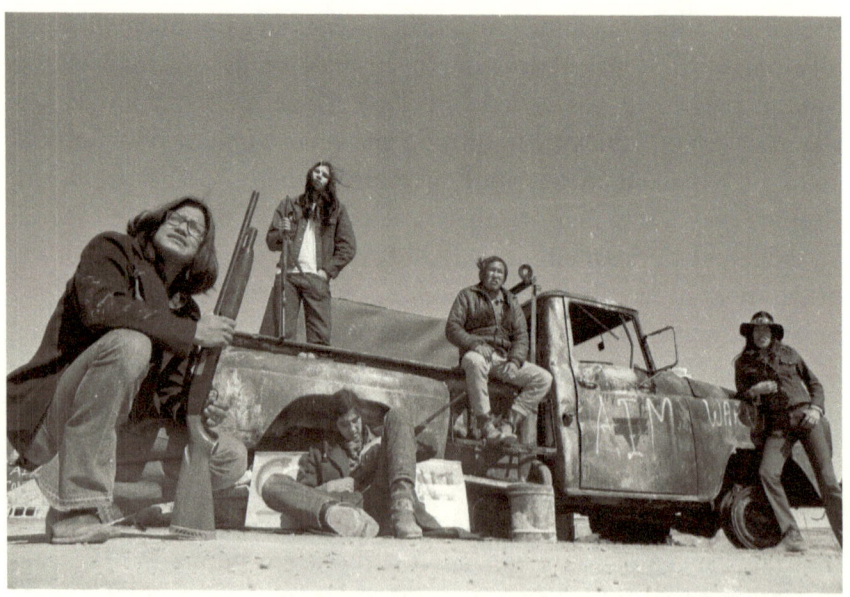

Indian militants roadblock during Wounded Knee siege 1973

Every morning I had to pass two roadblocks to get to Wounded Knee, one manned by the FBI and another, a mile farther, controlled by AIM militants. The men at both roadblocks inspected our cars every time, as well as did full body searches. The Feds also checked the fuel level of our vehicles and warned that if we used excessive fuel inside the Indian stronghold, we'd be prosecuted for aiding and abetting them. We always told the Feds that sometimes the Indians siphoned gas from our cars when they didn't have an opportunity to steal the whole vehicle. The Indians would always ask, "What do you have for us today?" In return for entry, they demanded at least candy bars and cigarettes, small things they knew we could hide them among my cameras bags. So before leaving Pine Ridge to Wounded Knee, I would go to the grocery store, buy cigarettes and candy and hide them among my cameras.

Another menacing force I encountered during the occupation was Pine Ridge's tribal chief Dick Wilson and his heavily armed goon squad. Wilson patrolled Wounded Knee to prevent supplies from reaching AIM occupiers. Wilson and his forces hated AIM and wanted them dead and held no fondness for journalists publicizing the standoff. They were somewhat cordial and allowed me to photograph them, but given the opportunity they would assure my disappearance from their reservation. When the occupation ended violence increased on the reservation, with residents reporting attacks by Wilson's goons. More than 50 of Wilson's opponents died violently in the next three years. Power and politics on some reservations nurture evil with deadly consequences.

Firefights during the evening hours raged. The Feds and Indians exchanged thousands of rounds of ammunition, almost never hitting anything they meant to. Near the end of the siege, US marshals estimated that in one day of firefights they fired 6,550 rounds and the occupiers fired 1,875. The drama lasted for over seventy days, giving the siege an aura of the longest theatrical production in history. I came to know many of the Indian actors quite well, including two of their most famous leaders, Russell Means and Dennis Banks. They would often ask me if I got the pictures I needed, we'd discuss their tactics, and they'd assure me of their cooperation. They also tried to teach me about the plight of Native Americans throughout American history.

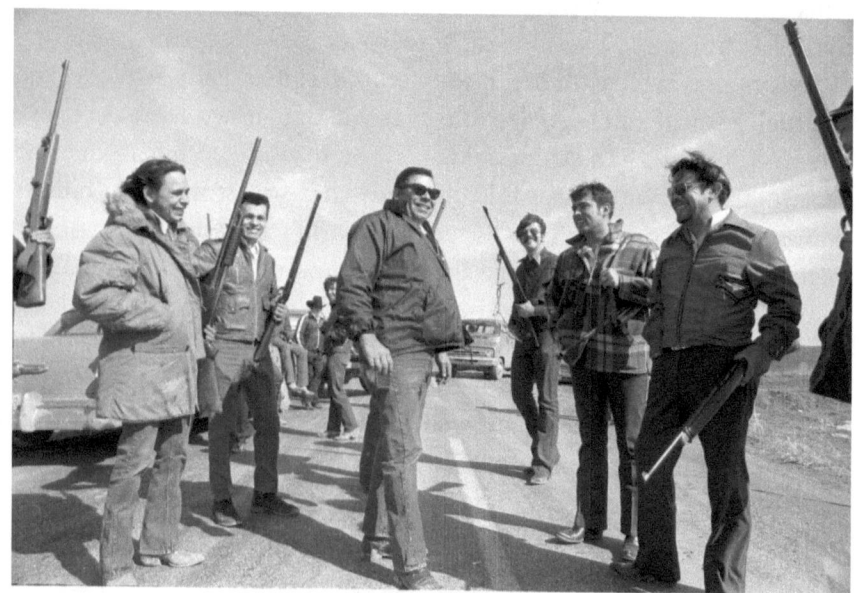

Dick Wilson (center) and his goons 1973

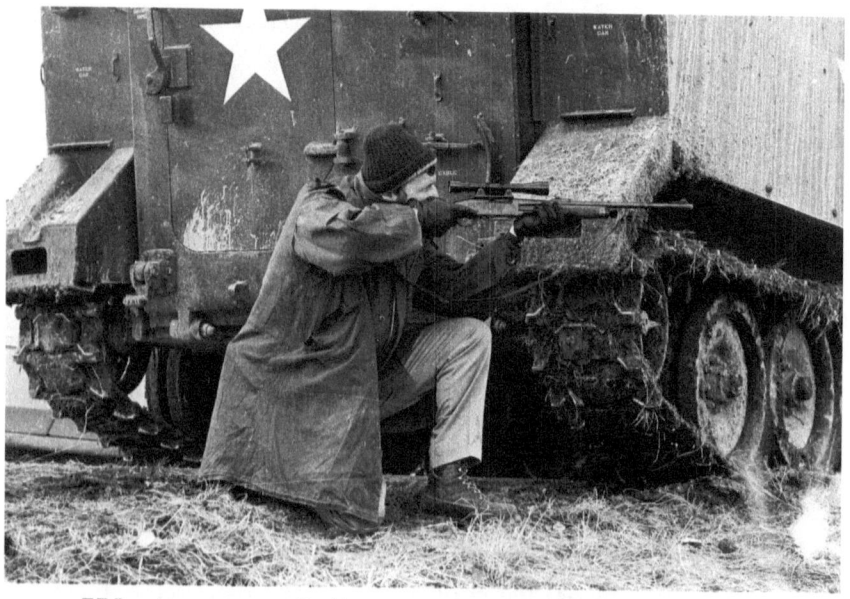

FBI sniper engages Indian occupiers at Wounded Knee 1973

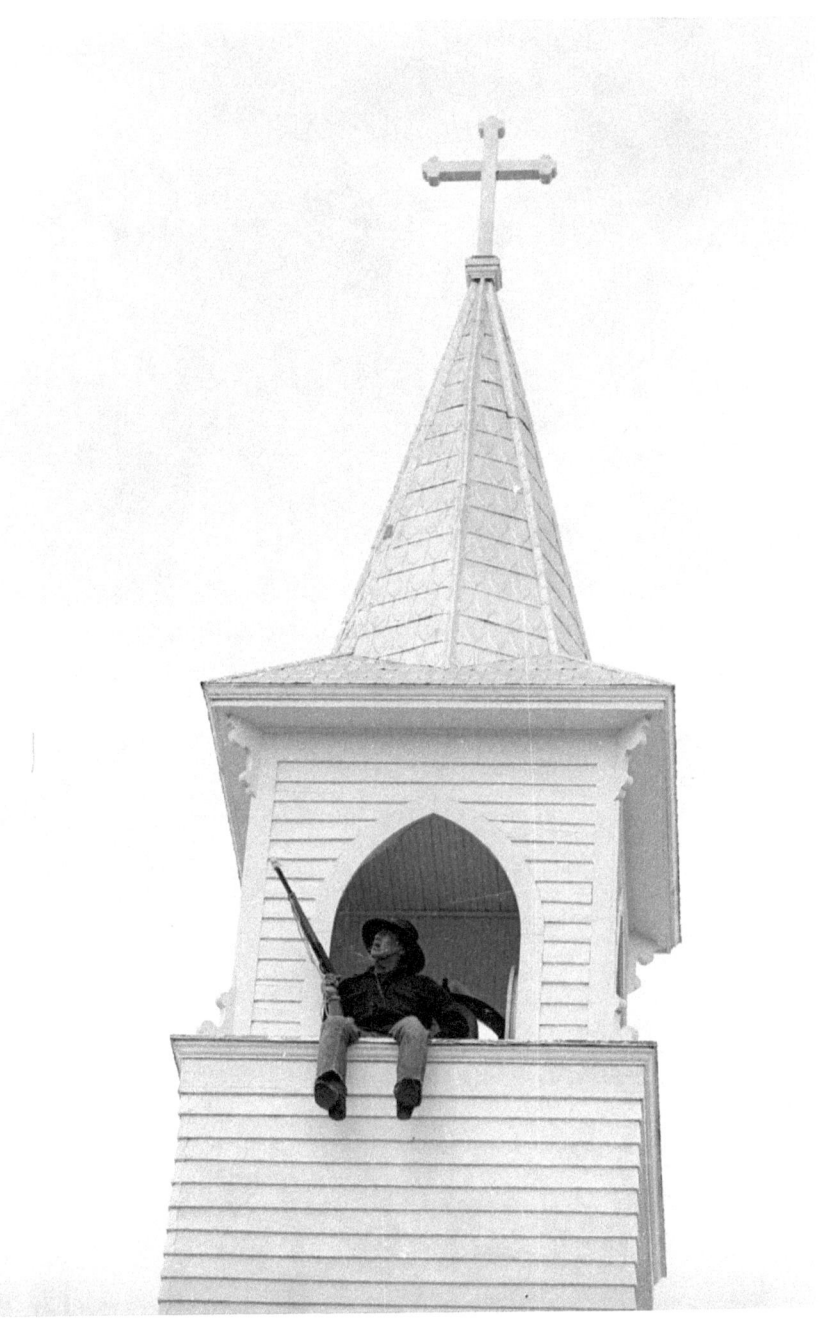

Indian with rifle on church steeple during Wounded Knee siege 1973

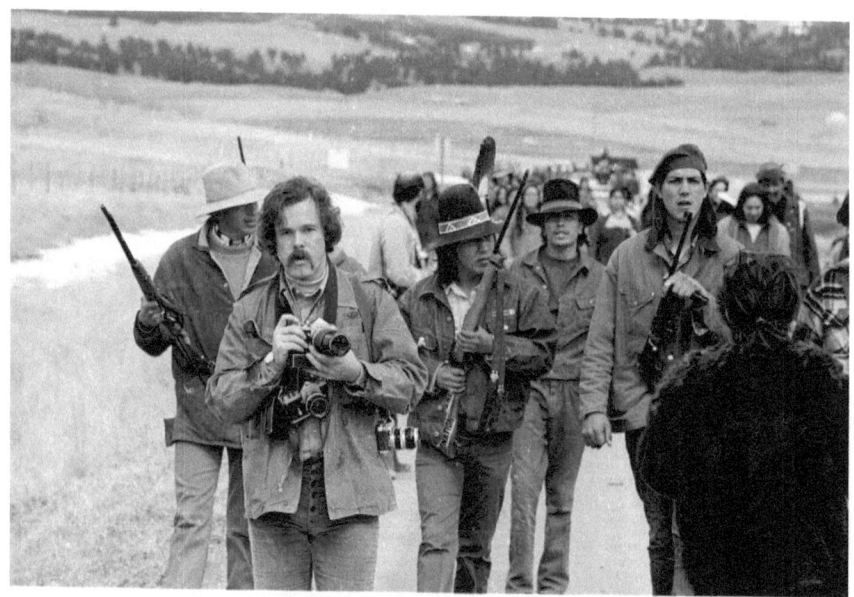

Jim (with cameras) with armed Indian radicals 1973

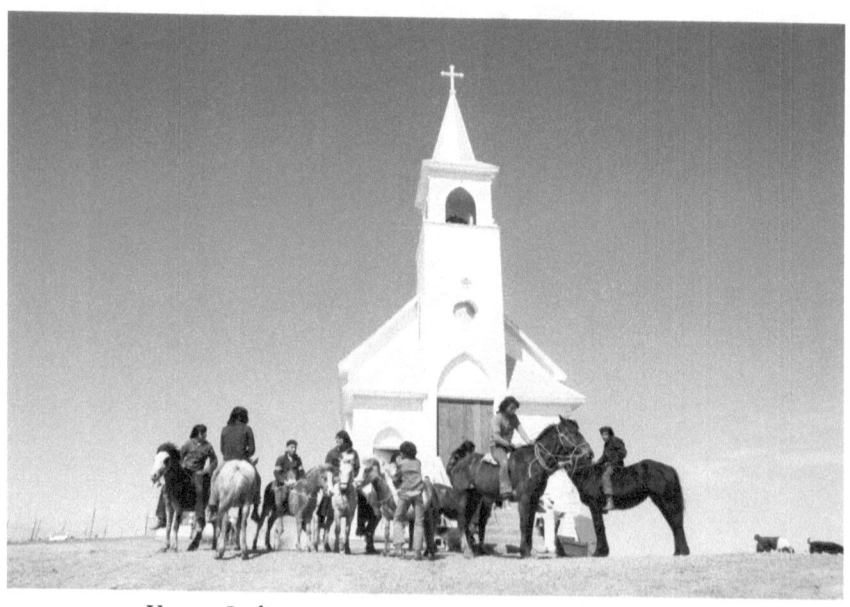

Young Indians on ponies at Wounded Knee 1973

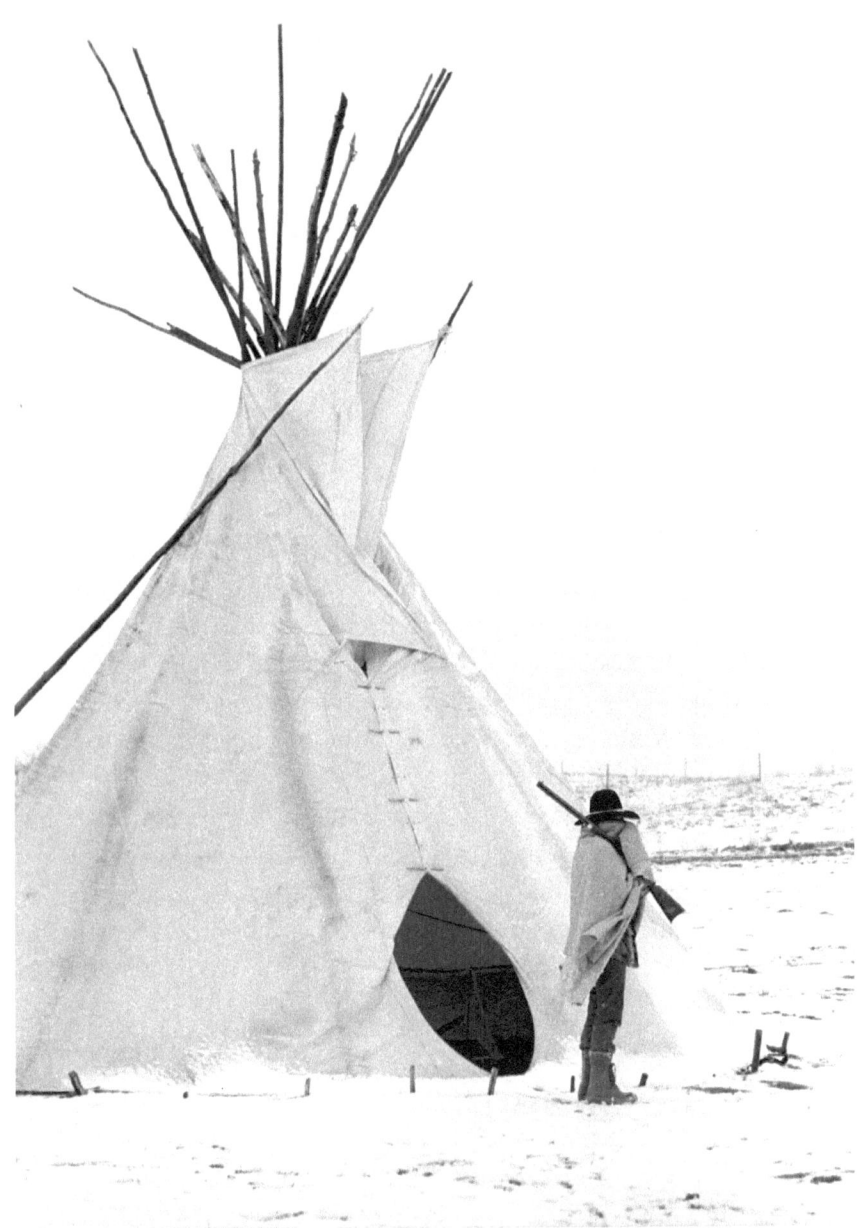

Armed occupier guards his teepee at Wounded Knee 1973

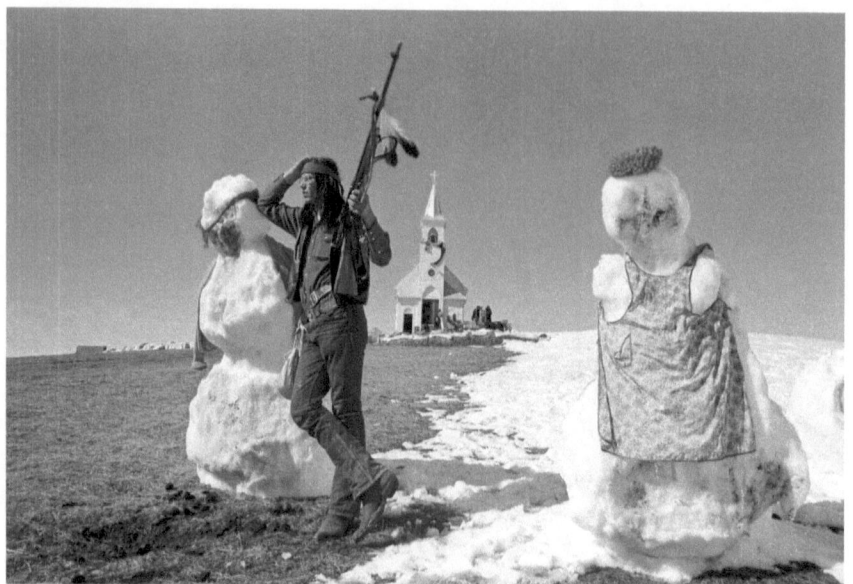

Armed Indian with snowmen at Wounded Knee 1973

Following the media sensationalism surrounding Wounded Knee, Marlon Brando refused to accept his Oscar for his performance in *The Godfather* and arranged for Sacheen Littlefeather, to speak on his behalf, as protest against Hollywood's treatment of Indians in films. Another Hollywood giant, Paul Newman, sympathized with the seizure of Wounded Knee and actually arranged to get supplies smuggled to the Native Americans.

As the Wounded Knee story wound down, UPI announced that they would be transferring me to St. Louis, Missouri to manage a two-person photo bureau. We had lived in a modest apartment for the last two years in Omaha and scraped together a down payment for a house in St. Louis. We wanted a yard for Priya to play in. We were glad to leave.

UNNATURAL DISASTERS

When we arrived in St. Louis, seemingly endless spring rains brought the worst flooding out of the mighty Mississippi in two hundred years. Flooded city streets claimed a few dozen lives. Each day, I ventured along the river in a boat, recording the residents sandbagging and protecting themselves from the rising muddy water. When the Midwest's frequent and violent thunderstorms rolled in to disturb the land's tranquility, they often left grim scenes in their wake, as when a passenger plane was downed three miles from its approach to the runway, clipping the roof of an apartment building and coming to rest in a wooded area. Eight passengers survived the crash; thirty-six died.

I sent my number two staffer, Art, to the hospital where the injured were taken, and I raced to the crash scene, heavy rain making the drive difficult. The carnage from the aircraft spread over a wide area of rain soaked, muddy woodland. Seats, mangled passengers and battered luggage hung from the trees. On one seat I could see an imprint of a passenger's scalp, strands of hair embedded into the plastic tray on the seat in front of where the passenger sat. I left unsure about ever letting a loved one near a plane again.

One evening a photographer friend named Jim Palmer, my competitor at the Associated Press, went out for drinks with me after a day spent covering floods along the Mississippi River. We talked through the evening, guzzling our time away. When the bar closed we drove over a bridge crossing the Mississippi to an after-hours joint near East St. Louis, an area as poor and dangerous as Detroit's inner city. We had no business going there.

We were the only white guys in the bar, though two young white women sat at the bar surrounded by several men. We didn't like the vibe and after one drink exited. A group of men had waited in the parking lot for us. They pulled knives on us. "Empty your pockets, honkies," one demanded. I had not more than a few dollar bills crumbled in a front pocket, but as I nervously pulled the wrinkled ball out the bills looked like a large wad of cash. One assailant grabbed it and they all took off running. A week later a young couple were robbed and murdered outside the bar. On the drive home, I started thinking about a need to stop my liquid consumption—nothing made my carelessness so clear as nearly being robbed and stabbed. It would take a cop nailing me for a DUI, or some other form of intervention to derail the binge drinking and derailing my life along with it.

On another hot day, thunderstorms pounded the city. I was dispatched to the discovery of three dead girls, found partially naked under a tree in a city park. Uncomfortable with the assignment, my heart started to pound; I didn't want to see another haunting crime scene of brutalized girls. Under a large tree lay three corpses covered by blue sheets. Police hovered. They were schoolgirls who had been returning home when the violent storm prompted them to seek shelter under the tree. When lightening struck the tree it instantly killed the girls. Some of their clothes had caught fire and burned their bodies. A horrible tragedy, but no traces of human evil.

• • •

In 1974, UPI transferred me to Minneapolis after only a year in St. Louis. Brijin and I drove around the chain of lakes running through the city's lovely homes and found a beautiful, safe neighborhood. Minneapolis, when not in the throes of its annual, six-month winter freeze when mounds of snow force the city to make sidewalks into tunnels, is a lovely city. Not much happens there in the way of national news, though; it's a city of sports, business, and weather. We found a lovely home, where Priya would have her own room, a yard to play in, and a lake to swim in two blocks away.

For the next two years I covered professional sports, namely the Twins, North Stars and Vikings. I started to like covering baseball for one selfish reason: running shoes. I got to know the Twins' legendary baseball great Rod Carew, who proposed a trade with me. Rod was a superstar and was showered by shoe manufacturers like Nike, New Balance and Brooks. He wanted photos of his action on the field, and would give me his expensive running shoes in return, as I'd taken to jogging around the lakes for exercise.

I started to think that floods were following me everywhere. From India, to Rapid City, to St. Louis, and, now, in Minnesota where the waters started rising. I was dispatched to heavy floods along the Mississippi River, in Red Wing and Rochester and, weeks later, I saw even more flood assignments in North Dakota. Occasionally, I'd cover the wreckage of twisters in Nebraska, Minnesota, and Wisconsin.

Priya had just turned three when her mom and I divorced, our relationship having long gone sour and festering. The "irreconcilable differences" were real. We had been drinking too much alcohol, far too often, and after an evening drinking we'd almost invariably fight. Our fights were not healthy affairs, working through issues. They were disasters that tore the seams of the relationship. She harbored angst about our daughter's death and blamed me. My own guilt had taken its toll on me. I do not think I blamed Brijin, but she felt the need to understand what happened, and I was the closest, most logical target to blame for the tragedy.

One of Priya's earliest memories was one such fight. She walked into the kitchen and sensed my anger from a fight with Brijin. She said to me "Just think about it, dad." Brijin and I crafted our own settlement and agreed to the terms of shared custody. I gave Brijin the house with no strings attached, and left. Priya and I spent many afternoons by the lake, a few blocks from where she lived with Brijin. I often photographed her and one showed Priya playing in a park. The Minneapolis Tribune ran it on their front page.

Loneliness sucked the life out of my small apartment, so I'd spend my time in all my favorite bars. One winter evening the police pulled me over, with the officer asking, "What's your problem? You ran a red light." I just looked at him and said, "I'm drunk." After he determined I lived a few blocks away, he just told me to go home and I drove away. Too many painful hangovers wore at my constitution. Mixing alcohol and Valium was plainly dangerous, and the anxiety attacks only increased, now enhanced with a sense of impending doom. I wondered if I would I lose it like my dad. I made an appointment with a specialist in chemical dependency at St. Mary's Hospital.

The counselor, a woman named Margie, expressed concern about my drinking pattern and concluded it was binge drinking, rather than all day, everyday alcoholism. She suggested outpatient treatment. She talked about her "umbrella theory." She added, "you have to remove the alcohol to find out what's going on underneath the drinking. You're concerned that you may be crazy, but we can't know until alcohol and drugs are removed." I liked Margie, a no bull woman and definitely very street smart. I chose outpatient.

In May 1976 I entered treatment at a local hospital, attending group sessions five days a week for four hours over four weeks. Minnesota was a mecca for recovering addicts. Movie stars, politicians, and others traveled there to dry out in world-renowned Hazelden and other facilities specializing in chemical dependency. As I was about to enter recovery I got the exciting news that I had again been selected to join the team covering the '76 Olympics in Montreal. Until now, it seemed I could do no wrong. With fear and trepidation, I called my regional supervisor, Ray Macchini, and told him that I wouldn't be able to work some evenings as I would be in treatment for chemical dependency. I assured him that the program would be completed in time for me to join the UPI team for the Olympics in Montreal.

Ray said not to worry, and I knew something bad was in the works. When Ray had used these words before, there was usually something I needed to worry about. We never had a cozy relationship and didn't like each other's style. In some ways, I felt bad for him; he had to manage me from 400 miles away in Chicago. Had he asked my mother about such a task she would've only said, "Boy, you just don't know. With that boy you just don't know. It wasn't easy."

Following treatment, I quit the drinking and the Valium, for twenty years substituting the habit for drugs with regular AA meetings. Margie also suggested that I attend meetings in a grief group. One thing I loved about AA meetings was a key element unfortunately missing in most churches. When people entered we all understood we were flawed regardless of rank or status. It mattered not at all whether you were a prominent attorney, on the top floor of a prestigious law firm overlooking Manhattan, or working under streets below cleaning sewers. We only needed to know your first name. Everyone was a garden variety abuser of chemicals with a broken past. Just like those attending church but maybe with a drug addiction. Those who entered the doors of an AA or NA meeting knew their lives were unmanageable. Those entering churches are also flawed, but may not realize the unmanageability of their lives. The 12 step programs understand that participants sedate themselves to cope in an unmanageable world like a lost, self indulgent child.

Margie invited me to a graduation ceremony to be held in the hospital the following week to honor the patients who had completed treatment. I planned to attend, proud to be on the road to recovery and a better life. But a call from my mother set me off immediately to Detroit. My dad had become unpredictable again, threatening violence. My brother Mike and I planned to meet and drive to see our dad, unannounced. Mike was flying in from DC where he was a police detective.

We surprised dad, who grew instantly agitated and, being a perceptive and paranoid man, knew why we were there. We talked briefly before he reached above a China cabinet in the dining room, grabbing a loaded revolver. We demanded he hand us the gun but he only glared at us and yelled, "You think you're tough." Mike moved toward him, like he'd done with others many times as a cop—though not always with success and never with his own dad. As I talked to our dad, Mike grabbed the gun. After a short discussion, dad said he wasn't going to do anything with the gun and we drove him to a hospital. He was put in a psych ward at University of Michigan's hospital in Ann Arbor, where he would be confined for several weeks.

We drove our mom back home and spent the night with her. My dad had been experiencing serious physical problems, which were exacerbated by his mental problems. My mom fell asleep on the sofa, Bible open in her lap, and I noticed several lengthy, unfinished letters to her son, all beginning, "Dear Paul," address unknown, pleading for her son to contact her and telling him how much she missed him. I felt like I needed to drink, but instead flew back to Minneapolis in time for my rehab graduation ceremony. I was deeply saddened by my dad's condition and my mother's agony over her first son's disappearance. She hadn't heard from him in seven years.

I first learned the Serenity Prayer in treatment and AA meetings. The words are beyond priceless: "God grant me the serenity to accept the things I cannot change, courage to change the things I can, and wisdom to know the difference." This has been my silent mantra repeated thousands of times over the years, right up there with the

Lord's Prayer. Knowing what you can and cannot change became the central guide to wisdom for me.

I had written several letters to UPI's top management in New York requesting a transfer to Washington DC, New York, or San Francisco, realizing that Minnesota's opportunities were limited. I thought my request should be granted, and my ego had been boosted plenty, as UPI's newsletter for employees had written only a couple of months earlier: "If Jim Hubbard is ever run over by a truck, it would take five photographers to replace his photographic contributions."

• • •

The evening before my scheduled departure for the Olympics, bags packed, Ray Macchini called to tell me I was being pulled from the assignment. Stunned, I asked why, and he replied, "We don't need your kind of problem there." I told him to put it in writing and thought about his implied message: "It's okay if you have a drinking problem, but don't tell your employer about it."

Within two days I received a letter, no doubt drafted by a UPI attorney, affirming I had been pulled from the Olympics. It went on to state, in part, "Be advised that if you should fail to make the grade, your job may be placed in jeopardy." UPI suddenly was hoping I'd be run over by that truck. They were quick to let one fall from grace. From this point on, work soured. UPI started building a case against me and sent more and more letters criticizing my performance. Whereas they had never shied from praise before, as I won awards and genuinely tried to do my job for them well, they could see no redeeming feature in me now. The letters continued for months and I responded in kind, arguing against the criticism in my burgeoning personnel file.

As a dues-paying member of the Wire Service Guild, our union affiliated with the AFL-CIO, I complained to officials about the ongoing conflict, feeling harassed by UPI management with threats to my job security. The Guild agreed. The war of words between the union, UPI and me intensified. I would have to be an idiot not to know my days were numbered, but I fought against a termination anyway.

In 1977 Macchini visited me in Minneapolis with the sole purpose of asking for my resignation, as he later admitted. He was impeccably dressed, two glittering finger rings worn below his recently manicured nails. He never got his hands dirty—reason enough to dislike him. He took me to the Little Wagon bar, a watering hole for Minneapolis newspaper employees, a block from the Minneapolis *Star & Tribune*. Macchini said, "If you don't resign, UPI will fire you even if it takes five years. Nothing can save you." I declined, and UPI and union officials continued negotiating, delaying UPI's hand.

Feeling undermined by UPI, I decided to uplift my spirits at one of my favorite restaurants, the Black Forest, which reminded me of the good times of Munich. I placed my order with a waitress named Sherry, who I'd seen many times when I used to sit at the bar. She was from rural Minnesota and, like many people of the region, of Norwegian descent. When I finished my meal I asked if I could take her picture—about as lame a line as a photographer ever delivered. She smiled and asked why. My response flew out before I could stop it from leaving mouth, "Cause you're a woman ordained with classic Scandinavian beauty."

We were off and running. On one of our early dates we spent the entire Fourth of July having a picnic at her friend's cabin by a lake in Wisconsin. Her friend also worked at the Black Forest, and as the day progressed they must've drunk gallons of German beer. I'd only recently completed treatment and was still attending AA meetings, and on our drive home I realized she was still tipsy. I thought of it as her business, while mine was staying sober. I knew it might be a problem, but felt strong enough to cope.

We married in Blooming Prairie, Minnesota, where Sherry grew up as one of eleven children. This time my bride wasn't pregnant and I tried to keep my eyes clear and my choices lucid. I was determined to make this one work and thought that a ceremony in a church would be a greater insurance than signing papers before a judge, like Brijin and I had done. As if in line with my own determination, the pastor required us to meet with him to discuss commitment and complications that arise over the years in every marriage. We had a ceremony in the Lutheran church where Sherry's family attended.

My daughter Priya participated in the wedding and I took some comfort that Sherry could help raise Priya as a stepmom. We borrowed some money from my parents for a down payment on a house only a few blocks from where Priya lived with her mom. I wanted to be close to Priya, and, perhaps atone for not having spent more time with her and with Brijjie when I had had the chance. I had become neurotically, consumed by the need to protect Priya from any danger, sometimes sitting in front of her house until the wee hours of the morning, frightened that her house would catch on fire, and that I would have to be alert to save her life. It didn't matter that I had been with Brijjie and couldn't save her.

It wasn't an everyday issue, but Sherry still liked to drink. She always indicated if she thought it was a problem she would consult with a therapist. We later joined a couples support group at a church we sometimes attended. The leader was skilled and the group seemed relaxed and open in our first meeting. One couple, Bill and Barbara, became instant friends.

Bill was a preeminent Scandinavian Studies professor at the University of Minnesota. Barbara was a well-known peace activist. They had a son named Jesse. We socialized often and Sherry went with Barbara to some demonstrations against the arms manufacturer Honeywell Corporation. Bill, who practiced Buddhism and years later committed suicide by setting himself on fire, liked to drink to excess. Barbara mentioned in a group session that she had concerns about his drinking. I believed AA had saved my life, and thousands of others trapped in addictive, self-destructive misery, and shared that information with Bill and Barbara.

Sherry announced she was pregnant. Our daughter Hanna, a blonde haired, brown eyed beauty, was born on October 14, 1978. Priya and Hanna became instant playmates and I took thousands of photos of them doing silly, playful things together. When I announced the news to my parents, my mom could barely keep steady between happiness and deep despair, "You sure are busy. I want to see her— have you heard from Paul? I sure don't know why he left all of us and won't contact us, it breaks my heart."

Dad's health deteriorated after he left the psychiatric unit. He developed diabetes and prostate cancer, undergoing castration surgery to slow the cancer. Mike and I visited several times as his condition worsened, sometimes bringing our families with us. Our last visit before my dad's death did not go well. He got angry over a minor incident, repeating the words he'd said with a revolver in his hands, "You guys think you're tough." He sat raised up in his chair, acting like he wanted to fight, and even went on about how I was being aggressive by sitting erect on the sofa across from him. Mike started yelling at him, and dad shouted at us to get out of the house. We made the long drive back to our homes, sad and embarrassed. I knew that Sherry's family was much gentler and calmer; they kept their feelings to themselves, which was alleged to be a value among Scandanavians.

KILLING FIELDS

Shortly before Thanksgiving 1979, I watched a news story about the horrible conditions along the Thai-Cambodian border. Pol Pot had slaughtered millions of Cambodians. The news showed survivors fleeing into makeshift refugee camps on the border, escaping with little more than the tattered clothes on their backs, at best carrying a tin pot or kettle through the mud and disease.

I had to go. Not to build my career, but because something had shaken inside me. This was something more than just work for the news, which employed a "shock and awe" strategy to draw eyes to paper. The hungry, sick and dying being cared for from humanitarian efforts would be my focus. There might be shock and awe, but that would not be the point. I had no papers to sell. UPI wouldn't send me; they already had Asian staffers at the scene and wanted me off their payroll—my career at this point could only be described as "survival."

The prospect of this trip felt like a revelation of purpose, what I had dreamed of as a little boy, to help "the least among us." I called Macchini and told him I'd be taking three weeks of accrued vacation time immediately. I started researching which organizations were operating in the camps to provide food, shelter and medical care for people sick and dying in the camps. I read a story in the local paper about the American Refugee Committee (ARC), a group founded by a Chicago businessman and headquartered in Minneapolis. They were right across the street from my office.

After work, I met the staff at ARC there and helped stuff envelopes with descriptions of the group's efforts and appeals for donations. The second day I carefully reviewed their materials and started to learn the scope of the work. I told them they needed photos to illustrate what they were doing. They were trying to recruit volunteers from the medical community to travel to the first operational refugee camp in Khao-I-Dang, near Aranyaprathet on the Thai-Kampuchean border. They'd already sent one team of doctors and nurses and were sending a second team in a few days.

I proposed a deal: if they allowed me to travel with the next medical team, I would provide pictures of them attempting to save the survivors of Pol Pot's genocide. The only string was that I'd be going as a freelancer, pro bono, not representing UPI. They agreed to send me with the medical team on a government chartered DC-10 humanitarian flight from San Francisco. A week later I boarded a plane in Minneapolis en route to San Francisco to meet the team. Fifty doctors, nurses, and one dentist would be on the long flight to Bangkok, no other passengers. We had enough room to play catch with a football. One nurse traveling with us was Joan Baez' mother, and we all met Joan when she bid farewell to her mother at Travis Air Force Base.

Children were dying daily in the camps often followed soon thereafter by their mothers. They succumbed to disease, infections and malnutrition. Soldiers were being shot nearby and the wounded brought to the Khao-i-Dang camp. The war between the Khmer Rouge and Khmer Serai guerillas kept up unabated. I ventured into the jungle one day, not straying far from the refugee camp, but heading inside Cambodia. I stumbled into an encampment where about thirty camouflaged guerillas were cleaning an arsenal of automatic weapons. They offered me a drink from a pot hanging over a campfire and I sat with them taking pictures, no one speaking. When shots rang out nearby, we hit the ground and each soldier grabbed his weapon. When I walked back to the camp a pickup truck sped by to pick up a fallen soldier.

Each day, over 1,600 frail refugees walked into the camp from the Cambodian killing fields, swelling Khao-i-Dang's refugee population to 80,000. Every night, as I left the camps, I knew that many of those I had photographed mothers and their small children, soldiers and young people, would die before sunrise the next day.

When I made it back to Minneapolis on Christmas Eve I made a vow: I would never return to my previous way of life after seeing that carnage. That Christmas, while Sherry, Priya and Hanna were happily opening gifts and enjoying our reunion, I knew I wanted to spend my energy ameliorating grim human conditions, to face suffering's haunting toll and work to end it.

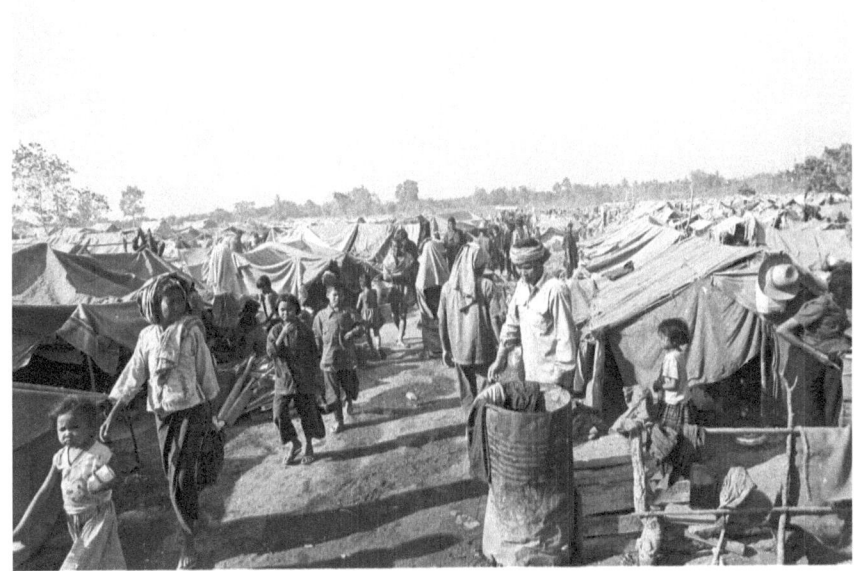

Refugees fleeing Pol Pot at makeshift camp on Thailand border 1979

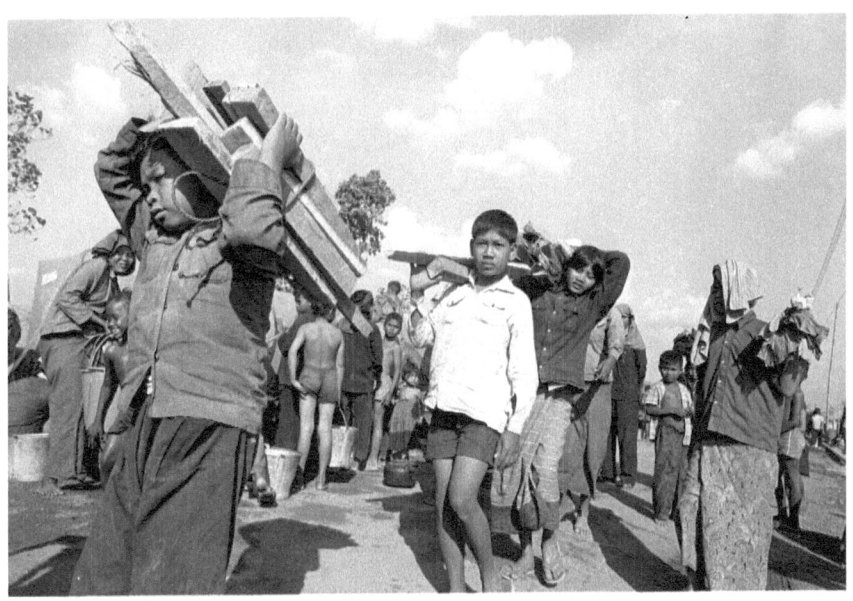

Cambodians arrive at Thailand border fleeing Cambodia 1979

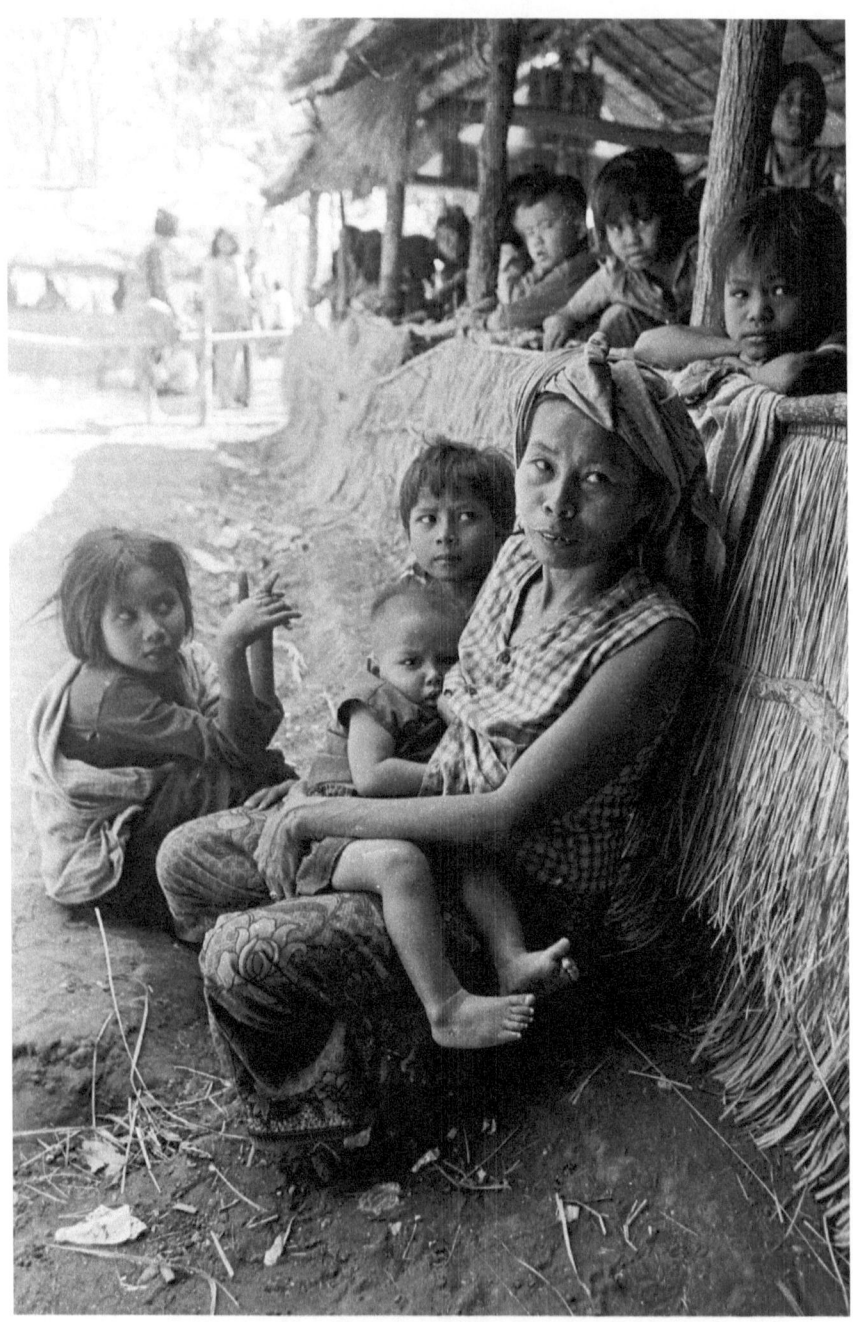

Cambodian refugees wait for medical aid 1979

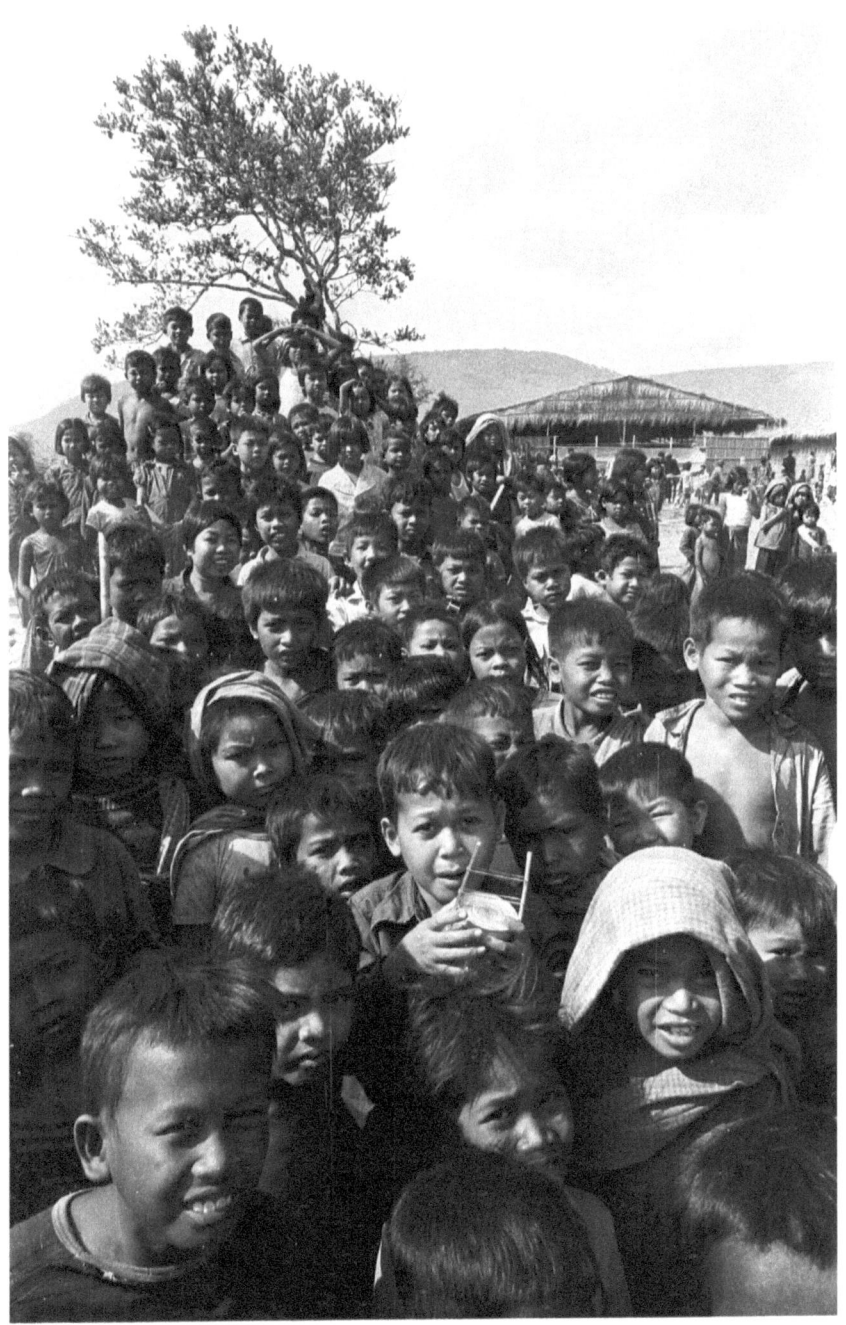

Cambodia refugee kids at Thailand/Cambodian border 1979

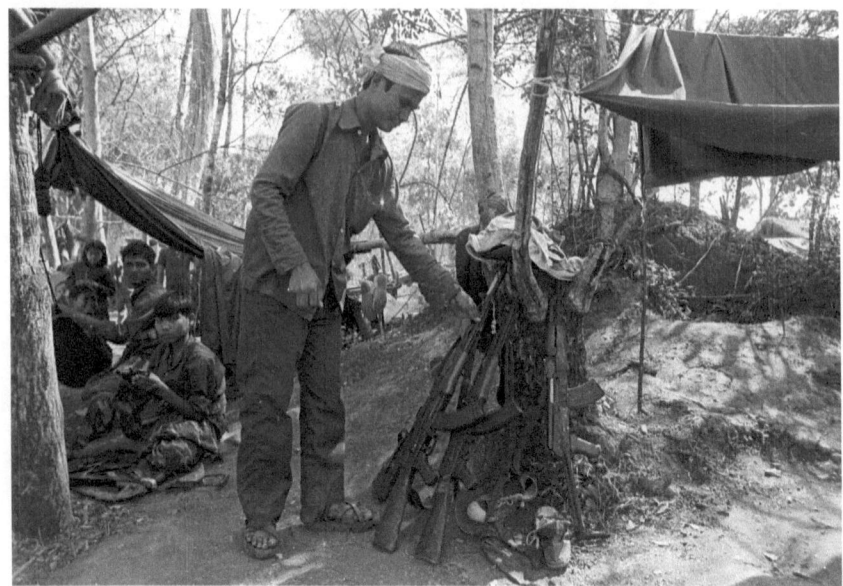

Heavily armed guerilla camp in Cambodian jungle 1979

When UPI learned about the trip they did what they always did: expressed their displeasure in a letter. They accused me of engaging in "advocacy journalism" on a "junket" to Thailand. Advocacy is a dirty word in journalistic circles, at least for the executives. Reporters, as the myth goes, are to be unbiased and objective, to not let feelings cloud their work. Executives, on the other hand, attend cocktail parties with top management and friends from other large corporations, and are frequently predisposed to accepting gifts and "junkets" to far away places. The largess, of course, requires a certain amount of favorable coverage for the generous corporations and their corporate heads.

Back in my days working for UPI in Detroit, my old boss and I were often provided luxury cars for vacation trips. We could always call our PR friends at any of the Big Three automakers for a free loaner in return for promoting their products. None of this was ever stated explicitly. I usually called the guy at Cadillac for the biggest four-door luxury ride he could throw my way. None of us ever took an oath mandating objectivity, though, when we signed up to become photojournalists. Heaven forbid that journalists advocate additional awareness for the genocide in Cambodia, on their own vacation time.

The battle to keep my job roiled on. In the interim, I enrolled in a few courses at the University of Minnesota, and finally graduated over a decade after enrolling in my first college class. I immediately enrolled in a master's degree at Hamline University in St. Paul. A year later, in 1980, I earned a Master of Arts concentrating on Third World Development. Soon after my mom called with bad news from home. My dad had been hospitalized and was in critical condition, the cancer was spreading. I flew to Detroit and sat by his bed for hours, dad laying unconscious, wired to monitors. My gut feeling was that he would die that night. I talked to him, expressed my love and forgiveness, and told him over and over how I had always wanted to be close to him. I don't know what, if anything he heard. I said a prayer by his bed and went across the hall to sleep on the only couch around. A nurse woke me up in the early morning hours to say my dad had died. Mike was with our mom, at home, and we gathered later to plan dad's funeral.

Mom lamented the decisions we had made during his breakdowns. "Where is Paul?" she'd repeat through tears. Both my dad and brother were named Paul. We sat with her for hours and she seemed comforted with a son on each side. The next morning I saw another letter she had written to Paul on the dining room table.

None of us had heard from Paul in over a decade. Mike had many police contacts who helped locate Paul's last known address. Mike dialed a number in Texas. It was Paul. Mike told him that our dad had died and if he wanted to attend the funeral he'd better hurry. Mike said it was like talking to the "man in the moon." He hung up without a response.

Growing weary of battling UPI's intent to rid themselves of me, I filed a complaint with the Minnesota Human Rights Department against UPI, alleging they were discriminating against me for being an alcoholic. Two days later UPI fired me. Once terminated, I filed a lawsuit for being dismissed in retaliation. The court issued a temporary restraining order reinstating me, pending outcome of the trial. I was put on a paid leave of absence until the trial's conclusion. My attorney, a man named Jerry Snider, was referred to me by a friend from AA meetings, who worked with him at a prestigious law firm. Jerry agreed to represent me pro bono, as he knew the case could set a new precedent. It would be the first alcoholism discrimination case in Minnesota history, perhaps in the US. The UPI team pulled no punches in the courtroom. They conceded the fine photography, but argued I was a substandard manager. They called me, "An artist in a businessman's world." I considered the statement a compliment.

At the conclusion of the five-week trial, UPI was found guilty and I won a total of $157,000. UPI appealed the decision to the Minnesota Supreme Court; it took another two years before that court would render a decision. Following my courtroom victory, rumors abounded that the case would open the floodgates for employees to sue employers for discriminatory treatment for chemical dependency. Corporations in the Twin Cities, which included some of the world's largest multinationals, would have to tread lightly around employees with chemical addictions. In 1982, UPI's founding family, the Scripps, sold the debt-plagued wire service to four businessmen from Tennessee for one dollar. All four were members of the Bahá'í faith.

It wasn't long after the sale that I received a phone call from one of the new owners. He asked me to meet them in a lounge at O'Hare Airport in Chicago. They greeted me warmly and were quite charming, helping take the edge off my nervousness. We talked for an hour. One mentioned that they had looked over my files and saw my denied request for a transfer. "Where do you want to go? You have mentioned in your requests San Francisco or Washington DC. Is that true?" he asked. I nodded and knew where this might be going. Perhaps Minnesota corporations urged the new UPI owners to get me away from the state with 10,000 lakes. The Minnesota Supreme Court was still deciding my fate and the new owners had decided to keep me happily quiet until the court's decision.

"Take a few days and decide which city and that's where we will send you," he explained. I decided to milk the offer and told them I would like to spend one week in San Francisco with my family, and an additional week in DC, and then I'd tell them my choice. They agreed, expenses paid, a bone thrown in that astonished me. Sherry was reluctant to leave Minnesota but excited for a new adventure. It was impossible to miss that the lawsuit had transformed San Francisco or DC from a pleasant, unaffordable dream into a very real possibility. When Sherry and I decided on DC, it turned out to be one of the best decisions of our lives. DC was a political city, a city of suits. We later discovered that the term "empty suits" is an amazingly accurate description for many elected leaders. San Francisco was a beautiful city and more relaxed, not as many suits, but we concluded that if I wanted to work toward social change, the nation's capital better offered that opportunity.

There was no welcoming party in UPI's DC offices. Management resented the transfer and my supervisor in the Washington bureau was a good friend of UPI's top executive, named in my lawsuit. He made it clear that it would not be easy for me in his bureau. The seven or eight staff photographers were split, some aloof, others friendly and uncaring about the recent problems. Over the subsequent years, I became familiar with the major power players at the Capitol and State Department, covering hundreds of press conferences and demonstrations. I was provided a congressional press pass to cover assignments on Capitol Hill, but a White House press pass required a fair amount of pestering about the rotation of staffers as each photographer was assigned to exclusively cover the president in the White House for a month at a time. This was considered the top of the ladder. I called the owners in Nashville who instructed me to report any problems I might encounter in Washington. I reported that management was preventing me from covering the White House and traveling with the president. Within a week I had a White House press pass dangling around my neck and entered the pressroom at 1600 Pennsylvania Ave.

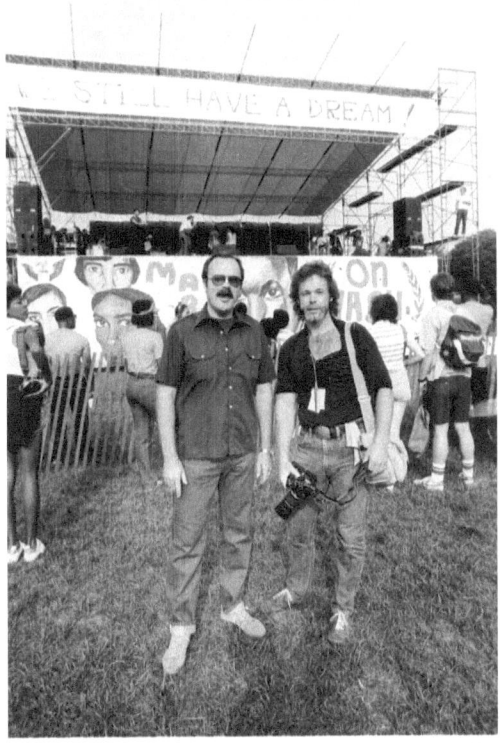

Mike(L) an undercover cop and me both working at the 20ᵗʰ Anniversary of the famous MLK I Have a Dream speech 1983

THE AGITATOR, THE DOG

My assignments were often with the "tight pool," aka the "death watch" or traveling pool that constituted a small group of journalists: a writer and photographer from UPI and AP and one cameraman and magazine photographer. Any romantic notions I had about pinnacles of careers were quickly dashed. Working in the White House—a place where everyone should apparently be important and harried with vital work that matters in every corner of the globe—was overrated. The monotony set in after a few days, it was always "hurry up and wait." Photo-ops were rare in the Rose Garden, the South Lawn or the Oval Office, and some days I never took a picture.

In the first month of my rotation time passed slowly and the seat of power started to feel an awful lot like the high school classroom, where I felt the walls closing in on me. I wondered if this was the prison my high school principal had mentioned I'd end up in. The first trip on Air Force One seemed special—this was travel with Ronald Reagan, the President of the United States, flying in the commander in chief's airplane is just like any other: popped ears, uncomfortable seats and bumpy landings. I will say this for Reagan: he had candy, white cigarette packs and matches for the press, emblazoned with the presidential seal. They were all great souvenirs, especially the white cigarette packs, and I kept a few in a drawer at home. One day I discovered three packs were missing and conducted something of a domestic inquiry. Hanna, my thirteen year-old daughter, had smoked them with her friends. I needed a safe.

What I liked best was being assigned to the presidential "death watch." I travelled for two weeks with Reagan to vacation at his ranch in the mountains near Santa Barbara, California, one of the loveliest seaside towns in the world. The press stayed in a luxury hotel at the beach, with only an occasional photo-op at the ranch. Trips like these, and the one in which we stopped in Los Angeles for Reagan to officially open the 1984 Olympics, made my work a vacation. While Reagan pushed a button to light the Olympic torch overlooking the stadium, we took photos next to him. We boarded military choppers after the lighting ceremony. I sat in the rear on the floor of the large flying machine with my legs dangling out the wide-open hydraulic door, high above the Pacific.

In less than a year the charm of Washington vanished entirely, but I didn't care. The majestic buildings, the power, the personalities— none of it carried any meaning to me. In fact, the people were usually a mix of spectacular pomposity and dullness; they sported the same clothes and hairstyles, and even their voices droned in the same way. Clones and empty suits.

The best picture I took at the White House occurred when President Reagan and British Prime Minister Margaret Thatcher walked out of the Oval Office into the Rose Garden to walk Reagan's dog, Lucky. It was a "photo-op" and when I pushed the shutter the dog leaped toward me. (Dogs have never liked me—this was almost bite number five from various canines.) Reagan looked surprised and tried to restrain Lucky, while Thatcher looked on, concerned. She may have thought, "Can't Reagan even control his little dog?"

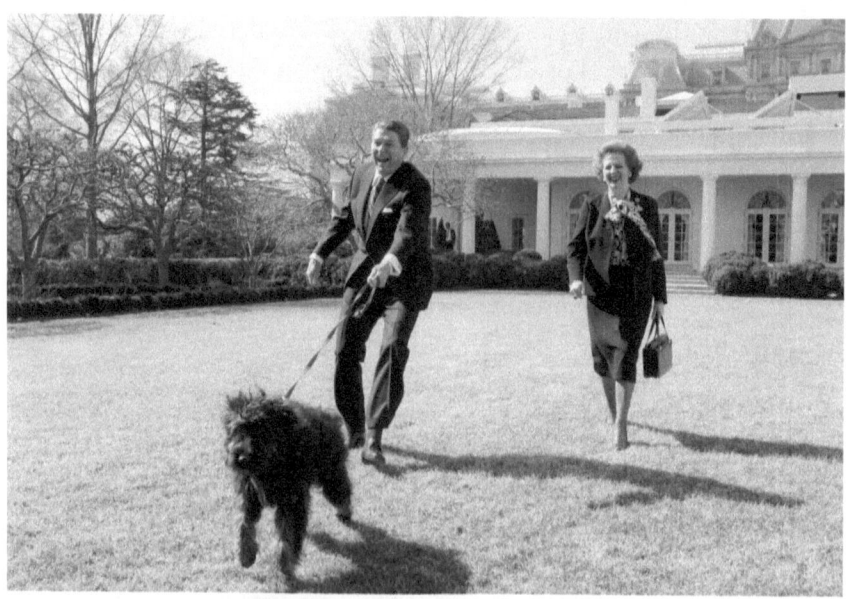

Reagan and Thatcher walk Lucky in Rose Garden 1985

One day, Reagan appeared for a news conference in the pressroom. He was asked about the homeless situation in America, which was gaining some attention; "homeless" was a relatively new term in the lexicon. He simply said, "There isn't a problem, although I did hear about a homeless family in New York." Hundreds of homeless people lived near the White House, outside the State Department and U.S. Capitol Building. Reporters and politicos alike walked by them everyday just to pass through the White House gate. President Reagan, the great communicator, ignored the people huddled in front of his home. Either he lied or his dementia had already limited his sight. Our scribes, the journalists from America's most important news outlets, neglected to challenge Reagan's assessment. This callous distortion reflected Washington's tendency to twist the truth and feed bogus news to Americans. Sadly, Reagan was the first but not the last president to deny the truth about homelessness.

On the way to and from the White House from the UPI bureau, I walked through Lafayette Park, across Pennsylvania Avenue from the White House, where hundreds of protesters have gathered over the years, and where homeless groups idly passed the days. I met a man there named Mitch Snyder, who had made it his sole mission to

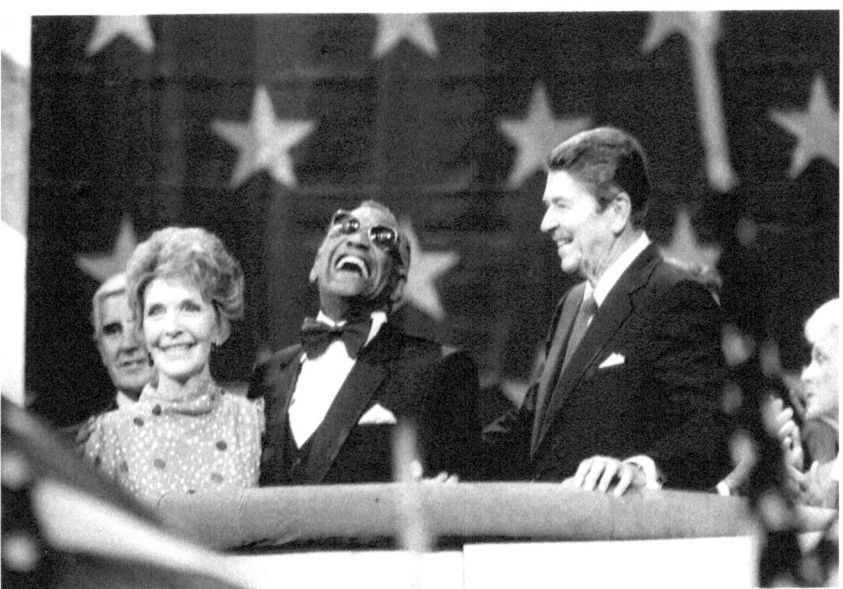

Ray Charles with Reagans at GOP Convention in Dallas 1984

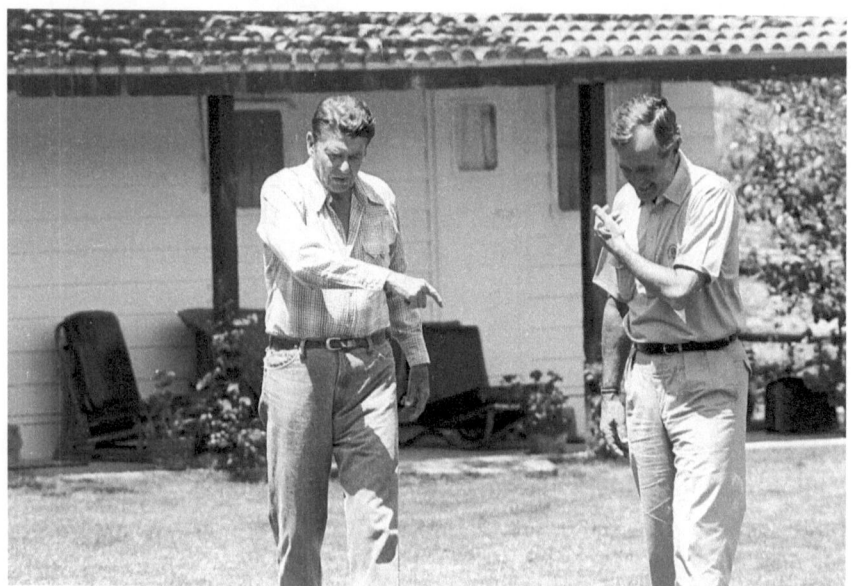

President Reagan, President Bush at Reagan ranch, Santa Barbara 1985

aid the homeless and bring awareness to their plight. Mitch always wore an old, green flak jacket and faded jeans and was an intense, articulate man with a fire in his belly. He was the most zealous and effective advocate for a social issue I had ever encountered. He was an ex-con who had spent a couple of years in Danbury Prison for stealing a car in Las Vegas. While in prison, Snyder met the legendary brothers Dan and Phil Berrigan, who were anti-war activists and priests. The brothers influenced Mitch greatly in prison, as they had many others. Anti-war efforts were Mitch's original motive for moving to DC, but he then turned to help the poor and homeless.

We got along instantly and he invited me to visit him at the Community for Creative Nonviolence (CCNV) building, an old city college unit a few blocks from the Capitol, and the largest shelter for the homeless. Mitch gave me the grand tour of the dilapidated shelter and I took pictures as we walked. The scene was quite grim; fallen humans desperate for a roof over their heads, even one infested by roaches and rats. In February 1983, a call came in from a coworker at UPI: the Minnesota Supreme Court ruled against the lower court's decision and found that UPI had had proper grounds to fire me, overturning the lower court's verdict. The ruling was unusual in that the ruling was based on the facts of the case rather than the more abstract definition of the law that the high court usually used as a standard.

Sherry and I stayed in bed for two days, immobilized. The nearly $200,000 we had counted on was gone, and probably my job along with it. I continued to report for work and neither management nor I said a word about my status.

In 1984 I decided to pursue a Master of Divinity (MDIV) degree in preparation for the inevitable career change and enrolled in Wesley Theological Seminary (WTS), a Methodist seminary next to American University. During the first few weeks of class we dove into the study of humanity and God. I was struck by this chapter in Galatians 5:19-21: "Now the works of the flesh are evident: sexual immorality, impurity, sensuality, idolatry, sorcery, enmity, strife, jealousy, fits of anger, rivalries, dissensions, divisions, envy, drunkenness, orgies, and things like these. I warn you, as I warned you before, that those who do such things will not inherit the kingdom of God." I was fascinated by and certainly familiar with snares of the flesh.

Renowned philosopher Dallas Willard, a professor at USC, said the four great questions humans must answer are: "What is reality? What is the good life? Who is a good person? And how do you become a good person?" These were the very questions I was trying to answer in my own life. In an Old Testament class we turned to Ecclesiastes 2:12-17: "So I turned to consider wisdom and madness and folly. For what can the man do who comes after the king? Only what has already been done. Then I saw that there is more gain in wisdom than in folly, as there is more gain in light than in darkness. The wise person has his eyes in his head, but the fool walks in darkness. And yet I perceived that the same event happens to all of them. Then I said in my heart, 'What happens to the fool will happen to me also. Why then have I been so very wise?' And I said in my heart that this also is vanity. For of the wise as of the fool there is no enduring remembrance, seeing that in the days to come all will have been long forgotten. How the wise dies just like the fool! So I hated life, because what is done under the sun was grievous to me, for all is vanity and a striving after wind."

There was enough in the above six verses of Ecclesiastes to beguile me for a long time. It was evident my studies demanded full-time, disciplined commitment. During my six years in the seminary I also learned that some of the skills required for effective ministry were not my strengths. For instance, that the task of managing a church, is the spiritual equivalent of running a business. Churches are often highly political, with congregants clashing over minor irritants. My own boyhood church in Detroit fractured over the pastor's credentials and nearly erupted into violence. There also are the required hospital visits, marriage counseling, and marrying and burying congregants. While I was reviewing my own possible path, the president of the seminary suggested to me that photography could be a form of ministry. Naturally, this appealed, and President Lewis then suggested that he might find a role for me in Nashville, TN with United Methodist Communications.

To keep busy and distracted from the looming sense of doom at work, I often visited CCNV and continued to photograph the homeless. On Thanksgiving Day 1983, UPI assigned me to cover CCNV's annual Thanksgiving Dinner in Lafayette Park—the one event each year that the media saw as an appropriate occasion to report on the poor. The wire ran three images, each depicting battered people having their turkey dinner with the White House serving as the backdrop.

Eventually, helping and documenting the homeless became my primary focus, the images of poverty reminding me of when our dad would drive us through Detroit's skid row. I also thought that if I wanted to understand the functionality, ethics, and values of a society, I needed to learn the perspective from people who are at the other end of wealth and power. Washington was the perfect place to view and experience the bottom-up perspective. The homeless people lived every day in front of the Pentagon, the Capitol, and the Justice Department—denied the promises of the American dream and more aware than most of the mirages therein.

I wanted to show my growing body of work about people who are homeless to as many people as possible. One of my friends told me about a national summit being organized for a weeklong symposium for architects who were addressing housing for the homeless, at the American Institute for Architects (AIA). It was a beautiful, huge building near the White House on New York Avenue. I contacted them and we worked out a way to show the photos at the conference, titling the exhibit "Portraits of the Powerless." TheWashington *Post* ran a story about the exhibit, and making a special point of highlighting the dichotomy between my career and my studies at the seminary. The story was right about two things: I tried to join journalism and advocacy in a way that provoked, and I had no idea what I would do once I acquired my Master of Divinity.

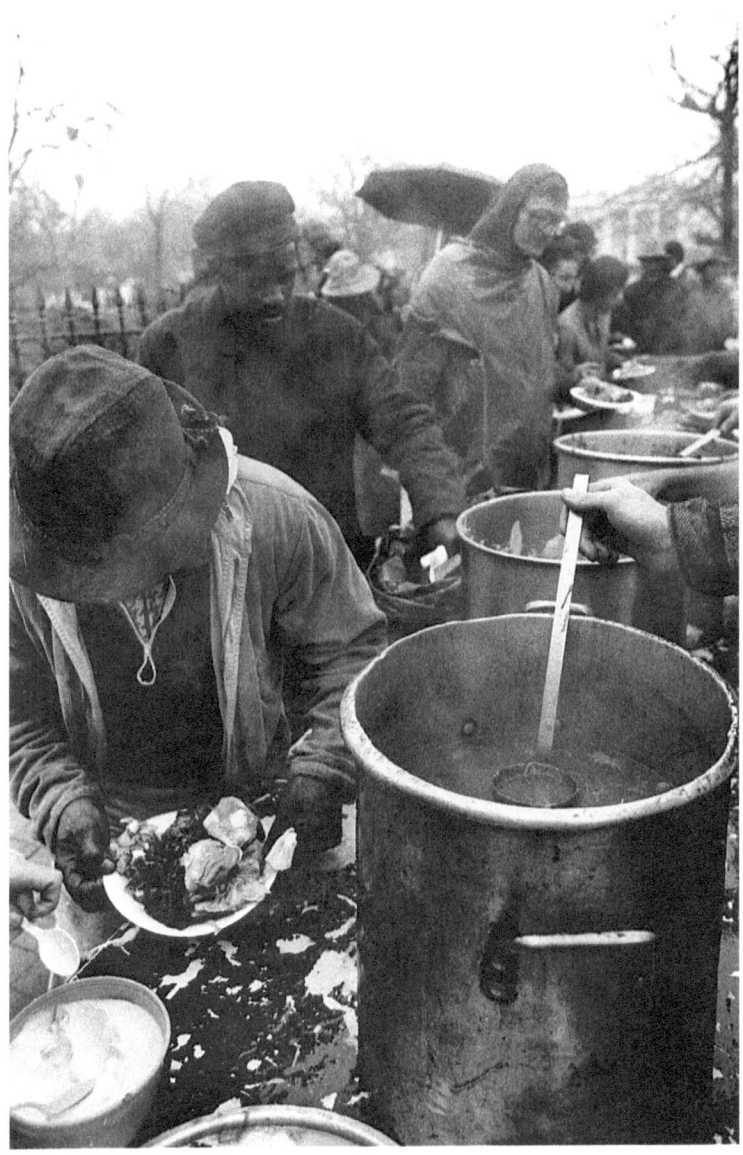

Homeless fed in front of White House 1983

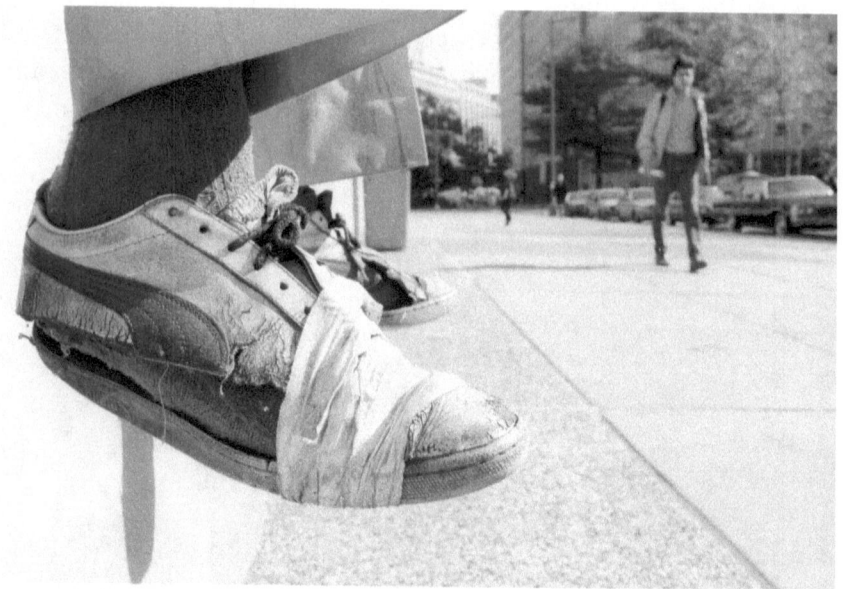

Homeless shoe 1986

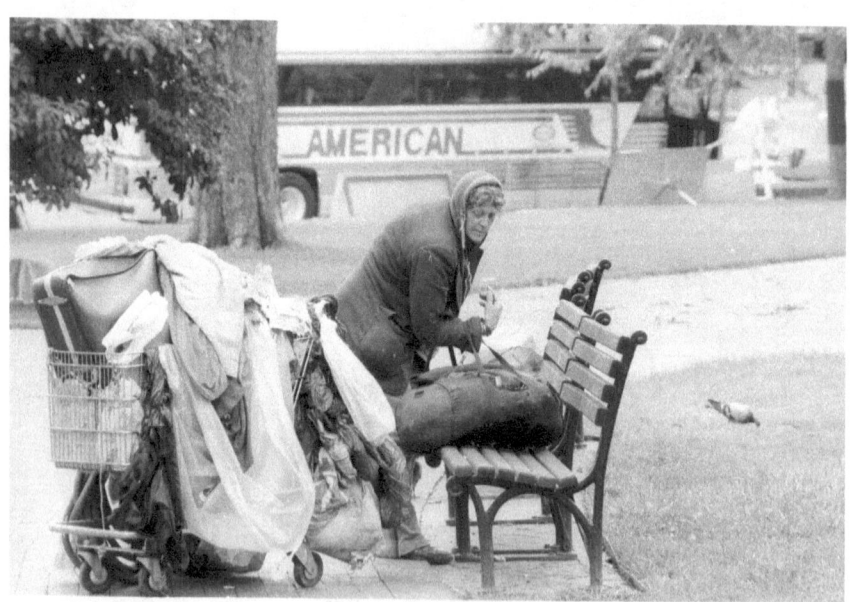

American homeless 1986

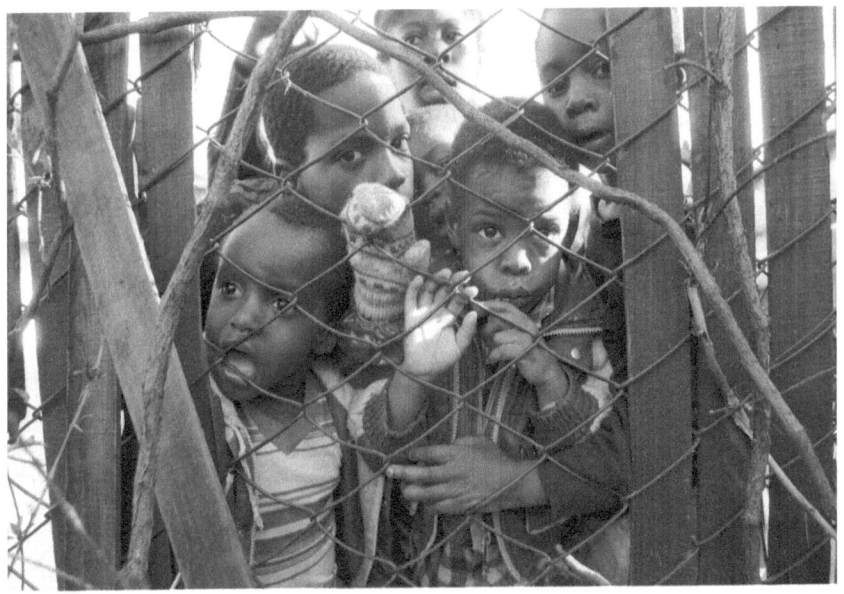

Homeless boys behind fence 1986

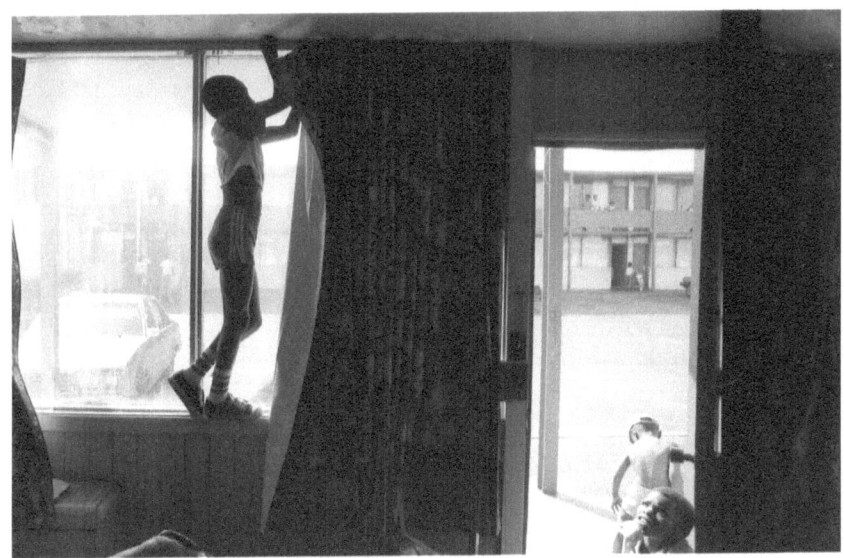

Inside homeless shelter 1986

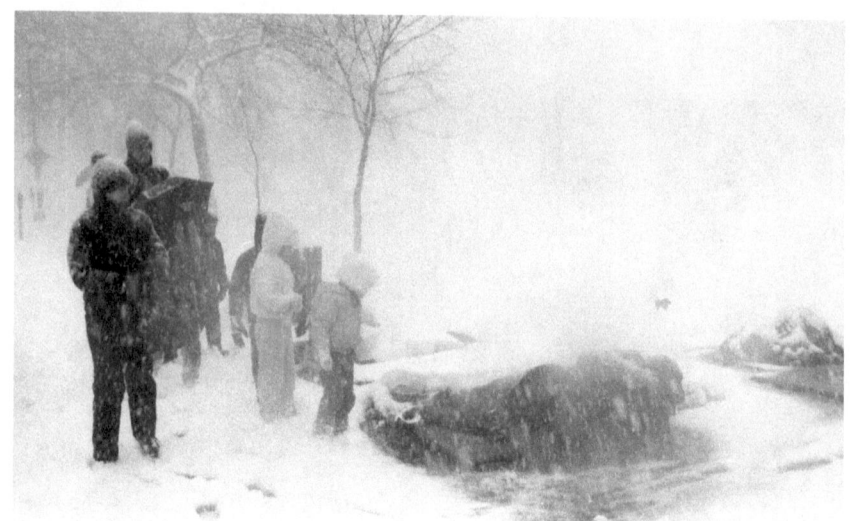

*Tourists look at homeless lying on grate in
blizzard, Washington, D.C. 1986*

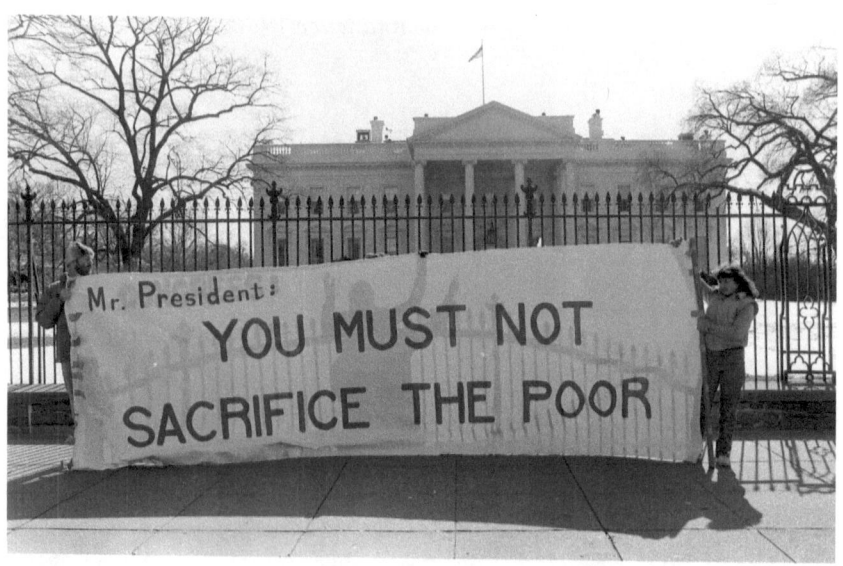

Protest at White House 1986

Mitch started to tip me about protests he and others had planned
so that I could cover the events. Once, they blocked traffic in front of
the White House and even scaled the fence. They were all arrested. I

was the only newsperson and had the only photos of these protests, and UPI started to grow suspicious. I tried hard not to romanticize the poor, like many do. Many of the homeless were just as corrupt, self-serving, and narcissistic as the people in Congress or riding the subway to work. They were just broke.

Other photographers started asking me for tips about taking pictures of homeless people, noting how they'd only get angry outbursts and threats when they tried to do their job. I'd tell them, "Just be friendly, ask them if it's okay to take a picture and then slowly ease into taking their photo." Over five years I had only had three violent encounters. One was with an elderly enraged woman with a shopping cart, who pulled a knife and moved to stab me. Thankfully, she didn't get too far. In another encounter in a park I tried to take a photo of a bearded and disheveled man. He pulled a large chain from his backpack and swung it at me, a near miss. Finally, standing near a small park in Dupont Circle, where small groups of inebriated winos gathered, a woman next to me pulled a long bladed knife from her handbag and stabbed another man in his belly. He fell to the ground and his small assailant dashed down the block. Several pedestrians stopped to help the victim and I followed the woman. Within a few minutes several police cars arrived and I pointed out the woman's escape route, unable to do much more.

I resigned from UPI in 1986, finally ending the festering anxiety that defined my final year there. My seminary required a one-year fulltime field internship, but Sherry and I were concerned about our economic situation. She started working fulltime in a Georgetown restaurant and I continued freelancing whenever possible. Much was about to change and insecurities crept in about whether Sherry was disappointed in my path as a ministerial student helping the poor. She would miss the opportunities to attend White House functions and consort with the powerful people most folks only read about. My daughters would lose their bragging rights. We would no longer celebrate the Fourth of July fireworks from the South Lawn of the White House. Our vacation-like adventures to California, with Sherry and Hanna on board the press plane behind Air Force One, would end. I felt guilty about not being home--like a person with a nine to five job.

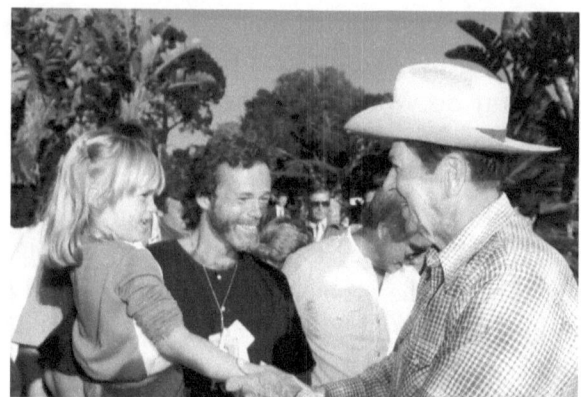

President Reagan, Jim and daughter Hanna, Santa Barbara, CA 1984

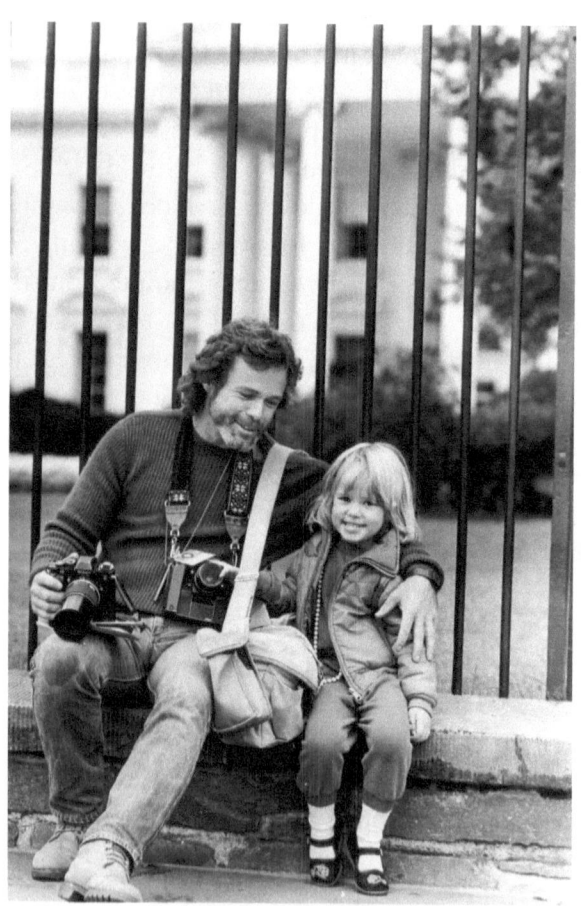

Me and Hanna in front of White House

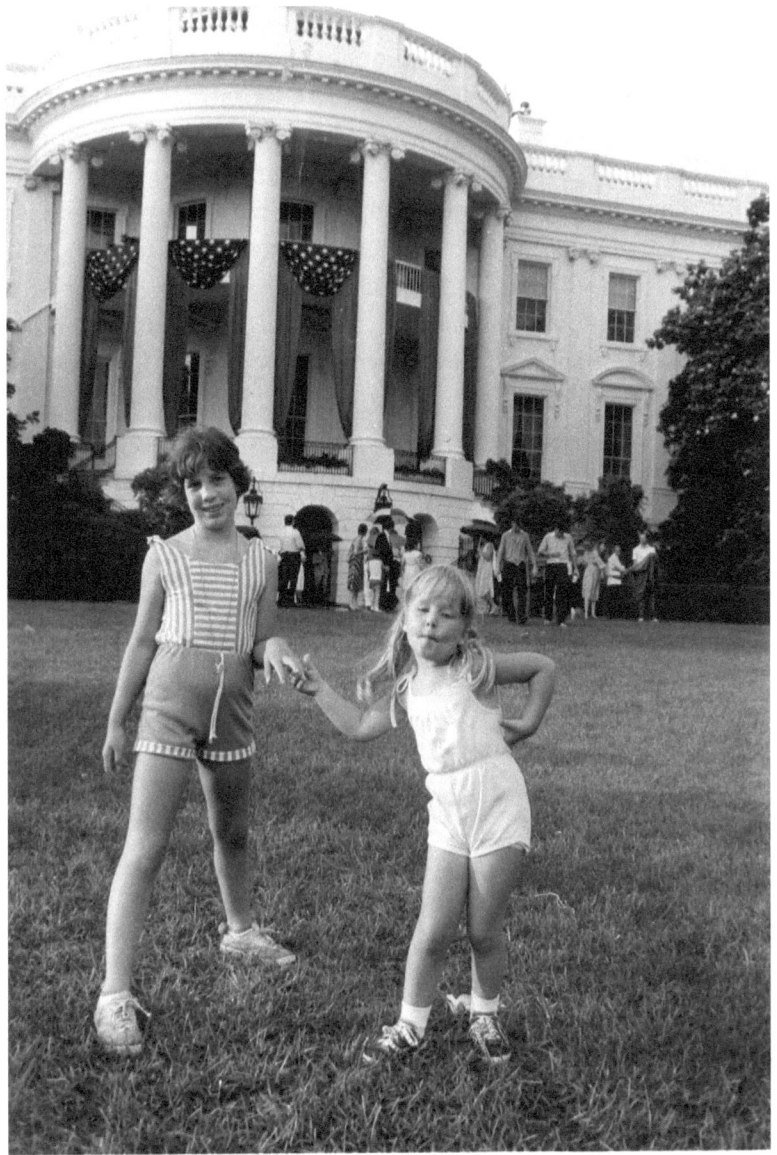

Priya (L) and Hanna pose on South Lawn at White House

I shared my troubles with Mitch Snyder and he told me a couple clichés I'd heard before, but this time they were not only valuable, but even profound: "Jim, when one door closes another opens. There's a surprise around every corner. There will be people who help." Mitch was right. New doors opened. Freelancing provided enough income while I was in seminary, and much of it came from word spreading that I specialized in poverty and homeless issues. This profiled me as a photographer with expertise, and contracts came in from governmental agencies, religious publications, and other nonprofit groups. The work finally provided the meaning and purpose I had hoped for, and had never quite found in the mainstream. Hollywood arrived at CCNV in 1986 to produce a television film with Martin Sheen starring as Mitch in "Samaritan: The Mitch Snyder Story," set at landmark locations around the nation's capital. Thanks to Mitch's endorsement, the producers contracted me for production and publicity photos.

Working on a film set mostly meant long hours standing around, but it was a thrill to meet the actors and Martin Sheen and I hit it off from the start. We had several long dinners together and when filming ran late into the night, I crashed on an extra bed at his hotel. We talked about anything that came up, from our kids to the work to religion and our spiritual philosophy. Martin suggested I write a book and I told him I had begun and he should too. He said, "I will endorse your book."

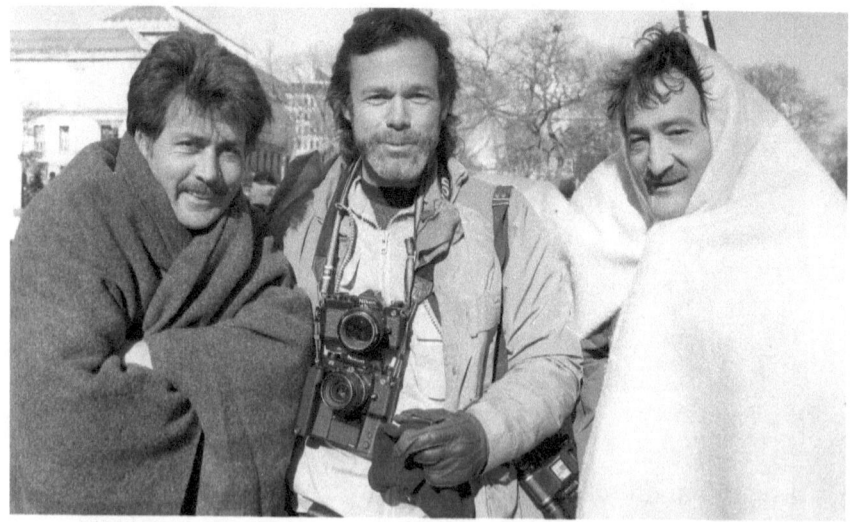

Martin Sheen(L) Jim and Mitch Snyder in Washington,D.C 1986

His son Charlie Sheen was the subject of a long discussion. I told Martin about my troubled life when I was about Charlie's age and that like Charlie I had also been thrown out of high school. I told him about Brijjie's death and my daughters, Priya and Hanna. He talked about what it was like working on the epic film Apocalypse Now and costarring with Marlon Brando as well as details about his heart attack while making the film in a humid jungle. A few months after the Snyder film was in the can, Sheen and I exchanged several letters for nearly a year. Years later, I ran into him at a demonstration in San Francisco. We hugged and reminisced about Mitch, the homeless, and our long conversations and letters.

THE PITTS

In my work documenting the homeless I learned a great deal about the DC system that allegedly provided them services. The Pitts, an aptly named hotel on the 1400 block of Belmont Street NW stood at the opposite corner of an old, three-story brick building named the Community of Hope. The Pitts was the intake shelter for all of DC's homeless, and once homeless clients completed intake paperwork, the staff at the Pitts secured temporary housing at substandard hotels and motels throughout the city. Some homeless families were sent to the Community of Hope, which gave them apartments for temporary housing.

When Cornelius Pitts showed up at the Pitts to metaphorically "empty the safe," he often parked his bright Rolls Royce at the front door. Sometimes he pulled up in his less expensive Mercedes 560 SEL. He usually kept his other three cars at home. Cornelius seemed to have been of a like mind with President Reagan. When hundreds, even thousands, of homeless families showed up at the Pitts Hotel desperately in need of temporary housing, he may have thought that forcing them to walk around an extravagant luxury car would fire their ambition to greater things, like owning their very own Rolls. If he had a message there, it was as simple and facetious as Reagan's: pull yourself up by your bootstraps and enjoy America's prosperity. Everything would trickle down.

But the city and the homeless were good to Cornelius. He was a close friend to DC's cokehead mayor, Marion Barry, and the city gave Pitts the sole-source contract to provide emergency shelter for homeless families—a contract that they renewed annually. It cost $3,000 per month for one small, squalid room at the Capitol City Inn. A private security agency, which may have been owned by Barry or Pitts, provided guards for the inn. The guards were alleged to have impregnated several women sheltered there, and were also known to sell drugs to the shelter residents. Taxpayer dollars went to Barry, then to Pitts, then to drug pushers, all in the city where the federal government controlled the purse strings and preached prosperity to all.

The two facilities were nestled in a predominantly African American ghetto. It was as dangerous as any in the US, and only two miles from the White House. Numerous open-air drug markets flourished and street violence was endemic. My brother Mike was a police detective in the area, and knew most of the "mopes" of the neighborhood, those still there and the ones he had sent to jail. During one of my visits to Belmont St, I stopped by the Community of Hope and met their director, Rev. Tom Nees, a Church of the Nazarene pastor. He lived a much simpler, less ostentatious life than Cornelius Pitts at the other end of the block. The Community of Hope operated a medical clinic for the homeless and had about thirty apartments for temporary housing. They had a small chapel inside, and every Sunday there was a spirited service, from which gospel hymns rang out into the hood during the early morning hours.

As I got to know him, Tom eventually offered Community of Hope as the place where I could fulfill my fulltime internship for the seminary. Most of the seminary students I knew were seeking internships in more upscale, traditional churches, not in a homeless shelter. Few seminary students wanted to intern in a poor, violent ghetto. But my focus for ministry was on homelessness and poverty issues, which seemed like an obvious choice, given the two thousand Bible verses concentrated on the poor. Tom and I decided that my job would be to counsel addicts, a demographic not in short supply in the neighborhood. I would also continue to take photographs for the Community of Hope to promote their various programs—a long awaited synthesis between my photos and ministry.

During the first week, I met several people in the neighborhood. The street was always teeming with people, especially homeless folks, many children, wandering up a hill, urban nomads, on their way to the Pitts, desperate for help. I met a man on the block I knew only as Shot, because not only had he been shot a time or two, he also liked shots, preferably of heroin or whiskey. He had a long history of drug and alcohol abuse, and it showed. He talked about how he had been clean from time to time but had never been able to stay straight for long. We were odd friends, him being a tall, skinny, black guy and me the shorter, husky white boy. But we both had a sense of how seductive it could be to live life carelessly.

One day we sat on the stoop outside his building and I asked him if he wanted to go to an NA meeting with me—if he wanted to *start* an NA group at the Community of Hope with me. He wanted to, and I said, "Our first meeting is next week." I posted flyers that announced the NA meeting and asked the area office of twelve-step meetings to post an announcement. We met the next Sunday in the small chapel at Community of Hope. Shot and I alone just sat and talked for over an hour. We said the serenity prayer and read the twelve steps from the AA Big Book. He shared with me his struggles with drugs and alcohol and I shared my story with alcohol. Following the meeting, we handed out more flyers in the neighborhood. We first called our little group Join Us but later changed the name to Joy Nuts—a better fit.

We had ten people the next week, and within one month we needed fifty more folding chairs. Some of the stories shared were powerful, describing human free falls into despair and substances. People described how they had become gravely ill, landed in jail, and lost everything. One small woman, Adele, described how she had regularly shoplifted in downtown department stores to support her habit. She had once placed an entire typewriter between her legs, under her skirt, and walked slowly out of the store undetected. Shot was transformed. Sobriety made him look strikingly healthier and happier. The program could work wonders, and Shot and I agreed that our recoveries were miracles. I said to him, "Keep coming back, the program works."

The seminary let me reflect on my life's evolution. While completing the required courses I read voraciously, especially the works of legendary leaders in education and religion, some of whom offered transformational approaches for the oppressed of the world. Among them, Paulo Friere detailed revolutionary modalities in the field of education and proffered the exclusive tools of the affluent to the poor, photography included. In both Biblical and secular studies I had been eager to learn why the world's inequities were so stark and common, what caused the chasm between suffering and success. Opportunities to learn more firsthand kept coming, this time from an agency in the South Bronx, called The Miriam DeSoyza Learning Center, which worked with handicapped and impoverished children. The director asked me to document their clients and their living conditions. For two weeks I photographed children in hospitals, living in wretched third world conditions of crowded small apartments. Many of the kids were physically impaired and others mentally.

Miriam DeSoyza escorted me to a South Bronx hospital where she wanted me to meet and photograph a very sick little girl. She was only two-years-old and had already undergone numerous surgeries. I felt a chill go through me when I first saw her. Much of her face had been severely burned and dramatically disfigured; the crime left her with only a partial face. She sat up in her bed, revealing that she was attached to tubes. She was happy to see us. I took her picture and her image has haunted me ever since I pressed the shutter. The girl's father had poured chemical lye down her throat, burning tissue and destroying her stomach and esophagus. When she vomited the lye burned her face. The capacity and scope of an individual's evil is immeasurable and conversely so is the good. Miriam DeSoyza struck me as a stern woman, driven by a mission. She personified compassion and mercy, and though she was tough she could bubble with generosity. When we left the hospital we drove through some of the neighborhoods in the South Bronx that looked like they had been ravaged by war—as had the face of the sweet little girl in the hospital.

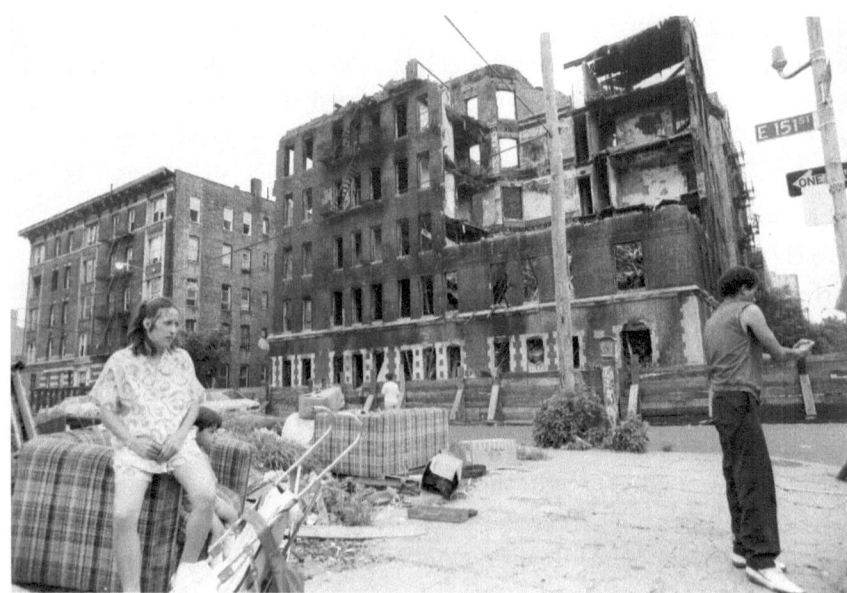

South Bronx street corner 1987

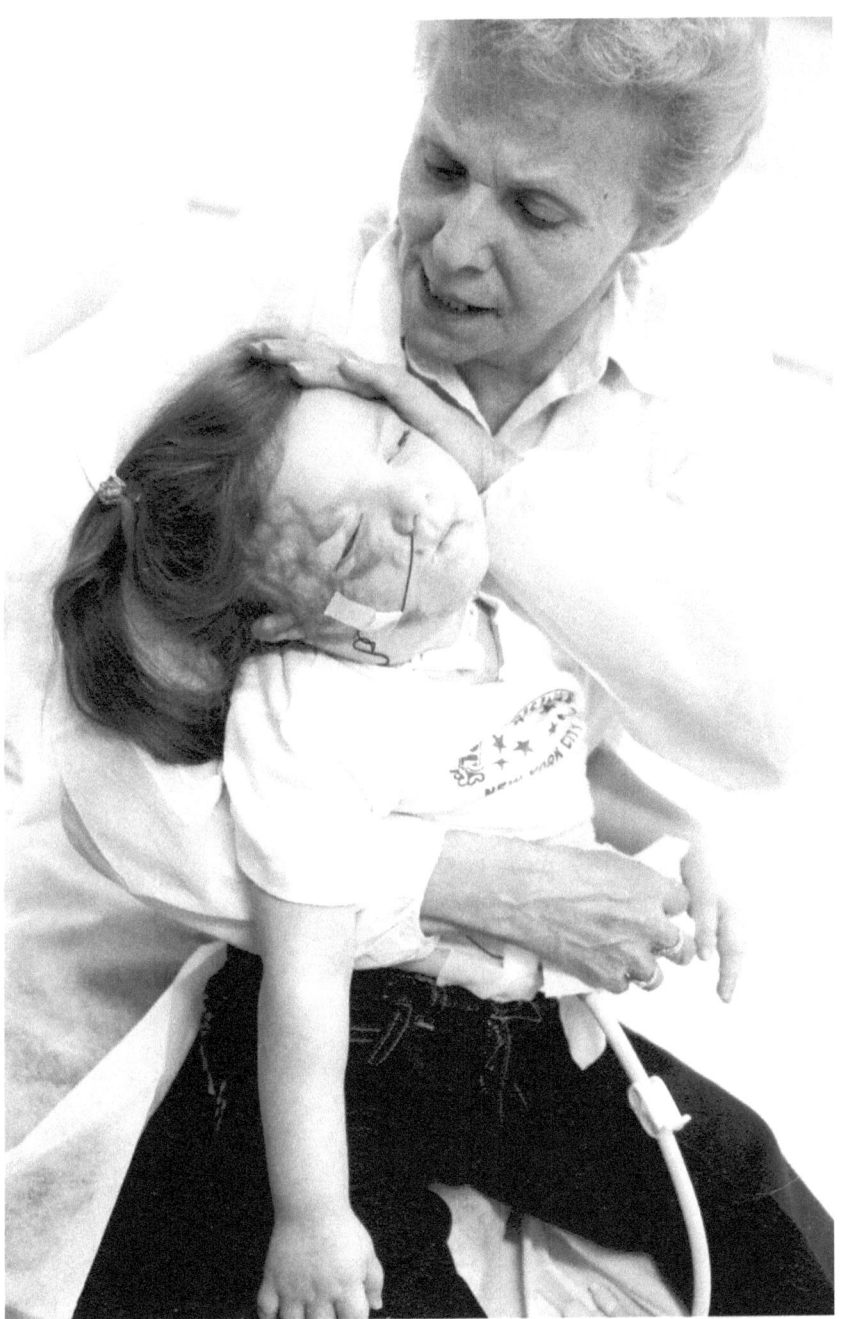

Girl in South Bronx with face burned by her father 1987

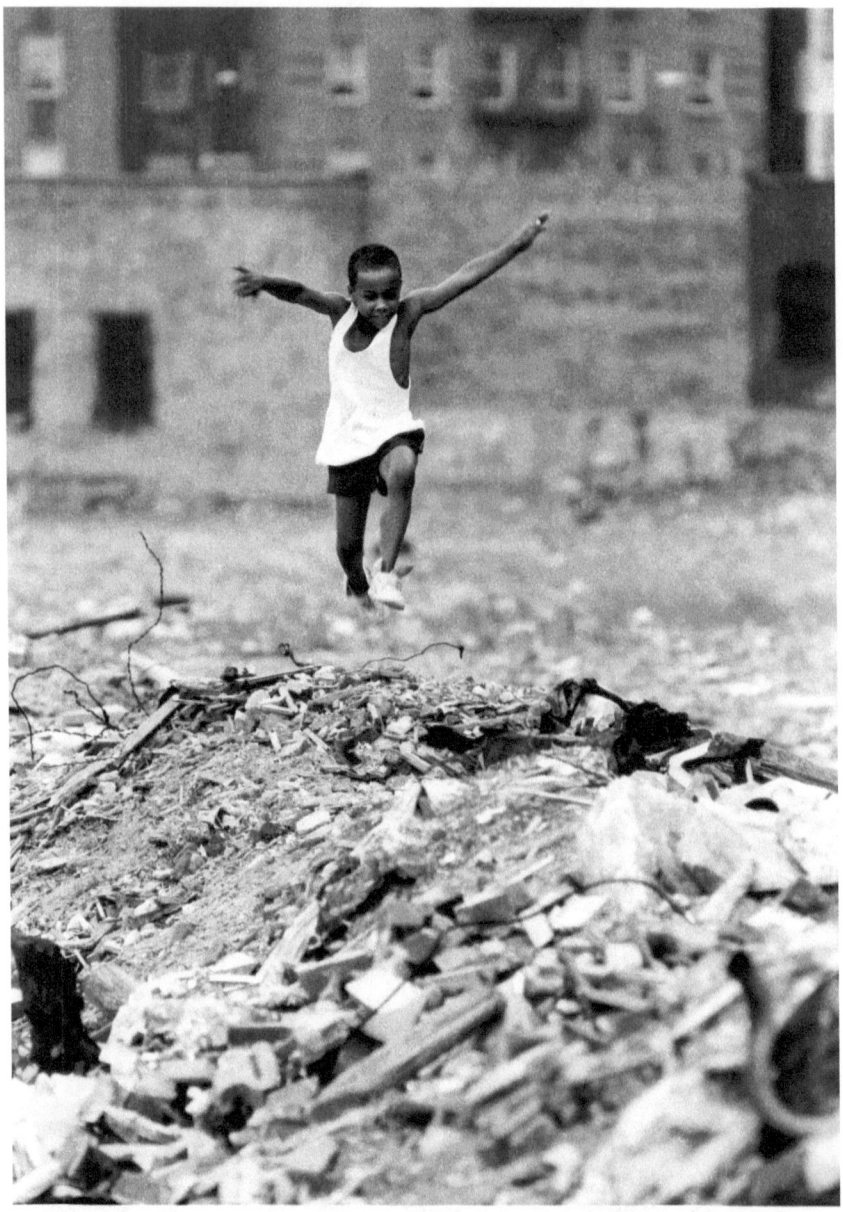

Boy Running in South Bronx 1987

That Christmas Eve as we sat down to a wonderful dinner the phone rang. It was Mitch Snyder. He asked if I could meet him in an hour at a Metro station. He and other homeless advocates were going to pull down the gates at several Metro stations by using chains hooked to pickup trucks so that the freezing homeless could find warmth and a place to sleep on Christmas Eve. I explained to Mitch I needed to be with my family. He seemed disappointed and tried to guilt me into helping. Mitch was a driven man and ironically could filter out the views of others when he didn't want to hear them. Years earlier, he had once told me that when other people challenged his strategies he'd never buckle. That declaration told me I would work with this man but never be too close to him. Mitch wanted me to photograph them tearing down the subway gates—a crime—and get the photos published the next day. "If I were to do that I might have to testify against you for the prosecution," I explained. I remembered being subpoenaed to testify against Indian activists following the Wounded Knee siege. He sighed and hung up.

On Christmas morning we exchanged gifts. My kids were showered with extravagant presents. I thought of the homeless kids and impoverished children in other countries who aren't showered with expensive presents. They often rely on discarded items for playthings like car tires and milk crates and empty cans.

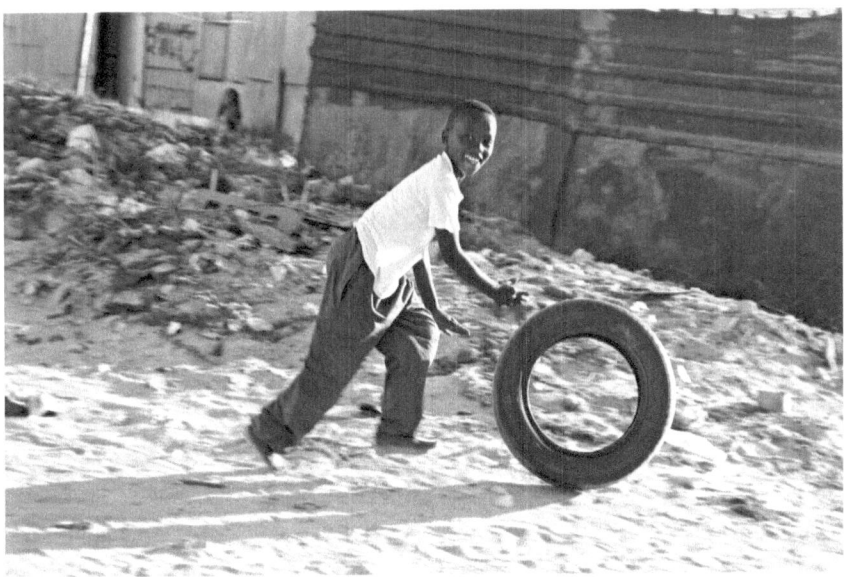

Kid rolls tire in Cape Town, South Africa 2006

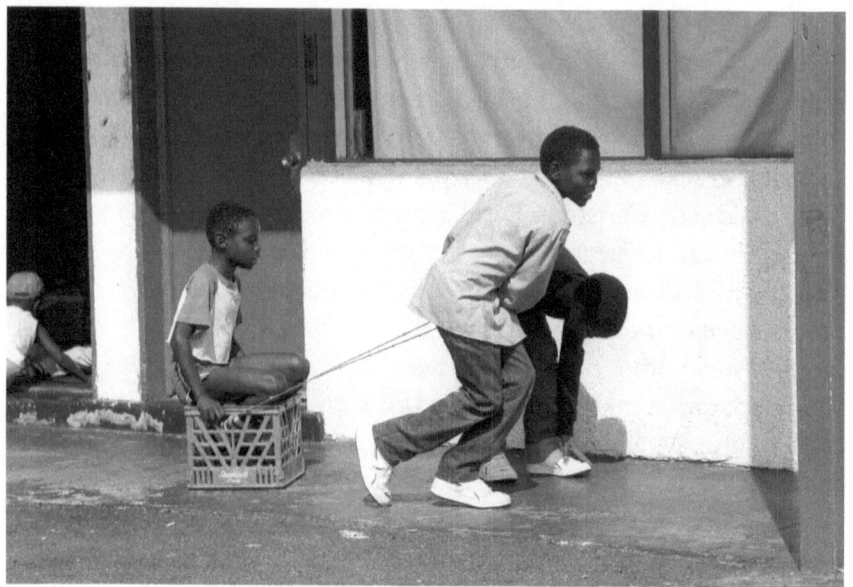

Homeless kids play with milk crate at shelter 1987

• • •

I wanted to launch a media center for kids at the Community of Hope. I sought Tom's blessing, and he told me I could do anything I wanted here, but had to raise the money myself. My plan was to teach homeless kids photography and writing skills, so that they could share their personal stories and bring public awareness to their plight. Every Saturday we met the children at the Community of Hope in our fledgling media center. We walked around the neighborhood on photo shoots. Some of the young photographers were talented and creative, and they got to work with volunteers who were staffers at *The New York Times*, *Newsweek* and *Time Magazine*. One of our most committed volunteer photographers was Fred Sweets, of *The Washington Post*. I had known him in St. Louis, back when he worked for the *Post-Dispatch*. Fred never missed an opportunity to help and managed our work at the Community of Hope.

A short time later a call came from NBC News requesting an interview with Maria Shriver at the Community of Hope. On the designated day, she arrived in a long black limo in front of the shelter. Several neighborhood residents stood on their stoops watching the

Kennedy celebrity enter the building, a symbol of power crossing the divide into a world of powerlessness. Maria and I sat in front of blowups of pictures taken by the children and me. She interviewed me for nearly an hour. She asked, "Why do you do this?" And all I could say was that there was too much sorrow and tragedy in this one block of the nation's capital. The children suffer, and I had learned in painful ways the immeasurable value of a child. Following the interview, I walked with Maria to her waiting limo. Several children gathered on the sidewalk to see her, and one child shouted, "Look, it's that famous woman from television with the picture man."

After Maria's show aired a lot of other shows called, and there was a slew of visits to titans of television in their natural habitats of New York and Los Angeles—lest I not forget Chicago, Oprah.

Sherry called me late one afternoon, after one of DC's news stations had contacted her about a homeless man named Willy, who had died that day. He had for years been a fixture on a sidewalk grate outside the State Department. I told her where she could find an image of him, and later a television van arrived to film the photograph. Willy had been seen by thousands of government workers and tourists, surviving the brutal summers and the freezing winters. He symbolized homelessness: a disheveled white man, unshaven with a long scruffy beard, in his fifties, and utterly non-communicative.

Sherry was amused, confused, and a little worried. "What's going on with your life?" She was perplexed about the strange outcomes spawned by working with the homeless, and she, along with others, thought I had become a bit weird. When I asked Sherry if she was becoming nostalgic for her home turf in Minnesota she shot back with the classic Midwest colloquialism: "You betcha." "Guess who called me today?" I asked. "Who, the media?" "Yep, *The Washington Post* wants Peter Carlson to write a cover story on homelessness in the magazine, and for me to do the photos." "That's good! And will they pay you well?" They would pay me quite well and I was reconnecting with Peter, the reporter who knew my life story.

Peter told me it would be the magazine's cover story entitled "No Exit." On our first day we went to the Capitol City Inn and Peter started interviewing people. I wandered the premises, looking for photographic prey. I already knew people sheltered in that garbage hole, and made the rounds to see if I could find them. I knocked on Vanessa Johnson's door, and she let me in and showed me her children's artwork taped to a wall. Her son Dion showed me Polaroid photos he had taken, while his mother stood there beaming. I sat and talked with the Johnsons for two hours. Then Dion and I walked outside, and I handed him my Nikon. We started shooting pictures together.

One afternoon Sherry handed me a letter, saying, "This looks important." It was from Majority Whip Tony Coelho, D-CA, in the House of Representatives. He wrote that he had read the story about me in the *Post*, and that he had stood before Congress to talk about my work. The letter explained he had taken the liberty of inserting the comments he made to Congress, along with Peter Carlson's entire article, into the Congressional Record of November 16, 1987. My ego soared. The letter went on to invite me to lunch with him in his office, which I didn't hesitate to accept. We sat down at an antique table in an alcove overlooking the Mall, in the direction of the Lincoln Memorial. A waiter in white pushed a cart up to our table. Tony asked about my work and said he'd like me to show him the world of the homeless. He wanted to visit some of the DC shelters. I told him I'd be happy to accompany him, and afterward called Peter to tell him I'd be escorting Tony to Community of Hope and Capitol City Inn. Peter wanted in, to see how the House Majority Whip responded to DC's underbelly. I told him, "Of course you're invited. It was your story that prompted him to contact me in the first place."

"You know, Peter, I doubt any politician on the Hill would be adverse to publicity, unless they're caught shacking up or doing some other shady thing." "Well, you never know about those guys," was all Peter said. Then I remembered camping out in front of former Senator Gary Hart's townhouse on Capitol Hill for hours with other newsmen, after he had challenged the media to catch him in what was alleged to be a steamy affair with a mystery woman. We tried. In April 1987 Hart had announced the beginning of his second presidential campaign. In less than a month a newspaper published a photo of the 29-year-old model Donna Rice, sitting comfortably on Hart's lap. Hart soon dropped out of the race. Politicians could be a unpredictable mix of bombast, piety and trouble, always tending to image.

Weeks later, Tony and his one-man driver-bodyguard picked me up in a black Lincoln town car. We drove to the Capitol City Inn where Peter would join us. No sooner had Tony stepped out from the car when a colorfully dressed woman wearing a hat the size of a tire ran up and hugged him. I introduced Ella, a flamboyant and well-known DC social worker who was known to swoon over the rich and powerful. Tony told Ella he wanted to take photos of the facility and some of its residents, and I introduced him to some of the occupants I had met during evictions. Ella stayed close to Tony while he snapped pictures. In my view Ella was a player, a big talker, and had missed her calling in politics. She knew the DC games inside out, and was especially familiar with the corruption in city's human services. She and I got along well, but I never trusted her and she easily could have had her own reservations about me.

Our little group walked around the scarred and unkempt shelter, which housed 200 adults and 700 children, one family to a room, month after month for years. The cost to the city was $3,000 a month per room and board for each family. No pool, unless you count puddles of bodily fluids. No pets, unless you count the pests. A sign in the lobby, where armed guards patrolled, advised: "Due to abuse of the ice machines the ice machines will be shut off permanently. – Management." Tots played on the sidewalk next to the busy street, and when the light at the corner turned red, teenagers darted out and attempted to earn spare change by washing car windows. Teachers from the elementary school serving the area frequently came in search of truant pupils, and often discovered that the children were embarrassed to show up in class because they were ashamed of their clothing and status in life.

Four children had died at Capitol City Inn, two murdered by their father, one of a mysterious illness, and the other hit by a passenger train travelling fast along the Washington-New York rail corridor, when some kids had been playing on the tracks directly behind the shelter. Drugs and violence were everywhere, sometimes propagated by the city-contracted private security.

On our drive home Tony asked me if I could travel around the country to document people challenged with handicaps. We signed a contract and I journeyed to six cities photographing the struggles of handicapped people, and even to Yosemite National Park to spend a few days with a disabled park ranger who had suffered permanent injuries after a fall climbing El Capitan. A few weeks later a second letter arrived from Coelho: "You can be sure that the memories I have from our shoot will weigh heavy on my heart and my conscience for a long time to come." A few months later another letter, again on fancy House of Representatives letterhead, arrived: "You should be proud of your efforts on behalf of the homeless, and now the work you have done for me with the handicapped." Coelho suffered from epilepsy—he authored the Americans With Disabilities Act.

And, as for Coelho, it was rumored he might become the next speaker of the House. The media started to report that he might be engaged in financial improprieties. He resigned from Congress in 1989. Like the politicians, my life had hinged on understanding the importance of images, though my work was about looking out at the world, and not about making the world look at me. But like Tony and Gary Hart, I, too, would learn the hard way what it felt like to fall from grace.

PART III

"All is vanity and a striving after wind."
— Ecclesiastes 2:17

NEEDLES, BULLETS, SHOTS

I decided to expand our Media Center's mission to some of the 700 kids sheltered at Capitol City Inn. Fred could oversee efforts at Community of Hope and I would oversee Capitol City. I had met two boys named Daniel and Dion who were obsessed with taking pictures, and both had already produced some stunning photographs. An energetic, cheery little girl named Charlene also joined in.

One girl, a cute as a button seven-year-old named Shavone, came skipping up one day and looked up at me and said, "Mister, can I take me some pictures?" Her smile won me over, and I asked her which room she lived in so that her parents could sign a permission/copyright form. The forms required a guardian's signature and were drafted because some of the people we would be working with might be difficult. The form's first sentence stated: "If you do not understand this form, need clarification, on any of the points, do not sign the form." Most parents had plenty of experience with DC's bureaucracy and had signed legal forms for welfare payments, housing and food vouchers and landlord, tenant agreements.

We marched into Shavone's messy room, where her mom was sprawled on the bed, looking comatose. She was not yet dressed for the day, though it was noon. Shavone shook her mom, yelling "Wake up, wake up mama, I wanna take me some pictures with the picture man." Her mom lifted her head and mumbled a few incoherent words. Shavone said, "It's me, me, mama!" Her mom was apparently too high to recognize her daughter, much less sign the form. "I'm sorry, Shavone, maybe next week you can join us," I told her as we left the room. She started to cry—yet another heartbreaker but not a situation entirely uncommon in the world of homelessness.

It had become clear to me that drugs and alcohol and a lack of personal responsibility exacerbated the lives of some of Washington's dispossessed. They often slipped into a spiral, poverty, despair addiction kicking each other always downward, fueling the destruction of entire families. Reagan's denial of homelessness didn't help anything. Nor did the callousness and corruption of DC's social services, which bordered on criminal neglect. Evidence of drugs and alcohol were visible everywhere we worked with homeless kids, on the 1400 block of Belmont St, and around almost every home I visited to pick up kids for our weekly workshops after they had moved from shelters. The housing was always substandard, often row homes or apartment buildings in poor, dangerous neighborhoods. Once, I picked up Dion and he introduced me to a relative who showed off a long, recently sutured wound from where a stabbing had sliced across his abdomen. When I would go to pick up Daniel in an apartment in the Anacostia neighborhood, I'd walk up a few stairs past a group of dealers. I knocked on Daniel's door at about 11AM, and there'd almost always be several people in his apartment getting high, his mother seemingly among them.

One Saturday when we arrived at Capitol City, the fire department had just extinguished a fire in one of the rooms. Yellow police tape sealed the area outside the building. A toddler was dead, unable to flee when her mother left her kids in the room unattended. The kids we knew stood solemnly behind the tape, snapping pictures while the investigators scoured the room. Ten year-old Dion kept saying, "It's sad, real sad."

After we had been working with the kids at Capitol City for several weeks, some of the Inn's staff and a few of the homeless residents became openly hostile. One of the older youths in our photo workshops told me that some people talked about me and wondered what I was up to. One security guard thought I might be an undercover cop, who often gathered intelligence on drug dealers in these neighborhoods. Two of the security staff stopped me one day while I was on my way out. "You know you can get hurt here, man, if you keep coming round. Some people don't like you coming and taking pictures, bringing those TV camera people with you. Who do you white people think you are?" It was alarming, but I'd been threatened far too many times before and was like water off a duck's back.

Every week I reviewed the photos taken by the kids from the last shoot. It became obvious that the pictures were becoming what could become a powerful exhibit depicting shelter lives. The images were not all sad, either. On the contrary, the images were a testament to happiness and the resiliency of the human spirit, especially in children. I selected ten of the strongest images and made an appointment at the Washington Project for the Arts (WPA), an alternative art space, to pitch an exhibit of their photography. The curator studied the 8X10, black and white photos and smiled immediately.

I told the curator, Phillip Brookman, that my primary objective was to bring attention to the homeless and that there was no better way to do it than through the eyes of children. Secondly, I told him that I wanted to get the kids to see themselves as important, as important as my own children. When working with the kids we often stumbled upon symbolic reminders of grim truths, like the countless needles and shell casings on the streets. The kids often made remarks about the violence, like "I heard gun shots last night" or "Did you hear about the killing on Chapin Street?" One youngster asked, "Why do so many people shoot drugs and shoot people with guns?" Another young photographer in our group was walking past syringes discarded on a street ravaged by frequent gunplay. He remarked, "We're shooting back." I stopped, turned to him, "Hold on. That's what this is all about. You're a genius. We are shooting back with cameras in your community, not bullets and dope. Lets call our project Shooting Back."

• • •

"What are you going to do after the show? Will you continue working with the kids? You can't just abandon them. Have you thought of having a permanent Shooting Back center for ongoing programs for youth? There are some legal issues that may arise like consent. Do you have consent forms to show and maybe sell the kids work? I hear there might even be a book deal. If you need help with funding you will have to be a legal, registered nonprofit." A friend barraged me with questions and qualifications over lunch. She had volunteered at our Saturday workshops and she knew the details of our fledgling organization. Like many attorneys I had known, she was a motor mouth.

"Let me finish my French Fries will you? Please pass the ketchup."

She handed me the ketchup and said, "Get it together man." I glared at her and replied, "Yeah, sure let's get it together and start a nonprofit. Will you help?" She was the first of three founding board members. I was the second, and Fred the third.

We filed the papers to establish a 501(c)3, a not for profit organization, and were approved. We decided to have meetings once a month and recruit more board members. Fred had a contact in a large prestigious law firm, Wilmer, Cutler and Pickering, which would later represent Shooting Back as our pro bono law firm. We asked them to draft consent forms granting us permission to work with and use the photographs the kids had taken. The terms granted both Shooting Back and the participants co-ownership for any photographs and writing created, granting both parties complete rights to use the materials for any use deemed appropriate, including media, books, films, exhibits, etc. Also included was the right for participants and or Shooting Back to sell the photographs.

Calvin Stewart was one of my favorite kids to work with. We discovered each other when I wandered into a small hotel housing homeless families. I had three cameras slung around my neck and shoulders, and he lived with his single mother, who worked for the post office. Calvin was older than the other kids, a well groomed, tall, and good-looking seventeen-year-old who also happened to be smart, well spoken and courteous. He took some of the most stunning photographs for the exhibit. When I met his mother, Veronica, I realized that she had a special commitment to her son and was determined to raise him right. She struck me as a grounded woman and a class act.

One day Calvin and I discussed our project and talked about the forthcoming exhibit. We were both excited. I blurted out, "We have to find some white kids, Calvin." He looked a little surprised but responded, "Yes Jim, I can see your point. All the kids are black and everyone in the photos is black. But this is DC. Most people here are black, except the white people who come in to work from the burbs." He was a quick study and I replied, "Would you come to the burbs with me? We could find some shelters and shoot some pictures and maybe help teach some kids." I asked. A big grin came across his face and he nodded yes.

We visited shelters in Maryland and Virginia and recruited some kids to diversify the exhibit and illustrate that not all homeless people are black. We discovered an old brick warehouse in Alexandria, Virginia, that had been abandoned and later been modestly converted into The Carpenter's Shelter, for temporary housing of the homeless. It was nestled next to a railroad yard used by freight trains. We met several kids who were eager to take pictures, most notably Chris and Norman Heflin, brothers who lived in a tiny partitioned space with another infant brother and sister and their mother and father. We told the kids we would be back the following week to start taking pictures.

DICKENSIAN SENSATIONS

New contracts provided sustenance for my family, and all the opportunities had to do with our society's poverty woes. Mitch and other organizers from around the country were planning a national march on Washington called Housing Now. They wanted to attract attention and pressure Washington policymakers, so Mitch and Democratic strategist Donna Brazille requested a meeting with me. The role they offered required extensive travel to twenty-two cities, to feature my images at exhibitions, all expenses paid, along with an honorarium. I agreed and we loaded our van with a portable exhibit of the homeless. Both Sherry and Hanna loved road trips, and this would be a long one. We drove to Boston for the first show, then set off to the south.

In Minneapolis, the prearranged venue was in an upscale shopping mall called Calhoun Square in Uptown, a trendy neighborhood near the chain of lakes. While I attached the pictures, mounted on foam core onto the portable display panels in the shopping center's lobby, I was interrupted by one of the center's well-dressed managers. He said that they could not allow the pictures to be exhibited due to the content of the images. I asked him, "What do you think they are dirty pictures, pornography?" He responded, "No, they are depressing and not appropriate for display in a shopping center."

By the next day about thirty of our activist friends gathered at Calhoun Square to protest against censorship. We had also alerted local media. A week after the Minneapolis protest an editor from the University of Minnesota Press called and told me he had read about the censorship of my photographs at Calhoun Square and wanted to publish a book of my images, titled *American Refugees*. The book would feature the photograph of the Fitzgerald family's eviction on the cover.

On the day of the Housing Now march and demonstration at the US Capitol, a busload of celebrities arrived to lead the march including Martin Sheen, Valerie Harper, Jon Voigt, Cher, Casey Kasem and others. Voigt and I talked a bit about how during the press conference before the march, he had welled up with tears a number of times. I had never seen anyone quite so emotional about the issue except those being evicted from their homes. The band Los Lobos played, followed by a litany of long-winded speakers. Afterwards, many of the demonstrators proceeded to Constitution Ave for an act of civil disobedience. We had planned to block traffic and face subsequent arrests. Sheen and I strolled together to block the street. He had been arrested many times before for acts of civil disobedience and encouraged me to participate saying, "Do it, it'll be freeing and good for your soul."

We were both arrested and taken in a bus to a police building and held for a couple of hours and later released. A limo arrived after our release to take Cher and her son to the train station for her trip back to New York. She offered me a ride to Union Station so I could catch the Metro subway home. We had a lively chat during the short ride, a fitting ending to a decidedly surreal day.

SHOOTING BACK

The original ideas for the Shooting Back concept germinated in part during my seminary studies at Wesley Theological Seminary. I was also inspired by an art book featuring children's drawings and poetry, created by the prisoners of a concentration camp called Terezin, near Prague. The book, *I Never Saw Another Butterfly*, was put together by Friedl Dicker Brandeis, who taught art and painting as therapy for children, and rescued 4,500 drawings that later served proof in Nuremberg. But the original seeds were planted much earlier.

As a little boy kneeled at his bed and praying for the sick, needy and afflicted with my mother next to me; something profound sunk into my heart, and a strange metamorphosis began that would take decades to complete. But my fate was sealed. Somehow, through riots, floods and politics, I would become a radical Christian. The ideas that were forming for what would become Shooting Back were inspired by those prayers, by those moments with my mom and the Bible, and, eventually by another book, too. God's special concern for the poor are stated over and over. His admonitions to the rich are searing and stern.

Christ was a radical wake-up call for humans—God's concern for the poorest and worst among us turns the world's order upside down. Thousands of years after Christ walked the earth, wealth, fame and power are worshiped as fervently as ever, especially in the United States. Another book that inspired me, *Pedagogy of the Oppressed*, by Brazilian philosopher Paulo Freire calls traditional teaching the "banking model," because it treats the student as an empty vessel to be filled with knowledge—as if a person were a piggy bank. He argues that pedagogy should treat the learner as a co-creator of knowledge.

My career amply illustrated the world's economic injustices.

In seminary I tried to learn about how to combat these injustices not just practically, but spiritually. The idea of co-creating learning resonated in me. I would do whatever I could to bring the tools of the privileged to the poorest of the poor. They deserve just as much as anyone to memorialize their lives in photography and art, to learn that their lives have as much worth and power as any, despite their struggles. Many of the kids in our programs referred to me as the, "picture man" or "Master Butt Chin"—some of them thought my clef chin looked like a butt, and when film crews started hanging round I wasn't terribly anxious to get that onto a national broadcast. A former NBC News producer named Robin Smith often visited our program, and she wanted to bring her crew and to film the work for a television documentary. PBS backed the idea for a half-hour documentary titled *Shooting Back: Photography By and About the Homeless.*

The only funding available for Shooting Back came out of my pocket, other than the in kind donations from the photo labs that processed the film and made prints, and a few photographer friends who donated an ample supply of film. During one workshop, I walked around the shelter with nine-year-old Daniel, and when we spotted a kid about six-years-old complete a back flip, Daniel shouted "Wow," and ran toward the gymnast. He asked him to do it again so he could take a picture.

Daniel took a photo but said he had not included the kid's legs in the frame. I said, "Daniel sit down." He looked down at the parking lot's hard, dirty asphalt. He sat down reluctantly. I squatted and sat down next to him. The gymnast stood in front of us and stared and prepared to do another back flip but first had to adjust his stained overalls. I said to Daniel, "Take his picture," and turned to the six year-old flipper and ordered, "Do it again."

We repeated this over and over again. The gymnast had done about twenty perfect flips in front of a dirty, battered concrete wall by the time we finished. I hoped that Daniel had taken the perfect picture. If ever given the opportunity the homeless gymnast could become a medalist in future Olympics, but opportunity was not a visitor to homeless shelters, so we tried to teach these kids the determination to work for it.

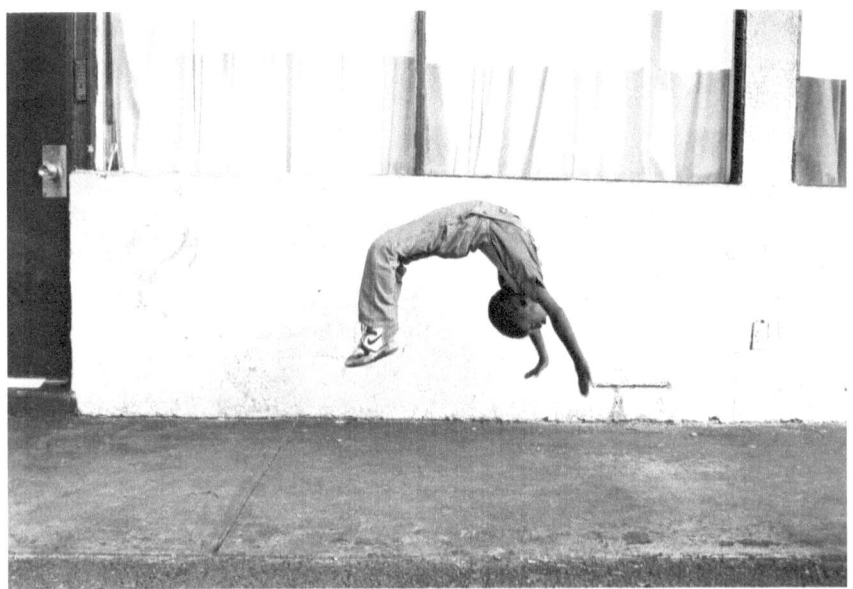

The flip photo shot by a 9 year old homeless child

Shortly before our exhibit opened, I received the sad news that Mitch Snyder had died. He had hanged himself inside the Community for Creative Nonviolence shelter where he worked and lived; he suffered from long bouts of depression, and when a long relationship with his girlfriend ended it pushed him over the edge. It was terrible that he would never see the Shooting Back exhibit. He was a troubled man but we had become friends, and I knew he had internal struggles.

The exhibit opened on a grand scale in September 1990 to a huge crowd and was the second most popular show in WPA's history. More than 10,000 people attended the show and WPA raised more money than ever before, with donors including some of the largest foundations and corporations in the US. But the real cachet for investors came from the worldwide press coverage of the Shooting Back phenomenon. I laughed while I watched Charlene and her mother Patricia laughing and dancing across the gallery's hardwood floor, bumping into each other and many of the art patrons. Charlene had been one of our most energetic and creative photographers at only eleven-years-old.

It was one of the most publicized global photo exhibits in recent history. After the show, some of the kids and I travelled to Perpignan, France, to present our exhibit at a prestigious international photo festival called VISA. The exhibit went on a three-year tour across the US. Our literary agent Anne Edelstein orchestrated a book publishing. Legendary *Life Magazine* published the photos in a seven-page story and Daniel's perfect photo of the kid doing a back flip was featured on magazine covers across Europe. The show travelled to Japan.

Daniel's photo was called "The Flip," and has been used for diplomacy. The US State Department's Office of Art in Embassies Exhibitions sought permission to obtain a large print, which they framed and hung in the embassy in Kinshasa, Democratic Republic of the Congo.

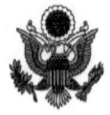

Embassy of the United States of America

Kinshasa, Democratic Republic of the Congo

May 1, 2013

Mr. Jim Hubbard
1630 Shell Avenue
Venice, CA 90291

Dear Jim,

I am writing to let you know how much my wife, Pamela Schmoll, and I have enjoyed having your work "Back Flip" black and white photograph on display in our residence here in Kinshasa the past few years. As you will see in the enclosed pamphlet, the focus of our entire "Arts in Embassies" exhibition has been on "voice", highlighting the importance of each individual's voice in moving towards a more just and peaceful world including the need to help those who are unable to speak for themselves.

We believe the exhibition, in which your work was key, was a great success and struck a chord here in the Democratic Republic of the Congo which, as you know, is beleaguered with longstanding issues of war, peace and human suffering. Hopefully, the exhibition played a role in the efforts of our government to help the Congolese overcome these challenges.

Please accept my sincere thanks for your generous contribution.

Sincerely,

James F. Entwistle
Ambassador

Enclosure: as stated

Letter from U.S. Ambassador to Kinshasa,
Democratic Republic of the Congo 2013

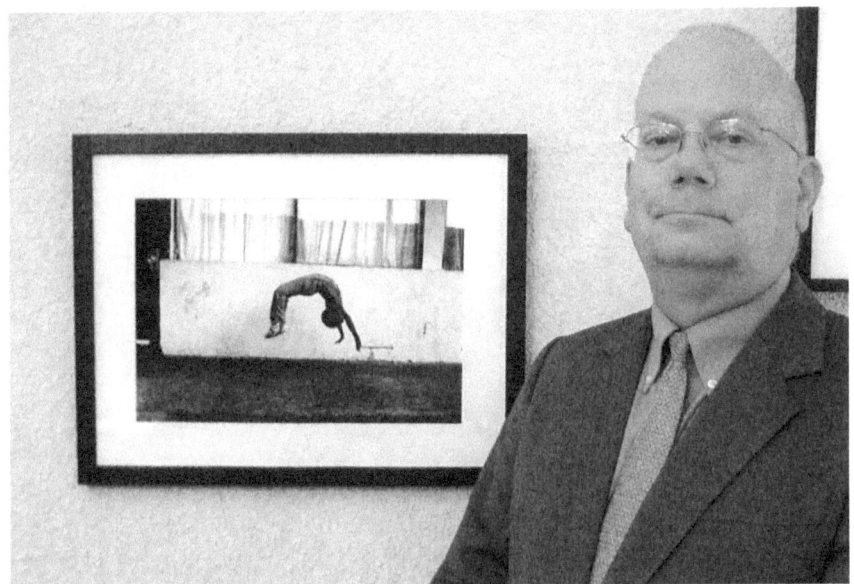

U.S. Ambassador James F. Entwistle to Kinshasa
next to iconic Flip photo 2013

Paramount Pictures summoned me to Hollywood to pitch a television movie deal. They wanted rights for my life story and the founding of Shooting Back. A second trip to Hollywood followed in the wake of a similar offer from NBC. On yet another front, a top agent from a speaker's bureau in Boston offered a two-year contract to join the lecture circuit. The studios assigned scriptwriters to conduct preliminary interviews with me. When the scripts were sent to me one of them described me as a guy wearing a flak jacket and sitting at a barstool. I couldn't help but be worried that Hollywood might invent some image of me as some humorous science fiction version of myself, full of distorted details and outright fabrications. I imagined a rehabilitated Vietnam vet who had hunted serial killers and was now working with kids.

I signed a contract with Jodi Solomon Speakers Bureau in Boston and they booked me in universities and colleges. I started traveling even more than I had with UPI, getting to over a hundred schools in two years. Sherry expressed concerns about my notoriety and whether all this attention hadn't inflated my ego. With so much adulation, I may have started sliding downward and begun believing my own PR, a dangerous thing to do. A little fame can be as poisonous as money and sex.

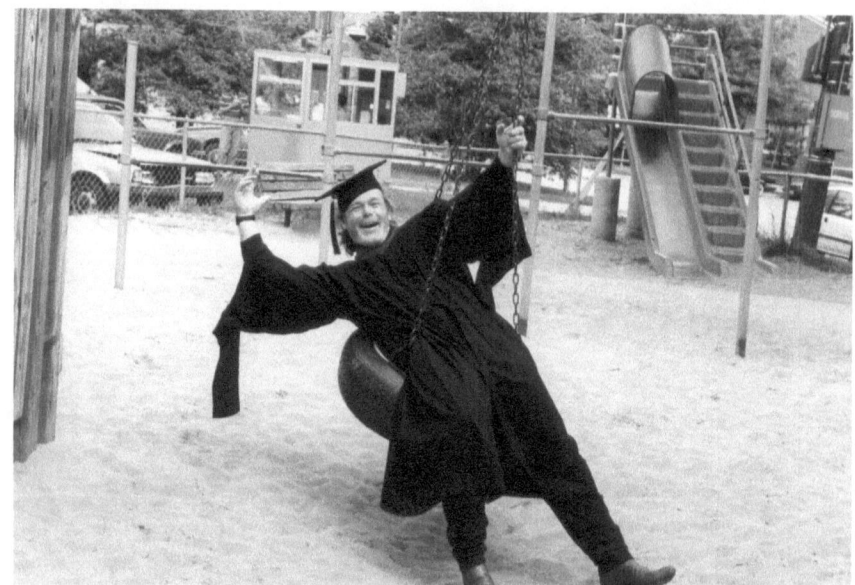

Jim just graduated from Wesley Theological Seminary 1990

BORED OF THE DIRECTORS

Shooting Back was riding high and the board believed they needed to safeguard the project from possible fallout. The members of the board I had recruited were inside the beltway elites or wannabes. They were a mix of attorneys, *New York Times* and *Post* journalists and art world highbrows who often called people, "dahling." What better group to guarantee ongoing publicity and legal protection when someone decided they didn't like me. It was a given that someone would eventually develop a distaste for me. Several would be on our board.

Our trouble began when the board spent a day with consultants who advised them of their responsibilities as board members of a non profit organization, They were instructed they were the governing and fiscally accountable overseers for Shooting Back to insure legal, tax exempt status. They heard the history of clashes between headstrong and wacky visionary founders and board members. Remember my dad and high school daze teachers and principal. They had all tried to exert control over me and failed. The board attempted to harness me but that was like trying to put their heads through the eye of a needle. In subsequent board meetings there were some heated, stormy discussions about the governing rights of Shooting Back versus my rights. Who gets the money? What is the separation between the organization and its founder? It was decided Shooting Back would continue to be represented by their pro bono firm, Wilmer, Cutler and Pickering, to protect the corporation's interests, but that I would need my own counsel for personal opportunities that might conflict with Shooting Back's.

Even though my salary was modest, I wasn't opposed to sharing the gold from movie deals—if there were to be any. The rewards dulled the fear that my life might be portrayed in ways that could be unflattering or inaccurate. Hollywood had no interest in protecting my image, after all—they were about drama and making money.

The board saw the issues more objectively. The contract drafts also sought rights to my daughter Hanna's life, and Sherry's. They would also need to sign papers, too, and it was finally at those blank dotted lines that I listened to my misgivings. They shouldn't have to endure to a scrutiny that might harm them.

During several meetings, Shooting Back's attorneys were on one side of the table, and I sat on the other with the agent and attorney whom I had met when she came to our exhibit. The standoff quickly grew adversarial, even though all parties wanted to agree to terms. Long story short, the conflict between the parties short-circuited any deals with Hollywood. For the next two years I was on the lecture circuit, and happy to see that no story about Shooting Back had any aspersion, which was more than a little unusual. I wondered when the other shoe would drop—there had to be someone either outside our circle or inside critical of our work or success.

Five months after the Washington opening, the exhibit appeared in a Lower Manhattan gallery. *The New York Times* ran a story about the show in February 1991 reporting, "Most people have never been inside a homeless shelter, but they think they know what one looks like. They have seen the typical media images of squalor and human misery. That is why the photographs taken by a group of homeless children in Washington are a revelation. What the 113 black and white photographs on display mostly demonstrate is how alive the people are, despite their surroundings." I loved that the 'newspaper of record' story implied that the intent of the photos was to humanize the homeless and foster the public's compassion for them in photographs taken by homeless children.

Calvin Stewart and I flew to California for an appearance on Gary Collins' *The Home Show*. Calvin was telegenic and did well on television, the spitting image of Dwayne Wayne, a character from the '80s black sitcom, *A Different World*. Three other youngsters often joined me for television appearances: Dion, Daniel and Charlene. They all lived or had lived at Capitol City Inn, before being given permanent Section 8 housing. We travelled to New York a few times and were accompanied by their mothers for early morning appearances on network shows. The kids were nervous yet thrilled when we appeared on television and were treated like stars. They were picked up in limos and stayed in some of New York's most elegant hotels, dining in the restaurants normally reserved for the rich and powerful.

Shooting Back was invited to attend and participate in Macy's 1991 Thanksgiving Day Parade and to be ambassador's at the Barbie Summit for Children at the Waldorf Astoria Hotel in New York where they would also have rooms for one week, courtesy Mattel. We selected four kids, Dion, Daniel, Charlene and Calvin, and Sherry and Hanna accompanied us.

We were to travel to New York by train. I picked up the two boys in the Shooting Back van but when we arrived to pick up Charlene we had not yet received a signed consent form from her mother Patricia. A woman came to the door and announced Charlene's mother was in St. Elizabeth's Hospital. The woman offered to sign the form right there, but I explained only a legal guardian could do so, leaving us with few options. Our train was leaving in an hour from Union Station to New York. I paused and took a deep breath and told Charlene to grab her suitcase, and then we raced to St. E's, a gargantuan, old brick building

I paced while we waited at the hospital. A very large female nurse led Charlene's mother into the waiting room—Patricia looked awful and out of it. I had seen her looking this way before, and heard she had a problem with drugs. Charlene handed her mother the consent form and slowly she scribbled her signature. Both her wrists were bandaged, covering the slash wounds from her attempted suicide. Charlene sat next to my daughter Hanna on the three-hour train ride; they talked and giggled the whole way.

The kids were showered with lavish gifts and mingled with other children from around the world. Charlene was given Barbie dolls and the boys received jackets, and all received gift cards for stores in Times Square. On the big day we got up early in our luxurious hotel suites at the Waldorf to participate in the parade, the kids living these all too brief adventures into a world totally unlike their own.

• • •

In 1992 I couldn't keep up with the travel for Shooting Back, and remember being bewildered and exhausted when someone told me I was the front-man, the face of Shooting Back. Tipper Gore and I had become friends years earlier, and we both shared a passion for photography and the issues of homelessness and poverty. Washington was about to welcome Bill Clinton as the nation's next president. I received a call from Hillary Clinton's office inviting me and some of the kids to a news conference.

Hillary had selected photographs from Shooting Back for one of the six official Inaugural Posters for her husband's first inauguration. She wanted us there to unveil the posters and receive our own copies of the large, beautiful prints. I took the same kids I had taken to New York, and we did what was becoming a familiar performance in front of the media. After the news conference Tipper Gore invited Sherry and me to attend the ceremonies and the Tennessee Inaugural Ball at the Washington Hilton. The night of the Inaugural Gala Sherry dressed in a beautiful gown—she was ecstatic, and fittingly gorgeous. We had a great time that night, but also would never want to attend another, having learned that the experience was uncomfortably reminiscent of being sardines squished together in a can.

Another wonderful travel opportunity beckoned for us, this a significantly longer journey for Dion, Daniel, and Charlene, who had become the most recognizable Shooting Back participants from media. They were the first kids offered the chance to go to France but declined after conferring with their mothers. We then asked Chris and Norman Heflin from the Carpenter's Shelter to come with us along, with their dad, Norman Sr. It was their first flight, and Hanna had to keep asking the flight attendant for more barf bags for airsick Norman, who vomited several times from his seat next to my daughter and wife. It was my family's first trip to France, and I was glad that they could come with me, feeling guilty at all the time I'd spent on the road away from them.

The Helfins accompanied Sherry, Hanna and me on a ten-day journey to attend and exhibit the Shooting Back photos at a prestigious international photographic festival in Perpignan, France, where the photos would be on display in a 12th century cathedral. Thousands of people attended from all over Europe. Shortly after our trip to France Daniel's mother called me, crying. "Jim, I'm very ill. Daniel loves you—would you take care of Daniel if anything happens to me?" "You mean for me to take him and raise him?" She said "yes," and I told her I would have to discuss the matter with my wife but I would help if at all possible. Nothing came of it. As far as I knew, nothing had happened to her, and the next time I saw her it was across a conference room table surrounded by attorneys, when she and two other mothers threatened to sue Shooting Back on behalf of Dion, Charlene and Daniel.

Later that year World Vision, a Christian nonprofit humanitarian agency dedicated to helping care for people in need around the world asked me to implement a Shooting Back style program with orphans in Romania. I recruited two freelance photographers, Steve Barrett, who had been a mentor in Washington, and Lauren a Minneapolis freelancer. We embarked on a far different adventure than any other we'd experienced.

We arrived at a bleak, foreboding and eerie building, with broken windows and a sign on the front door said, "Casa de Copii [Children's Home] #10." The orphanage housed fifty orphans, all boys. The director of the orphanage appeared, Victor Uta, followed by several boys and looking like he had walked out of central casting ready to don his cape and lurk for the camera. I became immediately suspicious of what went on when there were no visitors, but the truth is I didn't really want to know. I was determined to be low key and complete the project.

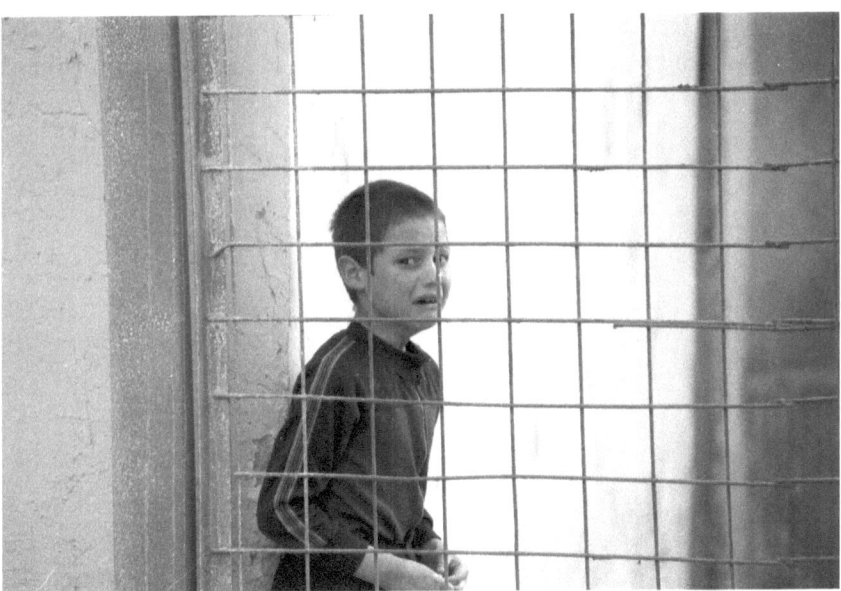

Romanian orphan in Bucharest orphanage 1995

The kids were surprisingly enthusiastic about the program, in stark contrast to many of the jaded and "shut down" kids I had gotten used to working with back in the states. The children spent two weeks photographing everything in sight, pigs on the farm, beggars rummaging through trash, crumbling apartment blocks and each other. We finished and headed home. We had had an incredibly exciting year, but I started to get antsy as fall descended. I wasn't enthusiastic about managing anything, even an organization for kids or for a cause. UPI wasn't exactly wrong when they criticized my managing skills; I needed to feel the passion for work, and that always meant being outside an office's walls. I trusted my friends to run Shooting Back.

The board and I continued to clash and following one heated meeting five board members resigned. One said as she huffed from the room headed back to her Georgetown estate, "Have a nice life." Fred Sweets and I looked at each other and broke out laughing.

The next day I called the police. I spoke with my brother Michael, the DC Metroplitan Police Detective who worked out of the Third District. "Mike will you and your friends join my board?" At our next meeting Mike brought several of his buddies, all journalists and attorneys. After introducing them to other remaining members Mike said "Do what you need to do and please provide us with a rubber stamp."

No Reservations

I conceived of a second Shooting Back project to raise the public's awareness. The people I had in mind were more hidden away from society than the homeless, but they also had faced profound struggles and a long history of injustices. I had first met them when I spent a couple of months covering the siege at Wounded Knee in 1973, where I'd learned of the poverty and despair on the Pine Ridge Reservation in South Dakota—long the poorest place in the US. High unemployment, violence, alcohol and drug abuse affected every family living in that countryside, and there was a terrifyingly high suicide rate for young people. Native Americans, having been crushed by external forces time and time again, were now vanquishing themselves, too.

It was time to make another change, especially because Sherry missed her home in Minnesota terribly. I empathized and in recent years had rarely been at home with her. She probably felt abandoned, and it looked likely that we were headed for a separation unless I picked up on my end. As it often seems among the people who feel called to missions, I unintentionally hurt the people closest to me in my quest to help others.

At our next board meeting I announced my new project and that I would be moving to Minneapolis for at least two years. The board received the proposals with mixed feelings, uncertain about my ability to help from outside the city and about the toll such a move would tax on the program. Relations on the board continued to strain with some members who hadn't resigned. A few months earlier, two members had asked Ella to join. I'm not sure why, but I suspected she wouldn't help. Ella was connected to DC politicos and when she heard about the new project in Minneapolis she expressed concerns about abandoning the kids in DC. Ella had often referred to the 700 children at Capitol City Inn where she worked as, "My children," and that especially applied to Dion, Daniel and Charlene, the mini-celebrities of Shooting Back. Dion and the others, though, had not been involved with Shooting Back for over a year. A few months later Ella announced she would be forming her own for-profit venture as manager of the three kids. I explained to her that would constitute a conflict of interest and requested her resignation. She didn't take it well, and left us with the inescapable sense that there would be trouble down the road with her group, which she called "Dion and Friends."

Sherry and I traveled to Minneapolis in search of a home in the neighborhood where we had lived years before. I was not excited to move back to Minneapolis. My mouth still had a bad taste from the Supreme Court's reversal of my lawsuit against UPI. In order to accomplish our goals on the reservations, we would have to get the approval of the tribal leaders who oversaw and controlled each sovereign nation. I travelled to eight reservations meeting these leaders in person, finishing my two weeks with approval granted at Pine Ridge and other reservations in Wisconsin, Minnesota, Arizona and New Mexico.

We bought a 27-foot Ford RV to live in and travel to reservations around the country. We also purchased a ten-passenger van for use in Minneapolis, to take Native Americans to and from the city and reservations. We planned to install a small darkroom in the RV to process film and make prints during production of what would be titled Shooting Back from the Reservation. Both vehicles required a co-signatory, and as no one on the board wanted to sign, I did. Though we were still figuring out arrangements for the new project, I would still return to DC to help out with the original Shooting Back, and the board had agreed to get me a small apartment there to use as my temporary home and base of operations.

We began work with Minneapolis youth in a small delapidated storefront space that we rented. I met Sammy Watso, a Native American activist and director of a gallery in a cultural center across the street from our place. I contracted with him to serve as an advisor for our project, and his son Thunder Watso participated in our Minneapolis workshops. I asked Sammy for his thoughts about putting cameras in the hands of Native American children and he responded, "This project signals more than just another collection of images. The photos by the children will capture Native life. It will be a collection of photos that sets us free. By giving the children cameras we can see the world we've left them, and they can begin to see themselves as the new keepers of the earth."

Sammy and I, along with our project manager Wes, hit the road in our RV for the 800-mile trek. When we arrived at Pine Ridge we introduced ourselves to the smiling young people and got to meet people with names I'd never heard anything like before, like Davidica Little Spotted Horse and Loris Few Tails.

The Indian project began receiving notable exposure early in our work both in print and broadcast media, most prominently when *The New York Times* gave us national exposure and featured a whole page of photos by Indian youth on their op-ed page. Europeans, and especially Germans, have something of a romantic fascination with Native American lore. Several journalists from throughout Europe contacted us for interviews about the project, and often sent reporters to the reservations. An attractive young German freelancer I'd met before, in Washington, visited us in Arizona. She spent several days interviewing the kids and their parents, tribal chiefs and me. While Katarina's views of reservation life were myopic, she had romance in her heart and was warm toward me.

WPA was eager to host another Shooting Back exhibit several years after their first. They secured large grants from Toyota, US West and a host of others to provide for the substantial costs we incurred while travelling between reservations for two years. They managed to supply sufficient funding to fly several Native youth from their reservations to the exhibit's opening, and a private meeting with President Clinton.

Our entourage of eight kids and four or five adults from a sacred drumming group in Minneapolis traveled to the nation's capitol to attend the exhibit. Davidica Little Spotted Horse and her group traveled from Pine Ridge, and I flew to Las Vegas and drove from there to the remote Hualapai Indian Reservation in tiny Peach Springs, Arizona, where we had also worked. Two kids and their mom's rode with me the ninety miles back to Vegas for our flight to the exhibit.

Early in the morning, before I started on my drive to the Hualapai Reservation to fetch the kids, the phone in my hotel room rang. The DC office manager Linda Posell called me and provided a phone number for a reporter who wanted me to call. Linda had been told to tell me the writer was on deadline. I dialed and the voice at the other end said, "Hanna Rosin, *New Republic*." I was aware of the liberal magazine and had read that Al Gore liked it, which wasn't exactly a ringing endorsement in my mind. I liked Tipper, but wasn't fond of Al, who struck me as a stereotypical Washington man—a pompous stuffed shirt. I had a bad feeling about the call.

I had heard that there was a reporter calling and interviewing people who had been or were currently associated with us. Some of them told me the story she was working on might not be favorable. She talked fast and I knew she was young. After more questions, I concluded she was also wet behind the ears. She wanted to know about consent forms that some of the children's mothers had denied signing. I said, "I'm in Las Vegas and need to catch a plane." She wouldn't describe her storyline when I asked, so I knew to use caution. A few more of her questions revealed some of her angles, like when she sought my reaction to a threatened lawsuit by three Shooting Back kids and their mothers. Guess who?

She tried to be blunt. "I need to see those consent forms." "Here's the deal, Hanna, do whatever you need to do, but I cannot get you the signed forms until I get to Washington. They're filed away in Minneapolis, where there's no one who can provide them to you. I can get them to you in a few days. But if you run a story denying they exist and that each is signed by every mother for any minor we ever worked with, you're a liar." I hung up.

I had often wondered when the other shoe would drop. Hundreds of all favorable magazine or newspaper stories? Where were the critics? The puzzle had nagged at me for a long time, but after that call I at least had an answer. She was at the *New Republic* and her name was Hanna.

On the day the exhibit was to open we had an early morning engagement with Bill Clinton. We could barely contain ourselves in anticipation of a private meeting with the man. The president's photographer took group pictures of us posing with Clinton, and one of the kids I brought from Peach Springs, a ten-year-old Hualapai boy named RJ, handed Clinton a large framed copy of one of his photos. R.J. Lewis, Jr, philosophical and articulate beyond his years, told the president something profound: "When I pick up a camera and look up at the sky, I go to a different dimension." The president said, "Wow, that's amazing."

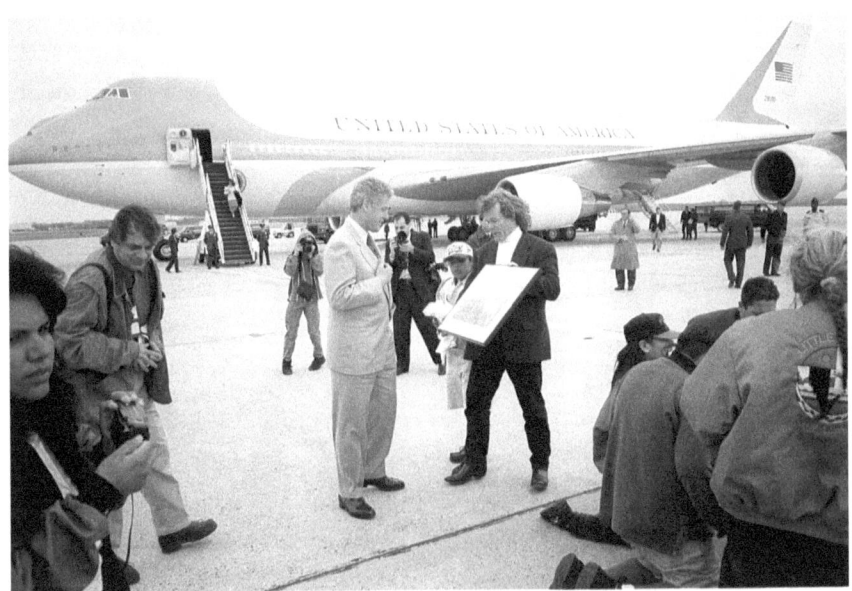

Jim presents President Clinton photograph from Shooting Back 1994

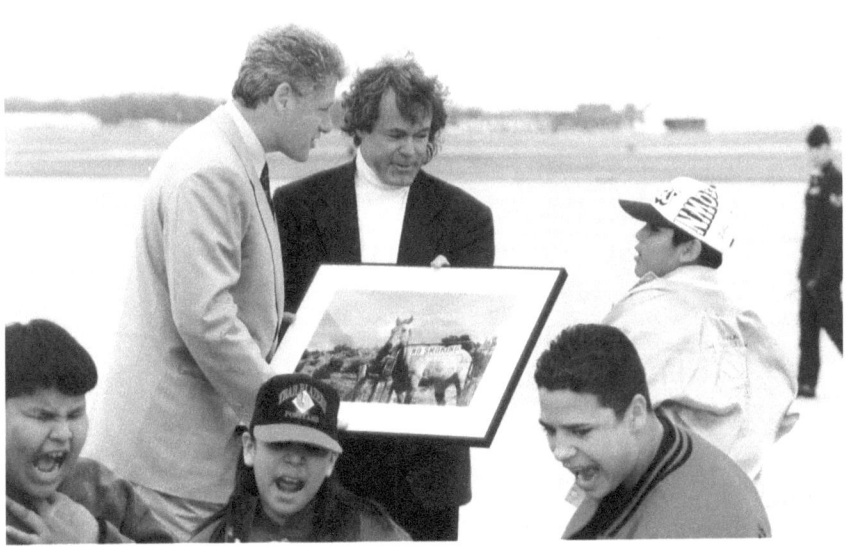

*President Clinton and Jim hold framed photo presented
to Clinton and shot by R.J. Lewis Jr.(R) 1994*

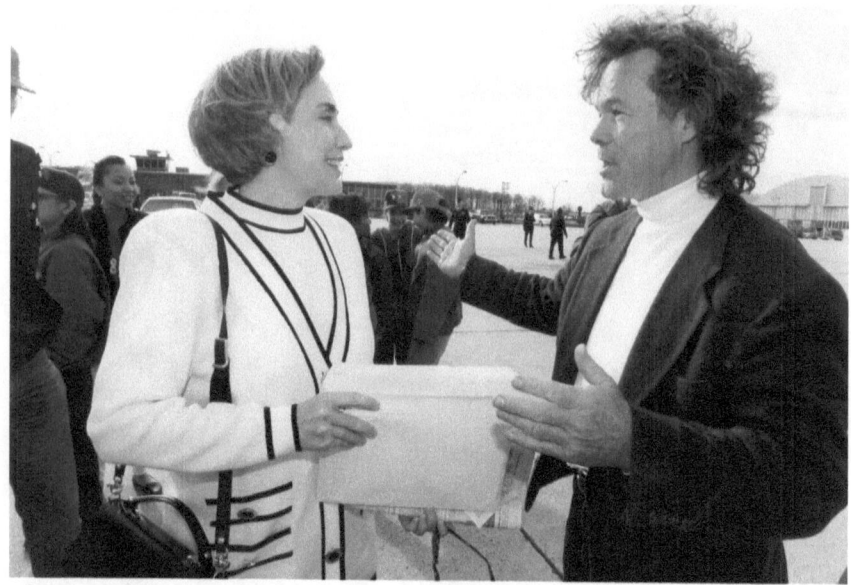

Hillary Clinton and Jim talk during meeting 1994

We were all jubilant on the way back to the hotel, only a few hours from going to the gala opening of Shooting Back From the Reservation. The kids soaked up adoration from the hundreds of art patrons and government VIPs in attendance. Two senators attended and attorney general Janet Reno made some opening remarks. But the board members and Linda Posell mingled uneasily—it was clear something was up, and that we had to talk.

SHOOTING BLANKS

Rosin's article was in the latest edition of *The New Republic*, and on the newsstands. Linda suggested we drive out when the reception ended to grab a copy. The kids were taken back to the hotel, and at an all-night bookstore we found the magazine with the long anticipated article, titled "Shooting Blanks."

Linda and I sat in her car and read the story. It was as negative as I expected, and the writer lied about how the parents of three kids from our program never signed consent forms, and about me telling her I could not produce them. The story said the three kids and their parents planned to sue Shooting Back because they had been robbed of tens of thousands of dollars in profits, remaining poor while I raked in fees from the college lecture circuit. It was obvious Ella had inspired the story. I felt bad for her, though—she didn't receive a byline next to Rosin's.

Linda suddenly let out a loud primal scream, startling me out of my own rage for a moment. My personal resentment, however, paled next to the sense of defeat at how the story would damage Shooting Back. I had never thought we'd be accused of exploiting poor kids. "We were finished," I thought. We remained in the car for another hour or so rereading the lies Rosin had constructed. "You know Linda, something like this was bound to happen. We haven't had any negative publicity. Now we do. It comes with the territory." She had stopped crying and said, "That's true, but these are *lies*." Linda's principles had been offended—she was always loyal, compassionate and committed, and I couldn't have been more grateful that she managed the office.

"Linda, do you remember Covenant House and its founder, Father Bruce Ritter?" I asked. She nodded, "I followed that scandal carefully. Thank God, we aren't being falsely accused of sexual inappropriateness, only the financial part."

Ritter was a Franciscan priest who began a one-man outreach to homeless youth in the 1960s and founded Covenant House in '68. Ritter and Covenant House were held in high esteem by the public until 1990, when he was forced to step down in the wake of allegations of sexual and financial misconduct.

It wasn't like I needed reminders, but Ritter's story and a long list of others were warning signs that those who wanted to help the poor faced certain perils, threats from the world and the dangers of temptation. I knew that some people had been correctly accused of wrongdoing and others were falsely accused, and hadn't thought myself naïve—at least not until that Hanna Rosin came along. I tried to do everything to insure that not only did our work actually help the poor, but also that Shooting Back staff were above reproach for any allegations of misconduct. We committed no crime or exploitation.

Before we departed Washington, the kids were given gift cards from sundry stores in a high-end shopping area on Connecticut Avenue, only blocks from the White House, and they got to enjoy a mini-spree there. Later that evening I flew back to Peach Springs with them, staring out the window at the low orange sun dipping under the horizon. I started to choke up thinking about the last kids who had gotten to enjoy such an adventure, three who I had cared about and were convinced to turn against me. People with their own agendas had used Dion, Daniel and Charlene as pawns.

Two weeks later, Linda and I met with the Hitachi Foundation. We requested a second year of funding for Shooting Back. They declined, citing the adverse publicity and a pending lawsuit. *The New Republic*'s story had done its damage. Funders run the other way and close the vaults to organizations tarnished in the media. A desire for vengeance continued to build inside me. I wrote a letter to the editor at the *New Republic*, in which I wrote that they had lied and given in to sloppy journalism. They printed it. Who would believe me? Most readers would blow me off as the accused culprit and would say anything, and I tried to turn away, to take a deep breath and be patient. Pray for guidance and direction.

An important chapter in my life had ended, or so I thought. I pondered some possibilities. I had sold clothes in men's clothing stores decades ago, and maybe I could try that again—assuming no one recognized me. I might have to return to something else I had done, maybe the construction work of my youth, the sort of business where my colleagues don't read *The New Republic* or watch PBS.

• • •

It turned out that I didn't have to do anything. *The Washington Post* took care of it. They were about to become my representative in the court of public opinion.

As had been the case when Peter Carlson called to write a story in 1987, another scribe from the *Post* called to write a story about recent events in my life. Judith Weinraub, a staff writer for the *Post*'s style section, the most popularly read section of the paper, wanted to schedule an interview. She wanted my reactions to the *New Republic* piece, and had already interviewed a number of other people about the article. She explained that some of the people she'd interviewed had said some unflattering things about me, and I responded, "If you want to know more about me you may as well read Peter Carlson's story." She said she'd read it, but for now wanted to know if I was bothered by the negative things people had said about me. I paused for a few seconds. "Judith, it's really not any of my business what others think of me."

She went on describing the newspaper's intent, "We plan to publish a lengthy article prominently on the front page of Style along with a photograph of you and the photo Daniel Hall took of a kid doing back flips. We want to provide a balanced story to our readers to make what they will of it. Just a couple interviews."

I still had friends inside the *Post* and called them to find out what the writer was up to. I was not about to agree to an interview that would slam Shooting Back, and me, all over again. I learned that the nexus for the story was what the *Post* believed were questionable journalistic practices that *The New Republic* had once used to berate the *Post* in a story. They had an axe to grind with the magazine, and the Shooting Back story gave them a window.

The story was printed on front of the Style section one month after *The New Republic* story was published in 1994. A sizeable portrait showed me next to the headline, "A Do-Gooder's Negative Image." I still considered the moniker an insult, but the rest of the article proved Rosin and her magazine had been untruthful, sloppy and biased.

The story opened with a line about how I was "not on your life a candidate for sainthood," which was more than fine with me, who knew my own sins all too well. Judith described me in the third paragraph as "single-minded," "demanding," "impatient" and "ego driven." She knew me better than I did, though some people I had clashed with, a few board members, for instance, might've also used these words. Working on news assignments on Capitol Hill, I once thought that if I spent too much time with these politicians I could become an arrogant, egomaniac just like them. It had happened.

But Judith also wrote that I had been "graced with a great idea." Shooting Back. She described the mess of *The New Republic* story and the flaring tempers involved, and went on to describe some of the conflicts on our board of directors. Two of the issues were about the copyright/consent forms and selling the kids' photographs, debates as to whether the money should go to children directly or to support the program. A third issue was more personal: what should happen to the income from the speaking engagements and any movie rights involving my life and Shooting Back.

Shooting Back's board of directors decided years ago that money generated from any photo sales would go into programs, not to pay royalties to the kids. "I suggested it," board member Fred Sweet's said in the story, the former *Post* photographer and *Los Angeles Times* photo editor. The most glaring deception in the entire story involved the mothers and the contracts again, and whether they signed anything or knew what they signed. Rosin echoed social worker Ella, saying to the *Post* reporter, "These are people who I'm sure never signed another form in their lives."

They had all signed more binding legal documents than I ever had—food stamps, welfare, and housing, to name just a few—forms they would have had to sign if only with an X. All of the mothers were enmeshed in DC's Human Services operation, an inept and suspect bureaucracy, no doubt, but one that still used reams of paperwork. Rosin either saw the world through rose-tinted glasses or was just out of touch with reality. She no doubt believes the poor do not share the seven deadly sins as the rest of society, both of us included.

After the *Post* story was published I received a letter from an influential Washington woman, who finished her note with the comforting reminder that "There is just no way you can please everyone out there, no matter how hard you work and how much you give personally and professionally. The other shoe had to drop." In an ironic twist, Hanna Rosin eventually left the *New Republic* to join the *Washington Post*.

• • •

A reprieve from Shooting Back woes surfaced when The United States Information Agency (USIA) recruited me to work with a program called Amerika Huas, in six cities across Germany. It was an opportunity to escape, briefly, to a place I loved and to do good work as intended, without the shadow of my troubles hanging over me. When I returned from the trip as a US emissary, I wrote a letter from Minneapolis to board members while negotiations continued with the disgruntled mothers. We had received several large grants, in spite of all the recent difficulties: a two-year grant from Prudential for $80,000, to create a technical assistance manual to help others launch Shooting Back style programs for kids; and a $10,000 grant announced from the National Endowment for the Arts (NEA) to produce the manual.

The ambassadorial journey to Germany put matters in perspective: Washington's endless games and toxic atmosphere had brought out my generosity and faith while also flattering my worst, egotistical instincts. The worst elements of my character and the city had poisoned the work, and my family life. We had to leave. We had a final meeting in a large boardroom full of attorneys. There would be no lawsuit. The three kids sat with their mothers at a long wooden table across from me. We all agreed to end our squabble. We signed a long document that my attorneys suggested I sign.

One morning while looking out my kitchen onto the street in Minneapolis, I watched as tow trucks arrived to repossess the RV and van, for which Shooting Back still owed debts. As cosigner on the vehicles, I realized the tow trucks were dragging away the vestiges of my economic security, pulling my credit rating down the street and out of reach. These years had been unkind to my relationship with Sherry. I really did not like being in Minneapolis. We drifted apart into our individual worlds; different friends, ambitions and daily contact made communication difficult. We increasingly couldn't see eye to eye without a shared frame of reference, like lenses shifting out of sync. But we hoped that in Minneapolis there would be a chance that in our home, together again, things could improve, and we could find it in ourselves to be worthy of each other again.

Back in Washington to pick up belongings from our office and apartment, I stopped for an early morning coffee, ending up staying there thinking about the strange experiences of life in the capital. It was difficult to believe the depth of my friendship with all those kids, and the subsequent pain of the fallout seemed surreal, the life of another man. I clutched the coffee and simply had no idea what to do with my life. But I felt grateful, at that moment. I had believed those words in high school that I would be dead by my twentieth birthday. I'd made it this far, but had no idea what could be around the corner.

• • •

Passages visited me in the coffee shop – or the author did, at least. The shop wasn't crowded, but I noticed a table with four well-dressed patrons, who looked distinctly like they were of the Capitol Hill crowd. As they left they stepped into a stretch limousine, and I saw a large black purse on the floor by their now vacant table. Feeling surreptitious, I glanced around and walked over, nonchalantly, to bring the purse back to my table.

Inside the purse a wallet contained both large and small bills, and the driver's license belonged to someone named Gail Sheehy, which I instantly recognized. She was the author of the book *Passages*, which I had read years earlier. I thought about turning the purse over to a Starbuck's employee, but decided to follow my instincts and keep it. How did I know what a barista might do with it? My mind raced about possibly meeting her. I walked out the door, carrying the purse, not forgetting to glance back toward the ceiling for the store's surveillance cameras.

I called the phone number on Gail's business card. Her assistant answered and said that Gail would call back. She called half an hour later. Gail thanked me and even went so far as to invite me to a party that night at a hotel, so that I could return the purse. There was no saying no, of course.

It was a lavish party at a five-star hotel downtown, flush with hors d'oeuvres and what looked like a class of people out of my league. Gail made sure all of the contents of her bag had remained intact, and she was kind enough to talk at length with me, asking many questions. She asked me to be part of a focus group for a television special she was producing, and once again, there was no saying no. Her office called me a week later: Gail had changed her mind—the plan now featured a new show, called "New Passages" to be based on her most recent book.

She wanted an interview, and to film me working with kids, Kate Jackson narrating. She scheduled a day to film me with kids and I recruited Chris and Norman Heflin for an impromptu photo shoot, telling them to bring their sisters. We strolled near the Heflin's home and the kids took pictures, giving Gail examples of the kids' work. The television special featured several people, mostly fifty or so, who had abruptly changed their life's direction that offered a passage into a second career.

By 1996, the interviews and TV shows and series of famous, attractive women with their production crews and attentive questions all became a bit much for me: I confess vanity. It was clear, though, that they were mostly doing their job and didn't always anticipate what my work entailed. Following an hour-long interview with Judy Woodruff, I asked her, "You really didn't know our conversation about Shooting Back would be political? What city are we in? Everything here is political." Judy replied, "I just thought it was about a children's photo project." I explained to her that the children took photos that millions around the world had seen, that informed those millions about a social reality foreign to them. Photos, whether taken by kids or adults, capture the frozen image of the world as seen through another's eyes. These kids' photos brought others into their lives, to see from inside their heads. To bridge these divides could only be political. Public reaction to the images could spark social or political responses; we could help children.

PART IV

"For by grace you have been saved through faith, and this is not your own doing; it is the gift of God—not the result of works, so that no one may boast." —Ephesians 2:8-9,

A Life's Gap

I returned to Minneapolis. During a Christmas shopping spree at the Gap, the day after Thanksgiving, I chatted with the young store manager, who asked me if I would be interested in working in his store for the Christmas season. He needed holiday help. I demurred about being in my fifties and unsuited for his younger clientele, even if the clothes I had on were clearly from the Gap. He laughed and said it would bring flair to the store's image. I filled out an application and described my retail experience decades before, but didn't mention the bit about being fired for grand larceny.

A few days later I punched the clock to begin work. When my daughters learned I was a store clerk at the Gap, they were embarrassed—until I told them about the discounts, at which point they simply told me the items they wanted, sooner rather than later, please.

At first, I loved working at the Gap, though I, too, was a bit embarrassed about my age. My love wouldn't last long; I forgot about the dullness of retail. Youngsters named Tammy, Heather, Brooke and Tiffany ordered me to fold clothes and replenish stock with names like Gap Jeans Trim Fit. It was mindless work, but a reprieve from managing Shooting Back, nonetheless. Several shoppers thought they had seen me on television but I always told them they must be mistaken. I quit when the holiday season ended.

There was nothing I held against Sherry. She was a wonderful woman but wanted a different life, from the one I was leading, and I had no sense where mine was even going at the time. I did work hard to be a good father for my daughters, but the relationship with my wife was frayed, and it wasn't good to be back in the Twin Cities. I moved out.

• • •

Around this time, a friend of mine from DC was in town visiting, and over dinner we talked about a recent story in a Minneapolis alternative newspaper. A young wannabe journalist had written a profile based solely on the *New Republic* story, and it fell somewhere between parody and simply sloppy work; the writer never so much as called, for instance. Stuck in my lonely studio apartment, my friend and I commiserated over a meal she made of cheese, vegetables and large chunks of sausage. With leftovers for days, I decided to put some of the food in a package and deliver it to the office where the reporter worked, as a spiteful reminder that if you want to write a profile you should probably talk to the subject.

An investigator from Hennepin County's prosecutor's office called and wanted to meet with me. In his office, he told me that a young reporter had complained about a package with uncertain contents. She was frightened. The materials within resembled human body parts, possibly intestines. The complainant named me as the suspect.

I admitted reading the story and explained that she wrote a piece of garbage, why not send some garbage right back to her? He looked stern and said that if I had sent the parcel, this meeting should be considered the warning before criminal charges. "Is food distribution a crime?" I asked. "You *are* a wise guy," he responded. He never asked directly if I had done the deed, but apparently thought it worth the time to try intimidation.

When I returned to my apartment, I looked in the refrigerator and was relieved to have saved enough sausage for lunch. Had I known Hanna Rosin's address when her story was published she might have received a similar package. Ironically, of course, the meal was quite good—but I confess a vindictive streak.

WESTERN VENICE

Emails and phone calls continued to arrive on occasion: some had questions and others offered work in photography workshops based on the Shooting Back model. When one such offer came from University of California Santa Barbara (UCSB), I responded quickly, recalling the old, happy days of visiting the city. We struck a deal wherein I would work with some of their troubled youth, including gang members, for a couple of months. I didn't even know they had gangsters or at-risk youth in a town I considered almost heaven.

All expenses would be covered housing provided. A publisher and trustee at UCSB offered her home in Montecito for the project's duration while she was abroad. Montecito, being a beautiful community tucked in the hills above Santa Barbara, was a community of wealthy people living in one of the best regions California had to offer. Tough job.

The kids I started working with were a stark contrast to the refugees in DC shelters and city projects, or the Native Americans on impoverished reservations. These California youth were predominantly Latino, and not quite as street savvy—but why would they be on the relatively calm and upscale streets of Santa Barbara? They had neither the edge nor the traumas developed early in life on DC's poor, violent streets. The Santa Barbara youth had challenges but on a much smaller scale, a microcosm of back east or on the reservations.

• • •

My old friend Fred Sweets had moved from Washington to Los Angles with his family and was working as a photo editor at the LA *Times*. When I had a break, I'd drive the ninety miles to LA and meet with him for lunch or dinner. He had become involved with a group called Venice Arts, a photography program for at-risk youth in Venice, a drug and gang infested seaside neighborhood. Venice Arts had been inspired by Shooting Back and used similar methods in their photo workshops.

Fred shared with me that the visionary cofounder of Venice Arts was embroiled in conflict with his board of directors, striking a chord of empathy in me. Fred wanted me to meet the founder and share some of my insights; he tried to set up a meeting but the Venice Arts visionary declined. Instead, I was about to meet the founding board member who had clashed with her cofounder.

Fred invited me to a party in LA, to which were also invited several Venice Arts board members. Seeing as my social life was in the toilet, I was pretty thrilled. One attendee, an energetic redhead, caught my attention and Fred introduced us. Lynn Warshafsky was an LA transplant from Milwaukee, Wisconsin, founded the board of directors, and incorporated the fledgling organization, making her a cofounder of Venice Arts. Later in the evening, she whispered, "I thought Shooting Back's founder was a black guy." I laughed and said, "I believe there might be some black blood in my family." She never exceeded two drinks and loved Scrabble—a promising start, and we promised to meet again.

A few weeks later we arranged a meeting in Venice, where she lived. Over dinner she told me of her woes with the other founder, and details about the project. She was a consultant to nonprofit organizations and astute about their funding, goals and games, and also happened to be a licensed mental health therapist. It was when she said she had once been a massage therapist, that I thought, "This has potential."

She shared that Venice Arts was new and struggling financially. In many ways, Lynn was my opposite—exactly the type of person I clashed with on the board of Shooting Back, but we were both committed to helping low-income young people, and opening doors for them that would have otherwise been locked. I thought I probably had more in common with the co founder of Venice Arts, but also suspected we would be far too much alike. The prospect of meeting someone with such a similar history and personality reminded me of a book I'd read long ago, for a psychology class at Wayne State University.

The Three Christs of Ypsilanti concerned Milton Rokeach's experiment on a group of three paranoid schizophrenic patients, at Ypsilanti State Hospital in 1964. The book describes the interactions of three patients, each believing he alone was Christ. The patients quarreled over who was holier and eventually started to physically fight, explaining their fellow patients away as being insane, or dead and being operated by machines. Two or three deluded founders of nonprofit groups for the poor might not have been so dissimilar, locked in a room together.

I invited Lynn to my temporary Montecito estate for a game of Scrabble, where she was surprised to discover that despite her confidence and skill at the game, I could beat her as often as she beat me. Over the next few months we met and played the game almost weekly. My daughter Hanna came to visit me for a week in Montecito and met Lynn. "Are you involved?" she asked. The all-knowing children.

My work in Santa Barbara soon came to an end, meaning I would have to leave the dreamlike, temporary home and face the cold world without a job or residence. Still licking my wounds, I felt desperate, remembering the words "Life is made or broken at the place where we meet and deal with obstacles," but struggling to feel them help. A glimmer of hope came in a telephone call from ABC that said the *New Passages* special would be airing in a couple days. I was delighted, having long thought that I'd been edited out. I called Lynn and told her about the show, inviting her to Montecito to have dinner and watch. Dinner consisted of a terribly made rubber chicken, and was terribly grateful when she politely didn't disparage it.

However, I knew Santa Barbara, as much as I loved it, would not offer the challenges I wanted in a larger, more diverse, urban environment. Los Angeles was the logical choice, and I soon moved into a home in nearby Carpenteria, a small, beachside community a few miles from Santa Barbara. I rented a small room from the owner, John, who had worked as a handyman at the Montecito house.

Lynn came to visit often and I asked John if it would be alright for her to stay the night. His question in turn made his feelings clear: "Do you think that's appropriate?" He was divorced and involved in a local church, and I wanted to respect his moral code—until I noticed he was bringing young men home late at night. When he hit on me

I knew it was time for me to hit the road. Lynn spent that evening with me, anyway.

My relationship with Lynn thickened like freshly poured concrete hardens on a new highway. When I needed to move out of John's house, she invited me to stay in her small Venice home until I decided my next move. Lynn was energetic and not only did she manage her small arts organization, she was a consultant for foundations and other nonprofits. She moved through life at high speeds, a tireless worker.

I started looking for work: the Venice Boys and Girls Club, a classified ad at the Southwest Airlines LAX ticket counter. Just about anything. Lynn sensed my struggle to find work and asked one day if I'd like to teach some photography classes at Venice Arts. I jumped. It was a kind gesture, and wouldn't pay enough to survive on alone, but with some freelance also dribbling in I could get by. What started as part-time work soon evolved into a full-time position as their creative director.

Neither Lynn nor I discussed our living situation, but it started to seem like I might be a permanent resident. We both had a propensity to just let things move as they might, without lengthy discussions. We shared similar views and values about many issues: serving the poor and the oppressed was the guiding principle of our lives. We had both voted for Clinton. Around that time, a Bible verse came to me, reinforcing my sense that Lynn and I had found something good: "Give justice to the weak and the fatherless; maintain the right of the afflicted and the destitute. Rescue the weak and needy; deliver them from the hand of the wicked," in Psalm 82:3-4.

We spent many evenings talking about social justice and liberation theology. She shared stories about politically active parents, who had brought their children to political rallies and protest marches. Her family was Jewish and secular, and held far different faith assumptions than the family I was raised in.

Devoutly religious people had stood shoulder to shoulder with atheists during many noble, justice movements in recent history, like the civil rights movement and anti-Vietnam war efforts. In many ways, the underpinnings for such efforts were grounded in Judeo-Christian values, which is not to say that Judaism and Christianity are identical. But they share an intersection of values based on the

Hebrew Bible (Torah), which were then brought into American culture by generations of Protestants, who have in turn been fundamental to American institutions and history. Both believers and nonbelievers have aspired to do good works and help the less fortunate or victims of injustice.

Our views about existence were fundamentally different and mutually exclusive. I hoped they wouldn't collide, but honestly did not give careful consideration to that possibility. Both Lynn and I were influenced by the beliefs of our parents. I knew an unquestioned faith over one's lifetime is a weak faith. I thought that over time, the chasm between our faiths would be bridged, as we shared more about the reasons for our beliefs and grew in our understandings—both of each other and existence, generally. But at that time my focus was on good works, and not faith.

For a Christian though, God's grace through our faith is fundamental for salvation. Had that been my primary focus when Lynn and I talked, I would have shared my views about faith. As the Bible states in Ephesians 2:8-9, "For by grace you have been saved through faith, and this is not your own doing; it is the gift of God—not the result of works, so that no one may boast." Faith is an inward journey blossoming outward into works.

From my earliest memories, I believed in God. If anyone I knew did not share my beliefs we simply didn't talk about the presence or absence of God. I had never been in a dispute with an atheist. I'm not sure I even knew an avowed or fundamentalist atheist. I had never given much thought to atheism or agnosticism. But the work was piling up and not leaving much time for contemplation. Several emails arrived weekly seeking advice about starting independent projects like Shooting Back. One day Lynn told me that I had a call from a television producer in New York, named Resa Matthews. My fears about being finished might have been unfounded.

• • •

When I returned her call she told me she was working on an A&E television special with former US Senator and New York Knicks basketball legend Bill Bradley. The special was being produced as a segment for an A&E Biography series titled "Uncommon Americans."

Resa explained that A&E wanted me as one of three people featured and that they would come to Venice to begin filming in a week. The call gave me a boost—my work and reputation might survive. Hope was renewed.

Fortunately, the film crew was able to document my work in a special class at Venice High School for mentally and physically challenged youth. I had only recently been contracted by Very Special Arts (VSA), an international organization headquartered in Washington DC, which had been founded by Jean Kennedy Smith to foster arts education for students with disabilities. The photographs taken by the kids would be exhibited in the VSA gallery in the nation's capital.

The A&E crew filmed life in our home, interviewing Lynn and me, and then spent a few days filming our work at the high school only a mile away. When they finished filming in Venice, Resa asked if Lynn and I could fly to Detroit—they wanted to film some old Motor City neighborhoods, and even interview my mother. Understandably, my mother was nervous about her first appearance on national TV: "Boy Jimmy, what have you gone and done now? This sure is something."

We sat down at my mother's dining room table for an interview, Resa looking around at the old family photos. "What was it like Lois, raising three boys in a small house?" My mother looked down. "Boy, you just don't know." Resa smiled and said, "Why don't you tell us about it." My mom responded, "Oh boy, it wasn't easy. They were a handful, especially Jimmy." She giggled. "He was a sweet boy, very compassionate and concerned. But he could sure stir up problems."

We returned to Los Angeles and normal life took its course again. In a simple ceremony, Lynn and I exchanged vows in a beautiful garden in Venice. We worked and lived together, officially a couple. And suddenly Lynn announced she was pregnant. As happens when a man and a woman jump at opportunity in their lives, this all happened unbelievably fast.

Our lovely, lively daughter was born March 8, 1998. We named her Sofie Rhose Hubbard Warshafsky, twenty-seven letters long. Don't even ask what happened there. And then, as if life were not complicated and quick enough, another person moved in: my mother.

THE BIG LIE

My mother had recently been diagnosed with dementia, which may have been Alzheimer's, and her health had fallen rapidly. Some of her neighbors called, concerned for her well-being, and reported that she had fallen and her shoulder and arm were badly bruised. After deliberations with my brother Mike, we decided to move her to California, where we could care for her and sell the home in Detroit. Lynn graciously agreed. My mother, on the other hand, was adamantly opposed to moving out.

Mike and I conceived a plan. We flew to Detroit and met at our mother's to assess her condition for a few days; it was clear that she needed to move posthaste. We planned to have her board a plane with me and return to California, with no return ticket. My brother and I would have to come back later, though, to unload fifty years of possessions and to sell the house. Our parents had felt the wrath of the Great Depression and learned to save everything.

The most astonishing discovery I made while clearing out my mom's house was in the basement cellar, where we would store canned and jarred food. I found jars filled with pennies, tuna fish cans, jams and things unknown to science hidden down there. Then I found an opened, half-full bottle of Seagrams. I thought we never had booze in the house—my father's rages, my mother's timidity—our parents had always scorned the bottle. I kept rummaging and I found other opened bottles that clearly had been drunk from. In the garage we found more, all in all thirty bottles of hard liquor stashed away.

I was shocked. My dad must have been nipping booze and hid the bottles in the house's crannies over the years. Could it have been my mother's vice? No way. This, too, could explain much about my dad's explosive behavior. I called Mike, who was also shocked, and concurred that the bottles were dad's handiwork, and not our mother's.

As disturbing as it was to discover my father's secrets, finding dozens of letters addressed "Dear Paul," in my mother's careful handwriting was more disturbing and shook me terribly. Over the years she had been writing to my brother, sometimes with long letters, others short. They were heartbreaking; none had been mailed. Neither she nor anyone else in the family had known his whereabouts since he vanished in 1969. One letter I found in a drawer was dated 1986. I read and reread the spiral-bound notebook leaves at my mom's dining room table.

> *Dear Paul,*
>
> *I am hoping that you receive this letter and will read it. Also I hope that you are enjoying good health and things are going well with you. Have tried to reach you at the number where I reached you quite awhile ago but was told that business number is no longer listed.*
>
> *After all these years I keep hoping and praying that I can see you and talk with you again. I love you so much Paul and was always so proud of you. You were and are so very special to me. I didn't love you anymore than I loved Jim and Mike, but you were our firstborn. I had more time to spend with you during the 3 years before Jim was born, then Michael 21 months later. Needless to say I was kept quite busy with three little ones for a long time. Whatever mistakes I made as I parent and failed in anyway with all of you I am very sorry. I have no doubts I made many mistakes.*
>
> *Your Dad was sick from 1972 to 1980 with heart problems, cancer and diabetes. He was not able to work during that time and that was a difficult time for him especially since he had always been so active and able to work. He had another breakdown in 76 and had to be in the hospital again. It was not an easy time for any of us no more than it was for us in 1967.*

Paul, I am asking you to please get in touch with me so we can discuss some things, I would help you with the cost of your trip if you will come up to see me—or I would meet you somewhere. There are things I would like to know about.

I am still staying in the home and so far have been able to manage. I Have not made any decision as to what change to make yet. Jim and Mike would like me to come nearer to where they are in the Washington area if I make a change. I am 72 now and probably should make a change while I am still able to do so.

Please let me hear from you, it would mean so much to me. I think of you, dream of you, and wonder how you are and what is happening in your life. You may have people in your life who love you and mean a lot to you, I hope you do. But there is no one in your life who loves you and cares, except God, more than I do.

I love you,
Mother

DETROIT CITY

After my mother moved in with us, she would often sit in the yard at the side of the house for hours. She would look toward the sky and say, "Isn't that the most beautiful sky you've ever seen, Jimmy?" Then she'd shift to flowers and ask, "Have you ever seen a more beautiful flower, Jimmy?"

She also incessantly asked, "When can I go home, Jimmy?" I always replied, "Soon, very soon."

It reminded me of the Bobby Bare song "Detroit City." The lyrics could have been written by my mother, "I wanna go home, I wanna go home, oh, how I wanna go home. Last night I went to sleep in Detroit City and I dreamed about those cotton fields back home. I dreamed about my mother, dear ole papa, sister and brother, I wanna go home, I wanna go home." She had always loved music by Frank Sinatra, Lawrence Welk, and the old gospel hymns, but something about "Detroit City"—besides our old home—fit her.

My mother swooned over Sofie, though, and they did everything together, even bubble baths together in our long tub. Unable to resist at the sight of such a sweet relationship, I started taking photos, which surprised even me. They showed the powerful love of family and the pleasure of life: a demented, feeble grandmother with her hyperactive, mischievous granddaughter. My favorite was a shot of the pair covered in bath bubbles, playing.

I sent some black and white 8X10's to an old friend at *Life*, who told me that the magazine had been thrilled to see them, and wanted to ink a contract to complete the documentary series spread in Life. My ego soared. A contract for *Life Magazine* was enough to make most photographers salivate. I was lucky enough to have had two.

They dispatched a writer to interview my mother and me. I could not have asked for better terms: no plane to catch, no far away place to learn—just the humanity of life at home. Some of the photos I took at this time are my proudest work. One photo in particular was a portrait of my mother. She held an antique mirror in front of her reflecting her lovely, wrinkled face standing in our garden.

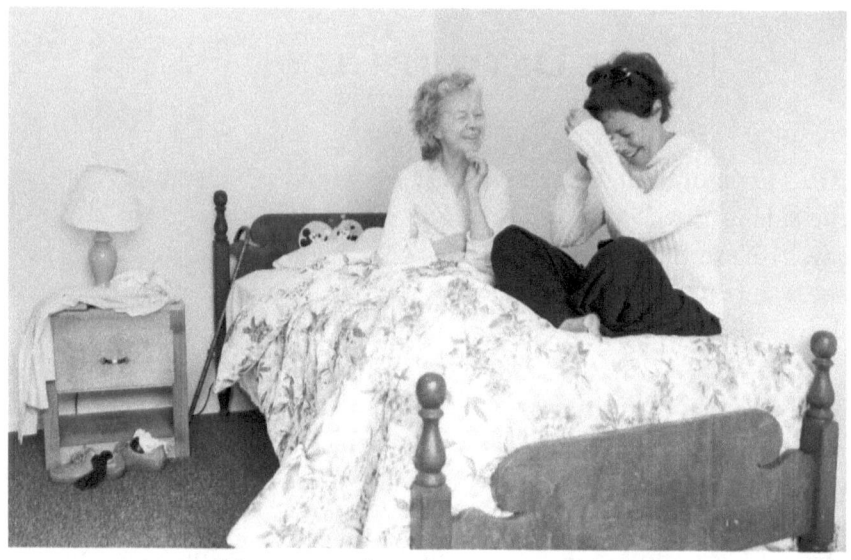

My mom with Priya in nursing home

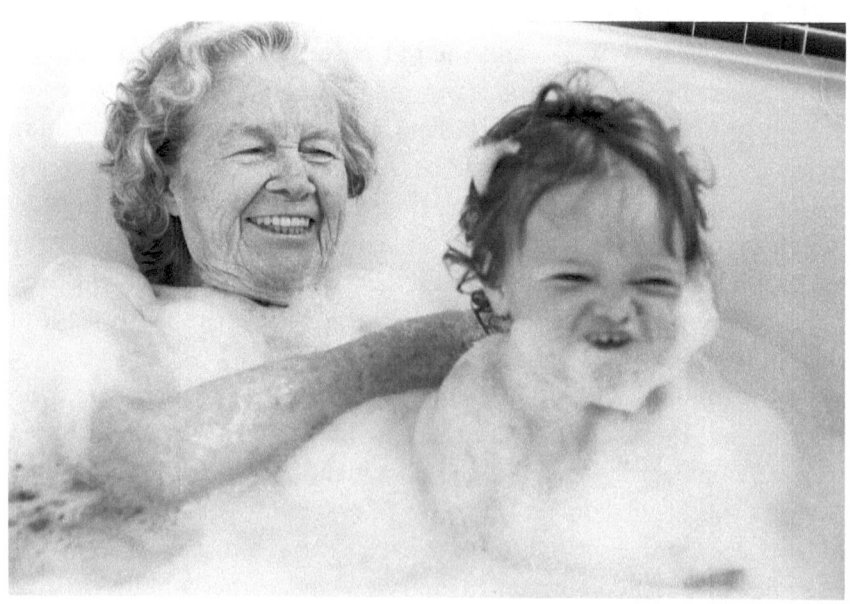

My mom and Sofie play in bubble bath 2001

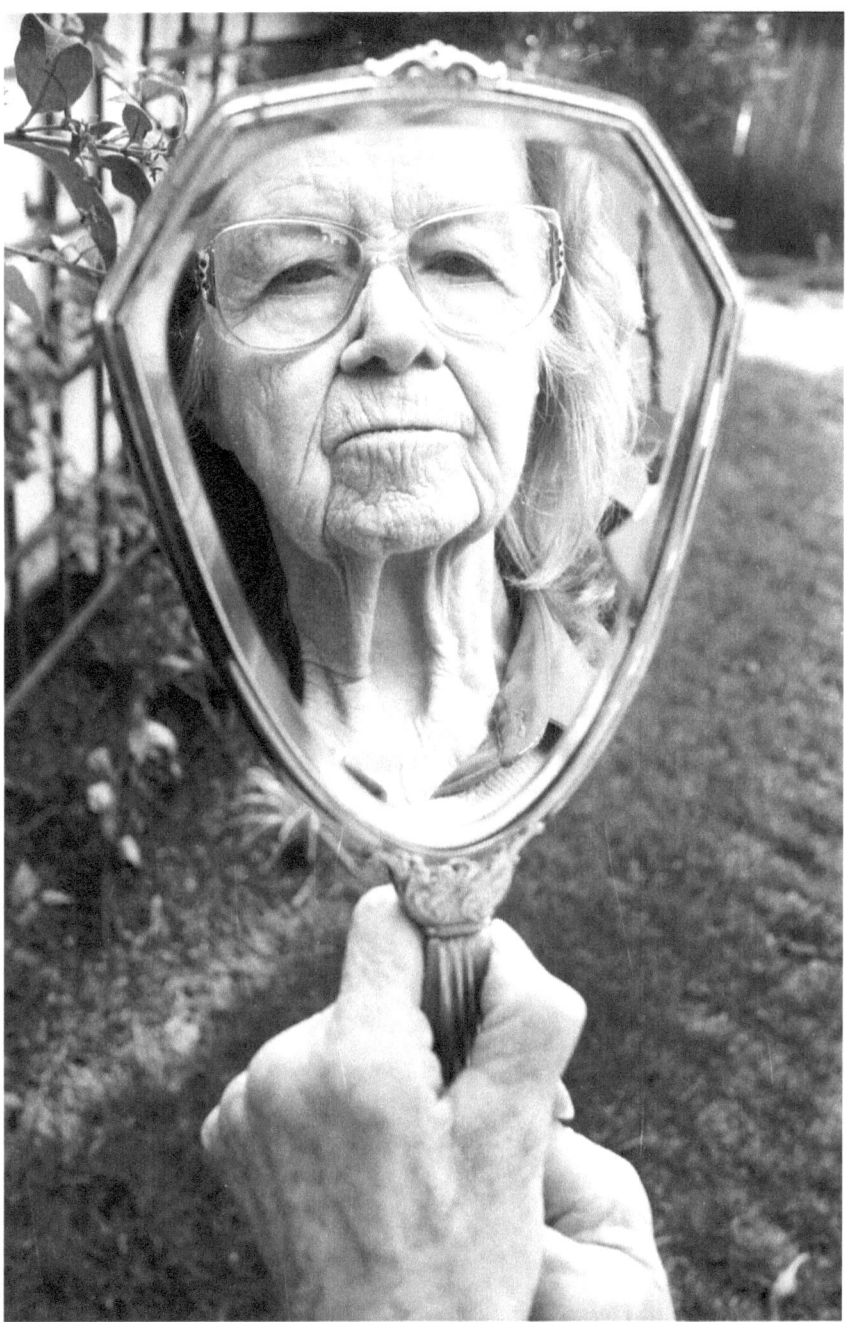

My mom with handheld mirror in Garden of Venice 2000

The Los Angeles Times purchased several for their magazine, to complement a story I had written about my mother, titled, "What My Mother Can't Forget." It was a difficult piece to write, as it focused on my mom's illness and enduring obsession with finding Paul.

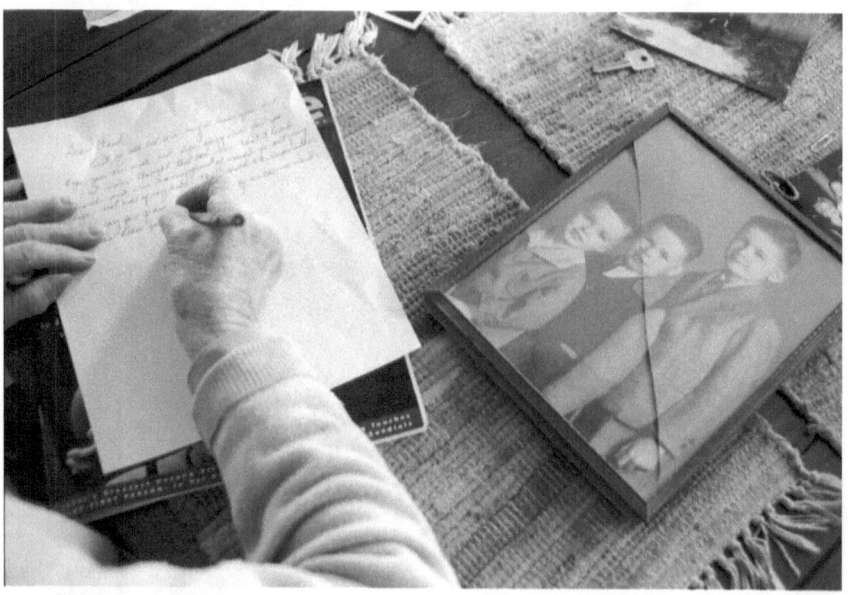

My mom writes letter to missing son Paul

One weekend, while up in the mountains teaching photography classes at Idyllwild Arts, I had a gnawing feeling that my mom was close to death. She had recently moved into a nursing home after breaking her hip, and I drove the two hours to get there as soon as I could, listening to that feeling in the pit of my stomach. We spent a few hours together. She was frail, tired and distant, like a stoic philosopher lost in thought. I hugged her, kissed her and told her I loved her. The next day I drove back to Idyllwild to teach, and the following morning the call came. My mom was dead. I raced back to Santa Monica and viewed her fragile, limp body, which was cold in exactly the same terrible way Brijjie's had been. The nurse told me that she held my mom before she died. She had whispered in the nurse's ear, "Lord, take me home." Then she died. I broke down and sobbed right there.

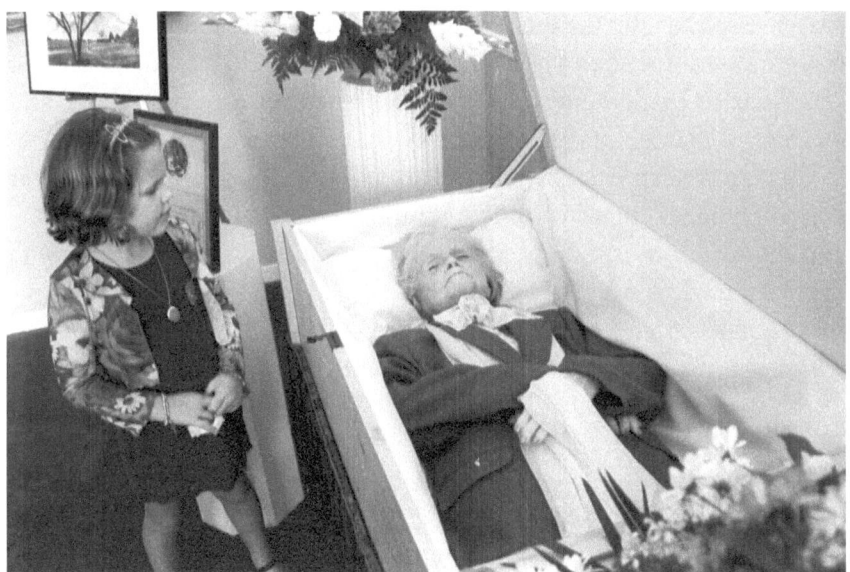

Sofie at my mom's funeral 2003

• • •

Life went on, though my mother's passing could make it feel like a crawl. A surprise helped distract me, though: one day an email arrived from Neal Baer, the show-runner for *Law and Order: Special Victims Unit (SVU)*. Over lunch he suggested we join forces and launch some photo projects in Africa, focusing on the devastation of HIV/AIDS. Neal was a medical doctor by training and an ardent humanitarian, with connections to NGOs that concentrated on global health issues around the world.

While Neal detailed his ideas, my mind went to my first trip to that gigantic continent. Lynn and I had gone there in 2001, travelling to Durban, South Africa with six LA young people to photograph and participate in the UN Conference on Racism. Our trip was funded and sponsored by the City of Los Angeles, but the conference was a controversial one—the US and Israeli delegations walked out.

I accompanied the young photographers to several street protests and demonstrations near the conference site. The strong anti-US sentiments alarmed the kids. Enraged protesters chanted and screamed angry epithets about the US and Israel, and the hundreds of tense, well-armed riot police standing at the ready were not an altogether calming presence, either. By the end of it I thought the conference had spread more intolerance than tolerance around the world. We departed for Los Angeles on September 10th, with one stop in Johannesburg and another to change planes back in the states, in Atlanta, Georgia.

We arrived in Atlanta on 9/11 at about 8:00AM, exhausted. Our travelling party consisted of Lynn, our three-year-old daughter, Sofie, and Lynn's mother, Dolly. The other kids and adult chaperones had departed for Los Angeles two days earlier. There was just enough time for a quick coffee and bagel before we had to board our final flight, which was due to depart around 10:00AM for LA. As one will at one of the world's busiest, most hectic airports, we stopped at the ticket counter to ask if our flight was on time. The agent looked on the verge of a breakdown and was barely able to form a sentence. I thought she might be ill. Suddenly she yelled, "There are no planes! *No plane is flying into our country.* All planes are grounded. All airports are now shutdown until further notice." I was confused. "But can we catch a later flight, tomorrow maybe?"

I looked around and saw what was the beginning of mass hysteria. There were rumors that there was an attack in New York and that an airplane had crashed into a skyscraper. I ran to a bank of hospitality phones just before hundreds of other people converged behind me. I booked a room (in what turned out to be a fleabag hotel—it didn't matter though, nothing really seemed to matter that morning) and we were out of the airport. Large numbers of police and national guardsmen were beginning to arrive as we left. There were rumors and later reports indicating that weapons had been discovered on some of Atlanta's outbound flights, including our flight to Los Angeles.

At the hotel there were already long lines. Rooms were scarce for the hundreds who were grounded, and huge numbers of worried, frightened people wouldn't even be accommodated in this dump. In another hour there wouldn't be a vacancy anywhere in the greater Atlanta area. The four of us crowded into the room and turned on the television and we were instantly horrified as were most people in the world.

We knew we didn't want to spend much time in this hotel. The next morning I called rental car companies, but there were no cars to be had in the city, only some rental truck outlets not far from the airport. When we got to the truck rentals, they could only provide us with a sixteen-passenger van, although there were only four in our party. They charged me triple the price for a one-way trip, which would end wherever we ended up, northward. Two days later we stayed with Lynn's best childhood friend near Mayslick Kentucky. Five days after landing in Atlanta we were finally going home again and caught a flight out of Cincinnati. The country would never again be the same.

Thankfully, Neal did not notice quite how far my thoughts had wandered, and he couldn't know that they had not gone to Africa but to the morning of 9/11.

Eventually we organized the projects in Africa. Neal was a man who could raise impressive resources, and we began to make strides. Our projects taught people to document their communities and the pressing health and social issues in them, using video and photography to heighten public awareness. We worked during two trips to South Africa and another in Mozambique with HIV/AIDS-infected populations; one of these projects, with thirty HIV/AIDS orphans, was particularly close to my heart. Neal produced an award-winning documentary filmed by a sixteen-year-old AIDS orphan, named Alcides: "Home is Where You Find It." Neal and I became friends, but it's hard to dislike a man with such an enormous love for humanity, and who works tirelessly to make real improvements in the lives of the suffering.

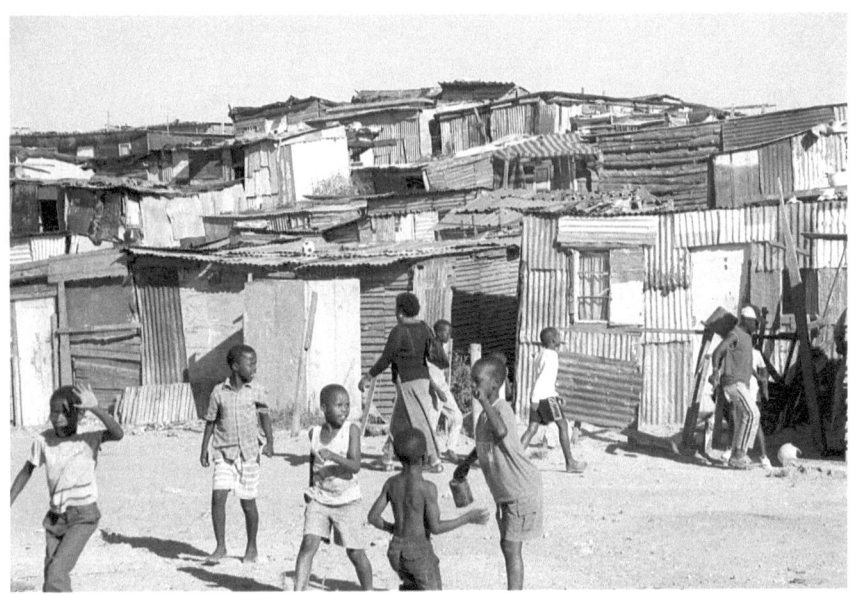

Cape Town shantytown 2006

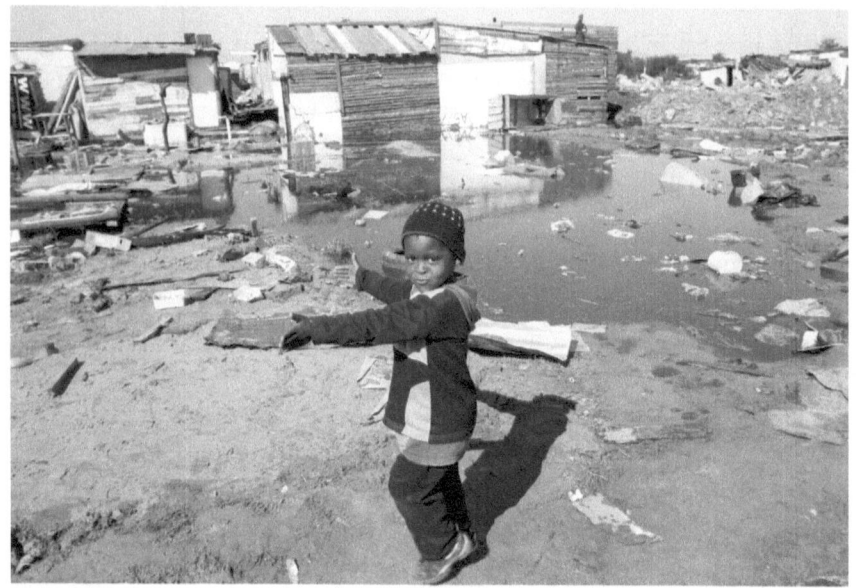

Boy shows his shantytown in Cape Town, South Africa 2001

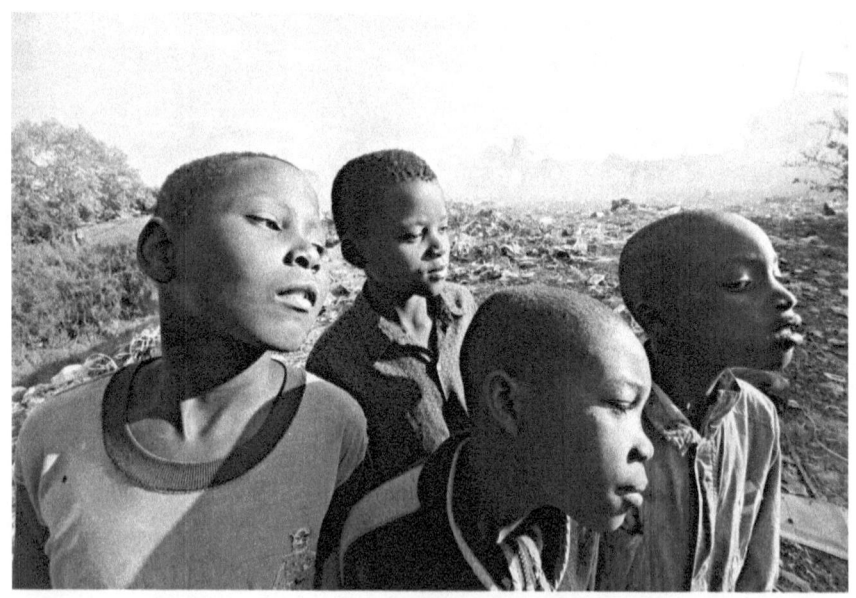

Boys pose near their home in Mozambique 2007

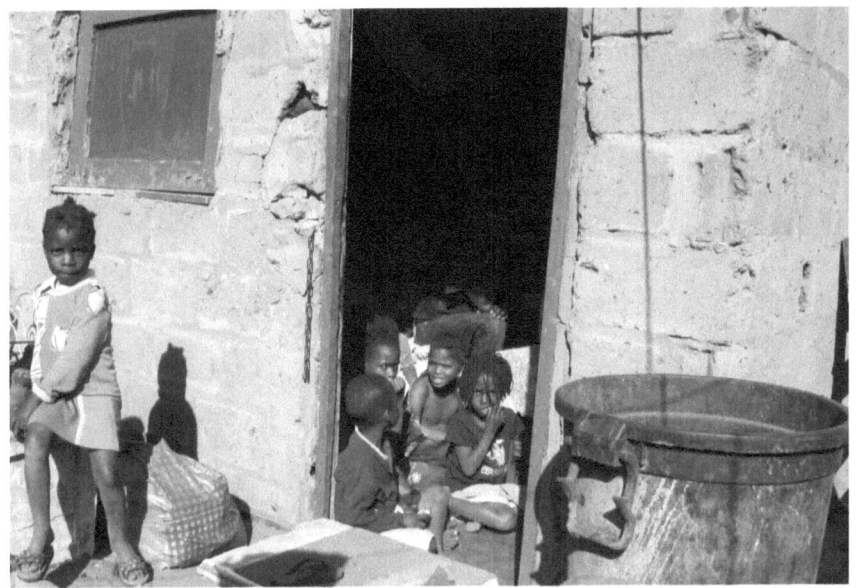

Kids at home in Mozambique 2007

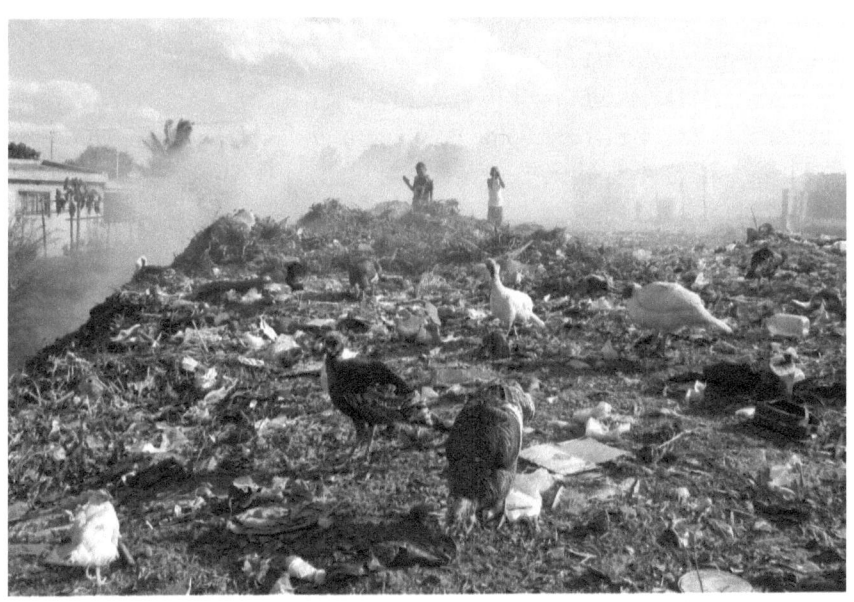

Kids play at dump near substandard housing in Mozambique 2007

During a subsequent lunch with Lynn and Neal at Hal's Restaurant in Venice we planned for other projects abroad. However, I learned about some of his biases. Neal was usually soft spoken and chose his words carefully. Before lunch was served Neal was preoccupied with politics and became more animated and chatty. He was upset about the Tea Party using several expletives describing his views. When I heard him say, "Those (blankety, blank) stupid Tea Party Baptists," my ears perked. "Neal, I'm from the Baptist tradition and I don't even drink tea let alone go to tea parties. I think the Tea Party has a more diverse following than just Baptists." I thought of Dallas Willard, a former Southern Baptist minister, who had written some of the most brilliant books I had ever read. I presume Neal may have meant stupid Christians. Regardless, I realized his faith assumptions were markedly different than mine.

I was humbled when the National Child Labor Committee (NCLC) called to say they planned to honor me at their annual Lewis Hine Awards ceremony. Lewis Hine was a giant in both photography and social reform. At their 2007 event I was to be awarded their Distinguished Service Award, and the first photographer to ever receive an award from NCLC. I was awestruck, flattered and humbled. Lynn, Sofie, Priya and I arrived at the Time-Life Building in New York, where we met with Neal and an actor from his show, Peter Hermann. Peter's wife Mariska Hargitay, star of Neal's show, planned to attend but fell ill. Years earlier, Peter had volunteered at Shooting Back in Washington, and at dinner afterwards I admitted that I was flattered he and Neal had come to the ceremony.

I continued to receive hundreds of emails over the years from people who wanted information or guidance from Shooting Back, and it was heartening to see that the idea and name had had such a long shelf life. Academics, social workers and reporters had widely acknowledged Shooting Back as a pioneer in its field, which didn't have a name at the time but is now known as participatory photography or photographic empowerment.

In 2006 Lynn, Neal, Geoffrey Cowan, former dean of the Annenberg School for Communication at the University of Southern California, and myself launched the Institute for Photographic Empowerment (IPE) for the new photography genre. Dean Cowan bestowed Lynn and me the designation of USC "Fellow." I was invited to join the faculty in the Annenberg School for Communications and Journalism at USC, teaching two classes. One—apparently the popular one, as it hits capacity quickly—is called Visual Communication and Social Change. The other class is titled Visual Communication of Death in the Digital Age.

DISPUTED TERRITORY

The name Shooting Back lived on. I wondered if I should take ownership, lest someone unsavory, like Ella, do so. Controlling use of the name Shooting Back might be prudent. I applied for a trademark with the U.S. Patent and Trademark Office, which was about as breezy and simple as assembling a car from paperclips. But I was glad to go through the lengthy filing process soon enough.

One evening my brother called and told me about a story on NBC's Nightly News, about Shooting Back in the Middle East. "They didn't mention you, so you might want to check it out. Don't you own the trademark?" Brian William's report had been about an Israeli organization called B'Tselem, which had recently launched a video advocacy project with Palestinian youth and purported to be affiliated with me. They called their project Shooting Back.

My interest piqued when I learned details of their mission. Not only had they infringed upon the registered trademark, they had linked my name to a program that put youngsters in a highly volatile environment—right in harm's way with headlines like "Cameras as Weapons" in the news in front of them. The kids were to document human rights violations perpetrated by Israelis against Palestinians. Their mission was fraught with danger.

I crafted a lengthy op-ed piece, and of course, I thought it'd be grand to see it in the *New York Times,* but I also knew it smarter to publish in a paper closer to B'Tselem's turf. *The Jerusalem Post* called. They published the op-ed, and also ran a photo and an interview. The legal games began between my new intellectual property attorney and B'Tselem's battery of lawyers from a New York firm. We went back and forth. B'Tselem later put a disclaimer on their web site indicating that they had no relationship with Shooting Back or me. They discontinued use of the name Shooting Back.

Not long after my op-ed piece was published in the *Jerusalem Post*, I received an email from Amman, Jordan. Sirin Masri wanted me to come to Palestine and work with thirty youth in a project she insisted be called "Shooting Back from Palestine." The participants would photograph life in Palestine for a travelling exhibit. "Do I have your permission?" and I liked her already. Soon enough we had not only settled on the name but made arrangements for the work. "You'll be quite comfortable when you're here," Sirin told me. Along with an assistant, I journeyed to Amman—my first trip to the Middle East.

I was thrilled to get to explore the Holy Land. When I arrived at the luxurious hotel there was a note in my room from Sirin. It was an invitation to dinner the next day with her and her friends—it turned out Sirin's family was enormously wealthy and influential in the region. "Get some rest," she instructed.

So I went down stairs for a drink and sat at a lovely outdoor patio overlooking Amman. The city was beautiful yet mysterious. Several women sat at a nearby table, some dressed in western garb, others in more traditional Middle Eastern clothing, colorful or modest shawls and covered features. They were all inhaling from four-foot tall glass hookah pipes. When they exhaled the smoke obscured my view of the city and rendered Amman, with its date palms and pleasant, dry heat, all the more exotic. But my impressions were undoubtedly also rendered strange by the severe jet lag.

I attempted to sleep but at 3AM I was wide awake and returned to the patio. It was empty. The view of the city put me in a magnificent trance. A loud call to prayer burst from speakers attached to a mosque across from where I sat. It was melodic and soothing and sounded more like a song than a prayer. I cherished the moment and followed the call. I said, "Thank you, God, for my life."

The next day I met Sirin and two of her lovely friends for a Middle Eastern feast at a posh restaurant in the Grand Hyatt's lobby. Several of the women, including Sirin, had studied in the US and had many American friends, and from their excellent conversation it showed why. We touched on a variety of global issues. Several of Sirin's friends, she offered, were Jewish, but it quickly became clear that the three women held strong and angry feelings toward Israel and its people. Sirin suggested that conflicts between Palestine and Israel had hurt her relationships with her Jewish-American friends.

I asked her about the 2005 suicide bombings, which had targeted three hotels in Amman, including the one we were dining in. She looked down and her shoulders drooped. "I was here that night with my friends. We were seated just across from where we are now. Some of them, my friends, were killed. I had just left the table and was in the restroom across the lobby when one of the bombers detonated. The explosives were attached to his body...It was horrible, it changed my life forever." I put my hand on her shoulder and apologized. Sixty people were killed and nearly two hundred injured that night.

Sirin arranged for a car, and a driver picked up my assistant and me the next day to tour the area. We headed toward Jericho and the Dead Sea, the low cliffs and pockmarked rocks rising as we dipped through the valleys and hills. Countless caves appeared in the rocks around us, each a portal into some dark mysterious past. After driving to the Dead Sea the driver asked, "You want to see Mt. Nebo?" We turned onto a desolate, dessert road. I got out of the car and stood on the vast, hot and arid Plains of Noab. The mountain took my breath away. It was a desolate and beautiful wilderness, on which the only other breathing creatures I saw were herds of camels. It was like riding a rollercoaster for the first time. Excitement raced through my mind and body.. All of a sudden a man appeared from out of nowhere and startled us. My assistant JoJo shrieked. The desert nomad motioned me to get on the camel for a bareback ride. "Hold on Jim," my assistant said while taking my picture on the camel.

"This is incredible," I thought, "Jesus, Moses, the disciples and all the Biblical giants traversed this rugged land?" I had read of them my entire life. Moses had ascended Mt. Nebo at the command of God in order that he might see the Promised Land that he was never to enter. He died at the mountain. It was in the plains of Moab, opposite Jericho and the Dead Sea, that the Israelites made their last encampment before ending the exodus from Egypt. That evening in my hotel room I said a prayer of thanks and read about Moses and Mt. Nebo in Deuteronomy.

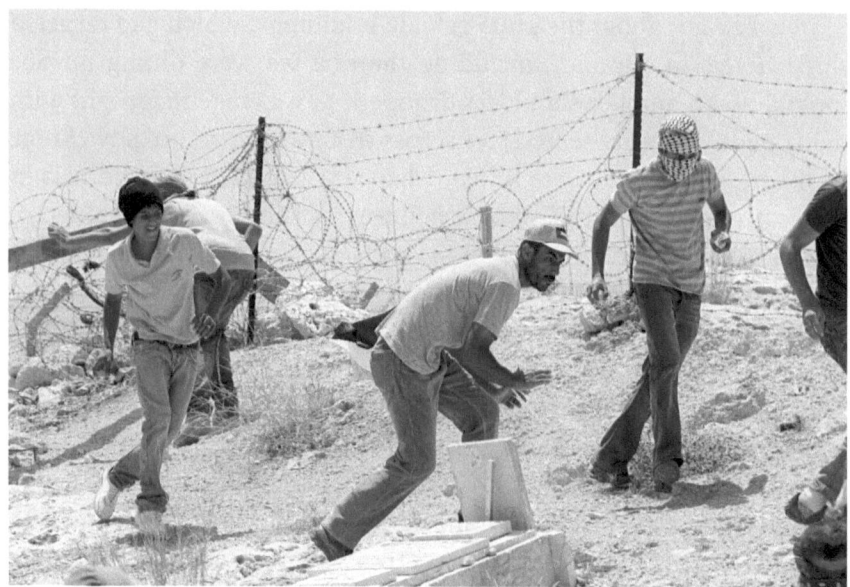

Palestinian protestors run from Israeli soldiers 2010

One morning, after we had worked with the Palestinian kids for a week in Jericho, a few of the kids and I climbed into a van in Ramallah for a half-hour drive up a mountain on our way to a weekly protest in Bil'in, a small town sharing a border with Israel, about fifteen miles up the bumpy mountain road. Israeli soldiers shot at us and attacked with tear gas, and protesters had been killed here. The Palestinian demonstrators taunted the soldiers with slurs, and used slingshots to fire rocks at them. The soldiers, however, were heavily fortified, armed, and hunkered down on the other side of an elaborate system of fences, some electrified prickly with barbed wire.

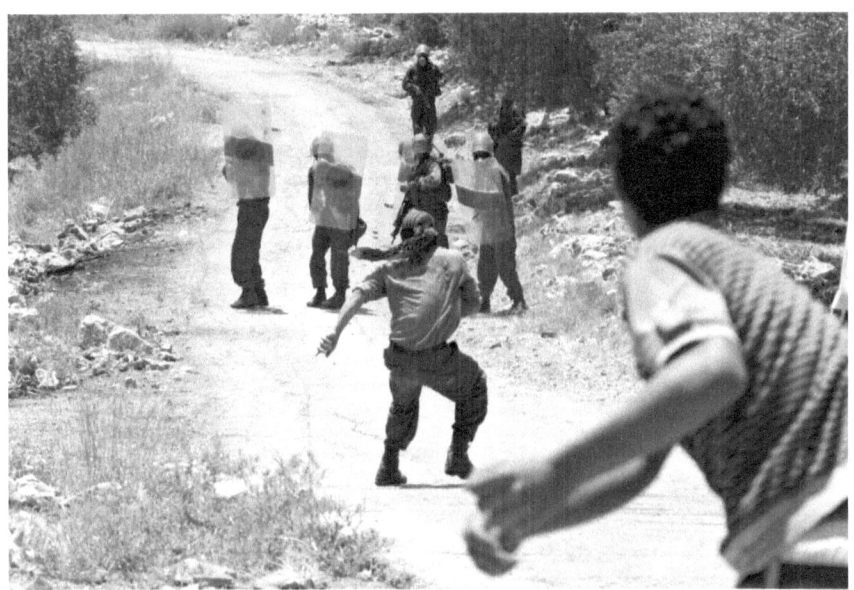

Israeli soldiers chase Palestinian rock throwers 2010

Being tear gassed in Bil'in reminded me of violent protests I'd been assigned to in the states. Even in the Holy Land a person chokes and coughs, eyes on fire, just like being pepper-sprayed in Detroit. No one is safe from the pain of violence, whether you're in Michigan or ancient disputed soil, and in our efforts to make peace we would do well to remember that we're all only human, one just like the next. Though the danger and horror varies and though we may disagree with each other, we're all still in this together.

PART V

"It is better to take refuge in the Lord than to trust in man." — Psalms 118:8

FINDING FAITH AT LOONEY LAKE

During one hot, humid summer, I met some of Lynn's family for the first time in Wisconsin, at a place called Looney Lake. Her parents were divorced, and her mother lived near Lansing, Michigan. Lynn had two blood-siblings and her dad had adopted two other children in a second marriage, meaning that family gatherings filled the cabin on the lake to capacity.

Lynn's family cabin was a large, log affair, resembling an upscale lodge, even, with expansive rooms and four bedrooms. A wooden sign hung above the front entry: "Looney Lake." Lynn's father, a prominent Milwaukee attorney, owned the forty-acre property, and the surrounding land was beautiful, heavily forested, and the lake full of jumping fish was surrounded by streams winding through the woods.

There's something to be said for being at the right place at the right time. My life was in dire need of renovation. Shortly after meeting me, Lynn's brother, Michael, said, "I don't know how anyone can believe in God." Perhaps an innocent comment, but oddly timed, to say the least; I suspected he'd heard I'd graduated from a Christian seminary. I wondered whether he was implying that I was stupid or warning me to not bring my faith into their family?

But I didn't sweat the difference at the time, as the family wanted to get to activities. Sadly, I was not in their league, exactly. Some of Lynn's siblings loved spectator sports and fishing, but I was fond of neither. Covering literally hundreds of sports events will drain you of every last drop of passion for a game. The sibling must have thought I resembled something of a vulnerable fish, and so cast his line and baited hook. The remark made me pause. When I finally brought myself together, I remember saying, "I do, and if you want to discuss it further, I'm available." The subject sat still in the water. Unbeknownst to him, his question sparked in me a dormant spiritual and intellectual need. It launched what I would call a faith journey, and it would consume the coming years.

It still astonishes me that an atheist's remark about God sparked my longing for a deeper spiritual journey. I would have thought some aggressive prompt for spiritual needs would have come from a Bible thumping, gun toting, Tea Party, Baptist fundamentalist Christian proselytizer. Or even a roving band of Jehovah's Witnesses at my front door. Indeed, I thought, "God does have a sense of humor. He introduced me to someone who doesn't believe, who then provoked a faith challenge." James 5:19-20 says: "My brothers, if anyone among you wanders from the truth and someone brings him back, let him know that whoever brings back a sinner from his wandering will save his soul from death and will cover a multitude of sins."

Lynn's brother had revealed his faith assumption. I don't know how he came to his narrative of (non)beliefs, though maybe, like many others, they came from his parents. My parents told me about Christianity when I was a boy and I believed them because they told me so. Church anchored my beliefs by expanding that story.

In other family gatherings I began to understand the ethos of Lynn's family, and some of the things that guided her formative years and even adulthood. Lynn had never said anything to me that belittled religion, and had only said that she had no interest in the subject. But the worldview she was taught at home was not one of tolerance toward religion. Between the two of us, we'd simply abstained from any discussions on the big questions of life that faith pursues.

But others would almost always say something negative or about religion and believers. It was not customary for me to back down from anyone who made a statement which I strongly oppose, or found insulting. But at the cabin I kept my mouth shut, not wishing to inflict discomfort on Lynn, her family, and all reunions from here on out. Instead, I said prayers asking for guidance, wisdom and humility. I needed to learn to love others, even those who scorned my beliefs and implied that I numbered among billions of stupid men and women otherwise known as Christians.

The more comments I heard, the more I wanted to know about what atheists *do* believe. They appeared to believe in nothing more almighty than humans or themselves, personally. I had never known any devout or outspoken atheists, or even given any serious thought to atheistic beliefs. Do they have a narrative that offered more hope and joy than the gospel?

I researched and learned from the leading and most outspoken atheist gurus: Richard Dawkins, Christopher Hitchens, Sam Harris and Daniel Dennett, aka "Four Horsemen of New Atheism." Christians trusted in the Holy Trinity meaning God as three divine persons. I read Dawkins' *The God Delusion*, and a resoundingly different book, *Atheist Delusions*, by David Bentley Hart, and essays by Hitchens and Harris. The Bible, after all, strongly encourages the search for truth, wherever it leads. It does not preclude scientific inquiry or studying the views of anti-theists.

Many atheists hold strong views about religion and its believers, and seemed to be most critical and obsessively irate toward Christians. I wondered if all atheists had read Nietzsche as children, aspiring to grow up and become personifications of rationality. Blaise Pascal said that the height of reason is to see its limits: "Imagination cannot make fools wise, but it makes them happy, as against reason, which only makes its friends wretched: one covers them with glory, the other with shame."

Details about Hitchens and Harris suggested that their thinking might have been somewhat impaired—and I don't say that solely because I disagreed with their existential views. Hitchens, by his own accounts, and his friends observations, drank heavily everyday. By 5PM he was probably too drunk to legally drive a car, but never felt incapable of instructing his readers what to believe, never too far gone not to share his unmatched revelations.

Harris grew up in a secular home in Los Angeles, with a Jewish mother and Quaker father who rarely discussed religion, though it was always a subject that interested him. He experimented with the drug ecstasy, and spoke about the powerful insights he felt psychologically. Some users experience bouts of confusion and problems with attention and memory.

As for Richard Dawkins, I agree with John Polkinghorne, a renowned British particle physicist, who said, "He's giving science a bad name. His book...is full of assertions, not argument, and it's incredibly naïve. I wish he'd just shut up." Dawkins and Harris have recently ratcheted up their rants, and most recently they've been against the Islamic faith. Christians can take a breather. Dawkins said it is a "given" that Islam is "an unmitigated evil in the world today." One blogger opined, "this is where Richard Dawkins and his army of blindly loyal followers will scoff, spit and curse like a seventeenth century congregation that's just been thrown a copy of *The God Delusion*."

Sam Harris joined the chorus, and was recently accused of racism, as the vast majority of Muslims are non-white. Harris, a white westerner, has become fixated on attacking their religion and advocating aggressive, even violent, tactics against Muslims. Some may start calling him a "cracker," a term I've been called many times, and that was hardly the worst I've heard. The epithet, by the way, was originally a pejorative for poor, rural whites from the south. My roots. You have to give Dawkins, Harris and Hitchens credit as they have collectively sold millions of books to a gullible, unanchored public, who are in search of a truth that can fit their secular life story. Too bad Hitchens isn't here to cash the royalty checks. God rest his soul.

Devout, fundamentalist atheist that he is, Dawkins has admitted that he has not read the Quran; he insists that he is sufficiently an expert to denounce Islam as the main culprit of the world's evil. He said that he has "not read the Koran, so couldn't quote chapter and verse, like I can for the Bible, But [I] often say Islam [is the] greatest force for evil today." How's that for a scientific research? One day we may not have to hear from him again, or Harris, if they anger the rare fundamentalist who might be as terrible as they insist. Danish cartoonist Kurt Westergaart drew a cartoon of prophet Muhammad in September 2005 for his newspaper; it was deemed so insulting and blasphemous to extreme fundamentalist Muslims that he has been living on the run ever since.

I thought of Dawkins and his cohorts when I read Proverbs 15:7: "The lips of the wise spread knowledge; not so the hearts of fools." And a question asked in Proverbs 26:12: "Do you see a man who is wise in his own eyes? There is more hope for a fool than for him."

But beyond the recent spittle directed towards Muslims, atheists have largely been obsessed with debunking Christian beliefs. Obviously, humans have free will and can choose whatever they want to believe in; I disagree with their beliefs but would never want to invalidate their rights. And I know well enough that thoughtful argument makes both believers and nonbelievers better. But their narrative offered no hope, and the tides of change were shifting with the vanguard of atheists. They now had the Middle East in their sights.

One last thing I found intriguing were the number of vitriolic comments made about the history of Christianity and the harm it has caused the world. The Crusades were mentioned far more often than atrocities committed by secularists Stalin, Hitler, and Pol Pot, and the de facto dynasty of North Korea. I never heard or saw a word about one of the bloodiest stories in history, the Mohammedan conquest of India. An estimated eighty to one hundred million Hindus were slaughtered, permanently disappeared or kidnapped by the warriors of Islam from 800 AD to 1700 AD. Millions of others converted to Islam at the blade of a sword.

The majority of history's wars have been conducted in the service of many gods. Most have been driven by the pursuit of profits or power, national or racial destiny, empire or the "greater good." Wars have been fought in obedience to ideologies without any thought of a god or gods. This is not to say that believers in "one true God" do not have blood on their hands. But Nietzsche despised Christianity for what it *was* above all else: its devotion to an ethics of compassion and morality. He hated Christianity for its concern for the weak, the outcast, the infirmed, and the diseased. He understood, though, the cultural crisis that awaited the world should Christian faith dissolve.

• • •

Years after Michael helped launch my faith journey, one of Lynn's nieces shared her wisdom and beliefs with me. She proclaimed in a banal comment that my religious views were based on "legend" and "myth." In my view, what she said was the equivalent of saying your beliefs are crap. This enlightened young woman earned a PhD in English Literature from a university in Europe and became an English professor at a New York university. I was certain she had gained her knowledge from her hermeneutics. Who was I to argue with the young enlightened exegete? She didn't seem to care that she had just thrown under the bus the research and exegesis of hundreds of Christian and non-Christian scholars, historians and archaeologists who collectively spanned hundreds of years

Offended, I wanted to ask what myths and legends formed her worldview. But instead I said, "If you're ever in the Middle East you may want to be careful not to insult the wrong person. You could lose your head, quite literally. You're lucky I'm a Christian." Had I prodded her further, she might have replied with a product of her postmodern education, "There is no truth, only truth claims." Our society cherishes the freedom to commit ourselves and practice any values of choice. But on one condition: they're not believed to be true. Many people view the Bible as a record of legend and myth. I returned to the profundity in Proverbs. In chapter 18:2: "A fool takes no pleasure in understanding, but only in expressing his [her] opinion." I'm grateful that their views fueled my commitment to deepen my faith.

Another professor of English shone as an example of a different kind of atheist from these hardnosed people I'd encountered so far. Rosaria Champagne Butterfield was a tenured, self-proclaimed radical, lesbian at Syracuse University, who said that Christians were "stupid, pointless and menacing...I thought of Christians and their god Jesus, who in paintings looked as powerful as a Breck Shampoo commercial model." She hated the mention of Jesus, but also realized that all major US universities had Christian roots.

She feels passionately about the ideas within Freud, Hegel, Marx and Darwin, and she strove to stand with the disempowered and the interests of her and her partner to speak of concerns for morality and compassion: AIDs activism, children's health and literacy and even dog rescue. She writes: "It was hard to argue that my partner and I were anything but good citizens and caregivers." As a postmodern intellectual, she operated from a historical materialist worldview, but Christianity is a supernatural worldview.

In interviews, and in a book she had written, Rosaria helped me better understand the beliefs of educated, secular, progressive, elite, nonbelievers. Dr. Butterfield believed herself to be a moral, good person and stood with the disempowered. She would have cringed at the possibility that all of us are complicit in some of the world's worst evils. She converted to Christianity and her worldview changed dramatically.

On the subject of feminine myths, it's worth noting that when the current executive editor of the *New York Times*, Jill Abramson, was appointed to that position, she announced: "In my house growing up, the *Times* substituted for religion." Her quote about the substitution of media for religion and the Bible in shaping contemporary America speaks volumes. The New York newspaper prides itself on being "the newspaper of record," but has it somehow become a religious substitute? Thank God I was not born into Jill's family—Sunday mornings sound like an empty affair. Sure, the *Times* features some interesting stories and commentary, but it's still what some of us in journalism used to call a "rag." Was the newspaper their Bible? What they believed in? Maybe their prophetess, Maureen Dowd, should visit Looney Lake.

I returned to the profound book of Proverbs: "Whoever trusts in his own mind is a fool, but he who walks in wisdom will be delivered," (Proverbs 28:26).

GARDEN OF VENICE

For several decades I had waited in eager anticipation for the next big news story to break. I had moved through the world too fast, often horrified at what I saw but running on adrenaline. There was never time for deep contemplation, but always time for a drink. Since the beginning, humanity has been hard wired to rebel against God. We all want to be our own god. I wanted to end my revolt. The garden is where I hoped and prayed to surrender fully to God.

Tolstoy, a man of complex faith and perceptive genius, said that, "In our world everybody thinks of changing humanity, and nobody thinks of changing himself. Let us be among those who believe that the inner transformation of our lives is a goal worthy of our best effort." I sought inner transformation.

I needed a refresher course in Christianity. I read dozens of books and was illumined beyond my wildest imagination. What surprised me was the burst of excited anticipation for each day of studying scripture and books of great wisdom. It felt like the adrenaline rush of chasing wildly after a breaking news story. Aristotle had said we are what we repeatedly do—we are creatures of habit. I committed to this habit and soon it was a vital part of my day. Pascal was right when he had explained what must be given up to wager that God exists, and that gaining infinite happiness in eternity can be gained even in our earthly life. His answers were purpose, peace, hope, joy and the things that put smiles on the lips of martyrs. My faith journey affirmed Pascal's promise, and more importantly, God's.

This would be a different journey, fueled by a commitment and not distracted by a career, as it had been during my time in seminary. I devised a plan. It would be conducted in my little, beautiful, yard, the place I love the most about my house, which I called the Garden of Venice. Among the flowers and trees there, there is one large Brugmansia tree in the middle of the garden. Its large, yellow-orange, trumpet-shaped flowers dangled from the tree's braches upside down.

The Garden of Venice was the same little expanse where my mom would sit when she lived with us, fascinated by the seemingly boring details. She was finitely focused, mystified only in the moment. "Isn't that the most beautiful flower you've ever seen?" she asked, incessantly. I imagined she was not unlike Eve when she first viewed the Garden of Eden. Each time my mom stepped into the yard it was like her first time. There weren't fruit trees. I only wish my mom had been the first woman tempted by the serpent. Knowing her, if she had been commanded by God to not eat the fruit of the trees she would have obeyed. We then might not be in the mess we are in today.

Memories of my mom motivated me to work on quieting my mind, letting myself be transfixed by my surroundings. I would have to filter out the world. It's easy to say that our culture is superficial—we all know that we idolize sports, Hollywood and unnecessary objects. We obsess about achievement and acquisition, and become addicted to technology that creates an illusion of human connection. But to move past just *recognizing* the superficial culture, and to actively filter it from your experience—this would be a challenge. This would not be an experience, to borrow from a recent book by an MIT researcher, titled "Alone Together." My mother hadn't been alone when she studied the blue sky or the angel's trumpets blossoms in our yard. She was in awe. She was with God, experiencing beauty and thankful.

My journey would require the mental discipline that I hoped would become habit. It would be like training for my first and last marathon. For the twenty-six miles, I set modest goals along the way, and after training for six months I finished the grueling run in just under four hours (three hours fifty-eight minutes to be precise). I had quit smoking six months earlier. This time, what I was trying to accomplish could have been done in a prison cell. The Apostle Paul and Diedrich Bonhoffer had both maintained and enriched their abiding faith in God while imprisoned.

My goals included contemplating and absorbing the messages from God's word; and integrating the model of Christ into my life—humility, compassion, meekness, forgiveness, and most importantly love for God and others, even my enemies. Most had not been my strengths.

Dallas Willard, a professor at the University of Southern California's School of Philosophy, has written some extraordinarily intriguing and stimulating books, and they were an enormous boon to me. In his book "The Divine Conspiracy," he offers, "consumer Christianity is now normative," and added, "the consumer Christian is one who utilizes the grace of God for forgiveness and the service of the church for special occasions, but does not give his or her life and innermost thoughts, feelings, and intentions over to the kingdom of the heavens. Such Christians are not inwardly transformed and not committed to it."

They remain imperfect, but all humans lack perfection. We remain unable and unwilling to do the good we know how to do. We remain governed by, or "slaves" of sin (John 8:34; Romans 6:16). We cling to and are dominated by such things as pride, fear, greed, impatience, egotism, bodily desires and allow for their control of our innermost lives. Christ offers a new life that abolishes the old. This is what I wanted and I had been a consumer Christian. Where would I turn for alternation of my soul?

• • •

Over the years I spent hundreds of hours in the garden. I read the Bible from cover to cover four times in four years—I would never claim to be a Biblical scholar. Reading portions of the Bible can sometimes be mysterious or awe-inspiring, cloudy or incredibly, brilliantly bright. It can be, as Saint Augustine said, like hearing the silence or seeing the dark. The richness, and directives found in what are called the wisdom books of the Old Testament, Psalms and Proverbs, are priceless jewels.

The Bible has estimated annual sales of 25 million copies, and has been a major influence on literature and history, especially in the West where it was the first mass printed book.

What about the Bible and its truths to impact the world? Jesus was clear: "You will know the truth and the truth will make you free." (John 8:32) The resurrection of Christ is the embodiment of Christianity, without which we don't have the rock to stand on. He defeated death. There are more eyewitness documents for the Resurrection than for anything else from the ancient world.

Regarding the veracity of the Gospels as written in the New Testament documents, there are more manuscripts than the ten best pieces of classical literature combined. There are upwards of 5,000 handwritten Greek manuscripts of the New Testament; the next closest work is of Homer's *Iliad*. The time between the original and first surviving copy of the New Testament is much shorter than anything else in the ancient world, at only 25 years. *The Iliad* has the next shortest discrepancy, at about 500 years.

For its breadth and depth, no religious or secular body of work matches the Bible for its impact in forming the moral bases of Western civilization and profoundly impacting Eastern cultures, as well, changing the course of the world's moral progress. It was this book that guided every one of the Founding Fathers of the United States. It is the book that formed the foundational values of every major American university. It is the book from which every morally great American, from George Washington to Abraham Lincoln to the Rev. Martin Luther King, Jr., got his values. Without the Bible, there would not have been Western civilization, or Western science, or Western human rights, or the abolitionist movement, or the United States of America, the freest, most prosperous, most opportunity-giving society ever formed.

The Holy Book inspired some of the greatest art and music the world had ever seen or heard. It offered the world unparalleled masterpieces of wisdom literature. The Bible gave humanity the Ten Commandments, the greatest moral code ever devised. It not only codified the essential moral rules for society, it announced that the Creator of the universe stands behind them, demands them and judges humans' compliance with them. It gave humanity the great moral rule, "Love your neighbor as yourself." It taught humanity the unprecedented and unparalleled concept that all human beings are created equal because all human beings of every race, ethnicity, nationality and both male and female are created in God's image. It detailed Jesus' Sermon on the Mount, the Beatitudes, which altered for billions of humans their conduct and the most profound sermon ever delivered to humankind.

It also taught people not to trust the human heart, but to be guided by moral law even when the heart pulled in a different direction. The postmodern substitute for the Bible is the heart. We live in an age where feelings are paramount, and an entire generation of Americans has been raised to consult their heart to determine right and wrong. But the heart and head and a whole host of emotions are deeply embedded in listening only to your feelings. There is pride, the root of all sin, self-interest and the fundamental desire we all have to make ourselves great, into a god.

Fools and those possessing an arrogance bordering on self-deification think we will long survive as a decent society without teaching the Bible and without consulting it for moral guidance and wisdom. Empty secularism has a growing grip on many western cultures, including the US. However, there is exponential growth in Christianity in Asia, Africa and Latin America. Many believers in those regions stay true to their faith at great personal risk. The Bible and Christianity have been and continue to be a threat to individuals and empires. North Korea persecutes Christians, and reports have said that the regime even tortures and executes them. A witness reported that a middle-aged woman was taken by state security officials from her home and shot to death—for having a Bible in her home.

UN studies, US governmental sources, newspaper accounts and documentation from churches, think tanks and human rights groups, found that in North Korea, Iran, Saudi Arabia and elsewhere, Christian conversion is severely punished, if not treated as a crime deserving capital punishment. In Egypt, Muslim mobs rampage through Coptic Christian neighborhoods, while in Nigeria, the radical Islamist terror group, Boko Haram, continues to blow up churches and slaughter Christians in their homes.

An Unusual Church

Finding the perfect church became one of my fantasies, though I knew it doesn't exist in any literal sense. The contentious split of my childhood church had indelibly, destructively, etched itself in my brain. But a church is its people, who are imperfect—sinners, not saints. It is a community coming together to worship God, and it shares a world of meaning, which is hard to do if you believe that life and the universe are essentially bereft of meaning. Church means a willingness to sacrifice for ideals higher than your own person. Religions create communities because they have a sense of the holy, and are thus capable of inducing real humility; churches acknowledge how small we are; yet they also redeem us from insignificance by the love and grace of God. Worshipping anything else—be it science, reason, class, race, country, wealth, power, success or fame—is idolatry. It's giving yourself up to something, and we get to choose what we give ourselves to: something earthly—ourselves—or something divine— each other.

I had been attending a Lutheran church around the corner from my house (like most sensible people, I hated driving in Los Angeles). I didn't feel a strong kinship there, but needed to be in the house of the Lord with other believers. The sermons were soothing, but felt like watered-down gospel. The pastor retired and they brought in a kid in his early thirties, fresh out of seminary. I listened to one of his sermons and knew I needed to find a more challenging church. I had heard about a dynamic preacher of the Presbyterian persuasion and attended a service they held in a local school's auditorium.

The senior pastor, Rankin Wilbourne, was not yet forty. He was a brilliant preacher who had garnered a wealth of biblical knowledge mixed with acute cultural awareness. He always introduced himself before his sermon, "Hello, my name is Rankin and I'm your teacher this morning." I was blown away by his message. After attending services for a year I joined the church, and Rankin introduced me to a wealth of books and films. Some books he referred to I had read before he was born, others I hadn't heard of. Every Sunday, the church's three services draws a few thousand congregants in their thirties to a building on the Santa Monica High School campus, where my daughter Sofie is currently a sophomore.

The church, Pacific Crossroads Church (PCC), is what is known as a "church plant" from Redeemer Presbyterian Church in New York City, where Reverend Tim Keller is senior pastor. Loosely speaking, Rankin is a Keller protégé. He could package a sermon with the best of them. Before encountering him, I would normally attend smaller churches, with old gospel hymns and people closer to my age, but I hungered for his insights. If I wanted a gourmet gospel meal, Rankin delivered the words. When he mentioned a book, author or film, I would Google it by the next day. Rankin is not the fire and brimstone type I had admired in my childhood; he was much quieter and more cerebral, but powerful, and more piercing.

A gospel-oriented church emphasizes that you experience the world as more than just what is material and observable. This does not mean that God is imaginary, but that because God is immaterial, we have to use our imaginations to *represent* God. It is having your imagination taken captive and reshaped by faith, letting go yet also actively experiencing the world. In church we sense our individual and humanity's broken condition. It's a safe place to allow ourselves to ponder good and evil, the songs we sing there are celebrations of our shared condition, together, forgiven by God.

Church can rewire us in a way that enables the goodness in each of us to triumph over evil. It's as if a circuit breaker—the device that protects against an overload or short circuit—were installed in our hearts not by an electrician, but the Holy Spirit to circumvent evil. God's circuit breaker disrupts the conduit of evil and redirects our heart to good. How could this happen? First we have the Ten Commandments, then when God appeared in human form, as Jesus, He taught us how to live the Beatitudes and through Paul's letters. When a person says, "I'm a good person," I sometimes reply, "I can see you are," because it's true—good resides in all of us, as do the seeds of evil. I have often wondered from where atheists believe the foundation of their ethics originated, whether they know it or not, that many Western ethical norms have largely derived from Judeo-Christian doctrines.

At University of California, Berkeley, a bastion for liberalism and secularism, researchers from the Human Population Laboratories of the Public Health Institute and the California Department of Health Services, found that people who attended religious services once a week had significantly lower risks of death compared with those who attended less frequently or never. "Maybe frequent attendees experience a greater sense of inner peace, perhaps because they can draw upon religious coping practices to help them deal with stressful events," according to the author of the findings. Adherents to Christian religions made up the bulk of the study participants.

Over two billion people seem to have a natural disposition to worship, perform rituals, sing and celebrate together, and feel our separateness momentarily dissolve into the experience of community. The trouble is: it depends on what we worship. Absent God, we tend to end up worshipping ourselves. In Matthew 22:37, Jesus says: "'Love the Lord your God with all your heart and with all your soul and with all your mind."

• • •

My church attracted large crowds and the pastoral staff suggested joining one of their small groups that met weekly. The idea for forming small groups in a large church was to connect people in a megalopolis like LA, and to grow spiritually through sharing life's triumphs and toils in an informal social setting. I attended a couple but was always the old guy, which wasn't uncomfortable, but simply needed more diversity. Call me an ageist. I shared this feeling with Orson Bean, an 84-year-old friend and fellow congregant who had been a long-time panelist on the popular television game show *To Tell the Truth.*

He said he tried a couple small groups and did not like being perceived as a grandfather by "a bunch of kids." Orson and I met for coffee and decided we would launch our own small group, which he wanted to name "the old-timers." I begged to differ and we renamed our group of two "Orson and me." Orson announced to the pastor there was a new small group of old-timers. We planned to recruit for our weekly meetings at Noah's Bagels in Marina del Rey, which seemed an appropriate name for a faith group's meeting place.

A film, television and Broadway actor and comedian, Orson laces our small group with some very colorful jokes. Neither Orson nor I grew up in the politically correct country we now live in, and he was influenced down to his soles, not his soul, by the crowd he once mixed with, which made him not unlike the greats of Henny Youngman, Rodney Dangerfield or Shecky Greene. The small group works wonders, and Orson and I have a "no holds barred" dialogue. He would tell me about issues that concerned him at home with his wife as did I. Orson's wife is a delightful woman with high energy like Lynn. Alley Mills, like Orson, has a show business background and starred as Norma Arnold on the popular television show The Wonder Years. We sometimes socialized as couples.

What better person to open up to than a star from *To Tell the Truth*? I've been lucky to find a friend with such candor, wit and faith, and know that should everyone find someone who complements their character, they'll discover the same sort of rich, rewarding and spiritually nourishing friendship. It was the first time I had ever sought this type of one-on-one experience except in AA or with a professional therapist. Matthew 18:20, " For where two or three are gathered in my name, there am I among them." We formed our group of two with assurance Jesus was with us.

TIME

I began every morning with prayer and a few moments of quiet contemplation. I often repeated the verse, "Be still and know that I am God." (Psalm 46:10). I carved time out of each day to sit in the Garden of Venice until all these little rituals were woven into the fabric of my life.

Solitude and silence in the garden was a great gift, and a new sense of freedom and peace surfaced. The seeds for the possibility of loving people began to bud.

Each day I read from a powerful devotional book, *365 Days with E. Stanley Jones*, which enriched Christ's messages. Jones was a legendary missionary to India, where he worked until his death at the age of eighty-nine, and where many considered him a 'Risha,' or 'saint.' I was introduced to Jones by his son-in-law, James Mathews, a Methodist bishop. I met Bishop Mathews while studying at Wesley Theological Seminary, where we became friends and he was a mentor to me. I spent many hours with him and his wife in their northwest Washington DC home.

While my studies of books had been in the analytical realm, my quiet hours of contemplation were devotional. They let me hear God's voice and obey His word, rather than the superficial conversations that are the discourse of our day, whether the subject is sports, success, celebrities, fashion or investments. Many people go their entire lives without truly experiencing or thinking about the depths of every day, and many people only experience these things in brief snatches. It seems to me that the need for virtual connections to other human's via texting, minute to minute, has become a form of insanity, a compulsion that imitates real connection without providing anything of value.

Prayer is essentially self-surrender. One learns to pray by praying. I began every day with the serenity prayer, followed by the Lord's

Prayer. Then I just prayed by believing God was someone I could say anything to. It takes practice, but I got the hang of it and offered thanks and began asking God to guide my direction, and for what I am to do. Sometimes I asked for help with talking to nonbelievers. He provided answers, but never with a loud burst of thunder or lightning bolts at my feet; He slowly lifted my old instinct to anger. Inner peace surfaced.

Prayer breaks the tyranny of self-preoccupation, absorbs you into God, and makes you interested in others. It's freeing. As E. Stanley Jones said, "Prayer is cooperation with God. Cooperation with Him in carrying out unfinished creative purposes. God wants to make us in helping Him to finish an unfinished universe. In prayer we do not have to overcome God's reluctance. We only have to cooperate with His highest willingness." Feelings of loneliness vanished.

I remembered the lyrics from a song sung when I was a kid, Just a Closer Walk With Thee. "When my feeble life is o'er, Time for me will be no more; Guide me gently, safely o'er To Thy kingdom shore, to Thy shore." The term feeble life was applicable to me and I believed all others. I thought of God often, and that alone improved my behavior and my life. The legendary Jones taught me about praying for others, even my enemies. He pointed out Acts 8:14-15, which tells of Peter and John going to Samaria, and prayed for them that they might receive the highest gift God had, the gift of Himself, the Holy Spirit. Selfish praying is not fruitful. Praying for others is.

• • •

I read the other current books authored recently and others from hundreds of years past. I stayed current with media articles. I was alarmed by the disturbing divisions between people, especially between proponents of science or religion, who increasingly could not seem to find room for discourse. Many people maintain that Christians are anti-intellectual and anti-science, which is, of course, patently absurd. There is no conflict between science and God. They are two entirely differing fields of inquiry, For example, the Augustinian monk Gregor Mendel was not only a Christian, but also believed in creationism. He also helped take the first steps of understanding genetics, with just a garden of pea plants.

Then there's Georges LeMaitre, a Belgian astronomer and cosmologist, and lo and behold, a monsignor in the Catholic Church who showed that religion and science, or at least physics, are in no way incompatible. This monsignor formulated the modern big bang theory, which holds that the universe began in a cataclysmic explosion of a primeval "super-atom." It was astonishing that these inquirers who served God, Mendel and LeMaitre, were giants in the sciences, advancing truth as they saw fit and without conflict. And let's not forget Galileo, a believer in science and God, who suffered for his achievements yet did not cease to believe himself.

Why then does the media never tire of trying to convince us of imaginary conflicts between science and religion? Too much of the media portrays a conflict between Christianity and science, exacerbated by the stereotype of Christians as gun toting, Bible-thumping, Tea Party idiots who believe in fairy tales, rather than science. This extreme group, which doesn't have anything to do with most Christians, has cast a shadow over millions of evangelical Christians. Many leading scholars and historians of science have formed consensus that science and Christianity have not been at war, but the notion has refused to die.

Albert Einstein thought: "The human mind, no matter how highly trained, cannot grasp the universe. We are in the position of a little child, entering a huge library whose walls are covered to the ceiling with books in many different tongues. The child knows that someone must have written those books. It does not know who or how. It does not understand the languages in which they are written. The child notes a definite plan in the arrangement of the books, a mysterious order, which it does not comprehend, but only dimly suspects. That, it seems to me, is the attitude of the human mind, even the greatest and most cultured, toward God."

The sciences might be able to explain the chemical make-up of pages and ink but will never be able to reveal the meaning of a book. The claim that science could ever provide a total understanding of reality as a whole overlooks the glaring fact that meaning, truth, beauty, morality, purpose, etc., are all ingredients in "the universe." The scientific method needs people to carry it out, and we humans live with the spirituality of beauty and morality every second of our lives. Scientific knowledge is derived from a tiny portion—just four percent—of the observable universe. Almost everything is unknowable. Jesus said that in his Father's house there are many mansions, thus we can speculate there may be room in the universe for millions of mansions.

"Some historians of science claim that the Christian doctrine of creation was central to the development of the scientific method. The concentration and diligence that go into inspecting God's work by a monk are hardly dissimilar from the rigor of the scientific method of a biologist or chemist. Childlike curiosity—asking, "How is such a thing possible?"—and childlike awe—exclaiming "How is such a thing possible!"—go hand in hand, and they complement faith. Science and religion have never been mutually exclusive, and they're not now.

But a handful of vociferous new atheists have apparently forgotten the joy of curiosity and rejected anywhere it might lead that they don't like. Dawkins, for example, believes the universe has "precisely the properties we should expect if there is, at bottom, no design, no purpose, no evil and no good, nothing but blind, pitiless indifference." Evolutionary biologist Stephen Jay Gould describes humans as "a cosmic accident that would never arise again if the tree of life could be replanted." According to these and other modern scientists, we are no more than selfish genes building selfish organisms.

Psalms 118:8: "It is better to take refuge in the Lord than to trust in man." Psalm 131:1-3: "O Lord, my heart is not lifted up; my eyes are not raised too high; I do not occupy myself with things too great and too marvelous for me. But I have calmed and quieted my soul, like a weaned child with its mother; like a weaned child is my soul within me."

• • •

Imagine Richard Dawkins and the minister of Westboro Baptist Church Fred Phelps attempting a discussion about religion or same-sex marriage. Both are rabid fundamentalists. We'd be more likely to see them in a boxing ring.

These days, we Americans live not only with political schismogenesis but also religious schismogenesis. A book titled *American Grace*, by political scientists Robert D. Putnam and David E. Campbell, points out that "recent years have seen the sharpest points of disagreement between religious believers, of nearly all stripes, and those who denounce religious beliefs of all types." Anthropologists' term for this type of opposition is "schismogenesis," which describes mirroring, escalating interactions. Whenever one side makes a move, the other side does the same, except to even more destructive, negative effect, like when a motorist cuts you off, you honk your horn, and then the other driver flips you the finger. Worse, like those horrible arguments with your spouse, where everything you say makes the other person dig in their heels more fiercely.

It is extremely difficult for believers to converse with nonbelievers. I have to reign in my emotions when someone berates or impugns my beliefs. Minds grow sensitive and wary, and quickly close down when it comes to dialogue with different, often difficult beliefs. But God demands that we love Him and love our neighbor, though it often seems that some neighbors are nearly impossible to even like, much less love. It is a challenge for me, but one I must continue working on. In Matthew 22:37-39, Jesus said: "Love the Lord your God with all your heart and with all your soul and with all your mind.' This is the first and greatest commandment. And the second is like it: "Love your neighbor as yourself." Scripture asks can God love me if I can't love others He created from love? I can't enter the Kingdom of God filled with hate.

In Soren Kierkegaard's book *Works of Love*, he equates God with love: "When a person engages in the act of loving, he is in effect achieving an aspect of the divine."

A Letter Long Overdue

Not too long ago I had been thinking how I disdained small talk, all those meaningless conversations that bubbled incessantly by each day. I realized I had to do some thinking: I may be as guilty as others in limiting my interactions to superficial, safe zones.

I knew that I had long loved to engage in life's meaning discussions but could rarely find another who wanted to venture along that road. Except at church. I remembered Peter Carlson's words: "he still lacerates his conscience with the kinds of questions that most adults long ago ceased asking themselves." Decades after that, I continue to ask.

On October 14th 2012, there was an email on my computer screen from Dennis Fitzgerald. I had not had contact with him in ten years. I read it and reread it, deeply moved that here was a young man asking me existential questions and wanting someone to talk to about the matters on his conscience. I considered this email serendipitous. It said:

> Hello Jim,
>
> Sorry it took me so long to respond. I have been working all weekend, and I currently work fairly long hours.
>
> I am still in Alexandria, though I am looking to leave this fair city, never to return again. Most of my family has moved away, my mother and my sister Amanda actually live outside of Portland now, so my reasons for staying decrease by the day.
>
> I actually find the "Greater Washington Metropolitan Area" quite loathsome; this having much to do with the caliber of the populace here, which I find to be in decline. Perhaps, it is as it always

has been, and I simply find myself losing my naïveté? Either way, I am preparing my exit strategy.

Other than the typical day-to-day tribulations, life has treated me quite well for the last several years. I am lucky enough to have found someone who I like to her core, and love entirely. We have one wonderful son, who is adorable and loving, and just makes my days brighter – though he can be quite a handful, particularly when he defecates in the neighbor's yard (he's a dog).

I have learnt much about the world that surrounds us, and discovered aspects of myself hitherto hidden by my cycles of doubt and self-recrimination. And so, I attempt to progress beyond myself, despite myself.

Did you ever struggle with anything equivalent? I only ask because most I have met would not volunteer this kind of information, but I suspect the experience is more commonplace than it feels.

As long as the subject has shifted, how are you? From what I can find publicly available on the Internet it seems things are going well for you, which I am very happy to hear, or read as the case may be. I suspect four daughters make for quite a handful themselves, albeit of a different sort.

Now, a selection of relatively invasive, yet innocuous questions: What have you done that you are most proud of? Why? Where do you see yourself five years from now? Why? What do you want most in the entire world, that you do not already have, and how likely do you think you are to attend/attain/ achieve/acquire/accomplish it? Why? What are you most afraid of? Why?

Please do not feel obligated to answer any of the above if you find them to be too invasive. If you would like, I would be more than willing to go quid pro quo with you.

It is difficult to get in touch with me right now, via the phone, partly because my work schedule is all over the place, and partly because I am in the process of moving, but things should settle down in by the end of the month, and then I will call you. I am actually stealing time right now just to write back to you.

I believe we were on the Leeza show around this time of year in 1993 (pretty certain it was the fall, and I graduated in the spring of '94). Thanks for looking for that. I only went looking for it myself because Olivia had asked to see it.

I hope this message finds you well,
Best Regards,
Dennis Edward Fitzgerald

I responded to the email and told Dennis I was finishing a book about my life, which could provide him with many answers for the existential issues he was raising. A few months went by and I called him. I am known for my short attention span on the telephone, but by the end of the conversation we had talked for nearly two hours, my new record, by far.

Dennis told me about when he met his father upon the latter's release from prison. A meeting was arranged at the Department of Human Services, where Dennis' caseworker could oversee the first time seeing his dad since he was two-years-old. The meeting was dramatic and difficult for Dennis, and he concluded that his dad was unrepentant. He even asked his son if he could hook him up with weed. His dad described how a dispute with Dennis' grandmother had escalated to the point where he stabbed his own mother in law multiple times, until her heart stopped. Dennis met his dad one last time to show him the neighborhood he lived in—without showing him his exact house. Dennis did not trust his dad, and was alarmed when his father asked his son why he lived around "spicks "and "niggers." Dennis decided he wanted no further contact with his father and hasn't seen him since.

I asked him how he felt the day he was evicted and I had showed up lugging cameras. He told me, "I was embarrassed and sad. I was also angry at my mother. I didn't want to be in the pictures and blamed her for us being evicted and becoming a public spectacle." After a brief silence I said, "I'm sorry I took your picture, Dennis, but I had no idea of any of the circumstances, or that you wanted to be excluded. I couldn't sense that you were distraught, apoplectic, even, but who wouldn't be on the day your family is forced out into the streets?"

"Right after I took your picture on the street, the Alexandria Humane Society arrived. They put your two pet cats in cages. I photographed them carrying the cats to their truck to deliver them to the local animal shelter. Your sisters were running behind the large man carrying the cages. Mary was grabbing his shirt, and she and her sister were screaming and crying. The cats were going to have shelter while your family was thrown to the street. Homeless."

"Did your mother make you sit with your family for the photos?" Another moment of silence. "My mother and other tenants were in a dispute with the landlord, and that lead to us being removed. She helped organize the protest, made signs, and wanted attention for what she thought was wrongdoing." When I had met his mother, Angela, she struck me as a tough, feisty woman. I'd liked her. Yelling and waving a sign, she clearly wanted attention for their plight. She had been more than happy for me to photograph her family sitting on all their worldly possessions. "I suppose she was fighting for you, trying to protect your family's rights. That's a good thing, right?"

"Yeah."

During the eviction, notorious homeless advocate Mitch Snyder showed up with a few friends, and I knew instantly who had anonymously informed me of the Fitzgerald eviction. I told Dennis that the family he was born into had perhaps made him a stronger person. "You can be proud of your strength and courage, which helped you survive some of what you experienced during your youth. Some of your strength may have been bolstered in church, when you heard a bit about Jesus and the gospel. You certainly met evil amidst good. Steve lured you into his demonic world and used you for his twisted ways. Evil roamed the halls of your church while others listened to their minister's good news. You didn't just survive, though, you turned out to be a thoughtful, caring man." And Steve went to prison for over a decade.

He told me another story and how the photograph I had taken of him during his family's eviction had continued to haunt and embarrass him over the years. The eviction picture followed him even when he was trying to woo a girl he had started to date as a teenager. She took Dennis to her lovely home in suburban Virginia and introduced him to her parents. They scrutinized him and gave him the once over for a few minutes. The father said he looked familiar, and asked about the church he attended, in case that might answer from where he knew Dennis. With no solid clues the dad, his wife and daughter walked to the kitchen, leaving Dennis alone for a few minutes. He glanced down at the coffee table and saw my book sitting on the table, right on the cover of which showed his picture, with his family, sitting on everything they owned. He put the book under his arm and walked out the door.

A Lucky Photo

An old photo I had taken continued to follow me for decades, and this particular photo didn't embarrass me like the eviction photo had for Dennis. The photo in the White House Rose Garden of President Reagan, Prime Minister Thatcher, and the dog, Lucky, elated me every time I saw it published.

In April 2013, my brother Mike called to tell me he was looking at the photo in the current issue of *Time Magazine*. He told me it was on the centerfold spanning both pages. He said, "I've never seen a magazine run a photo across two pages without even a border. I'm reading right now, 'Photograph by Jim Hubbard' in the lower right. Have you seen this, Jim?"

"No, I'm not a subscriber."

"Now you can say you do centerfolds, Jim."

"Yeah, that's it, I left the news biz to do centerfolds."

Mike's son, Michael Andrew, a former Green Beret like his father, took a cell phone picture of centerfold and posted it on Facebook. It was thrilling all over again; I had spent years shooting images and it was always a rush to see my photos published, but that this was the legendary, international *Time*, gave me goose bumps. I felt like a dog chomping on its first steak bone, or a kid with his first bike.

I had to wait a few days to find a newsstand with the magazine, but the feeling hit me all over again when I opened to the centerfold. I called my brother.

"You must have spent a few nights without sleep to find a copy."

"I'll admit, I was getting impatient to get my hands on one…I bought five."

It's unusual for one photo to occupy two pages in a magazine like *Time*, and the issue featured two other photos across two pages, one from Syria and one from China (of chicken feet). That's a lot of space where words could have been printed—the tides had turned. When I started in news, words reigned supreme, and the writer was the special child. Photographers were a necessary evil, to supplement the verbal craftsmen's views of the world. Now, the photographer's image is near the top of the pyramid. Visual communication, rather than words, have become deified, stealing space from the columns and speaking to 'readers' with images.

I wondered why the image had remained so captivating. It showed the two most powerful leaders of the Western world walking a dog, and I had dropped to my knees for a low angle, an unusual move, as most photographers would have stayed standing to get a shot more directly of the politicians' eyes and expressions. When Lucky leaped, the lower angle offered a more dramatic perspective of his lunge, whose suddenness caused Reagan to slightly lose his balance, and clutch Lucky's leash more dramatically. Thatcher walked at his side, smiling and mildly amused.

What the Secret Service may have uncovered in their background check was my unfortunate history with dogs, which have never much liked me. A thorough background check might have revealed that a dachshund had bit my behind, puncturing two tiny holes in my pants and body while I was delivering newspapers. After that, a German Shepherd tore flesh from my right hand, which left scars, and later still I had two more encounters with a pair of hellhounds. That information could have prompted the security detail to require a more securely leashed dog for the day's photo op.

For all I knew, Lucky might have even been an attack dog trained by the Secret Service to protect leaders of the free world. Or, Lucky thought he smelled some meat in my pocket. Bottom line, when I looked at the photo in Time Magazine, I was grateful. If Lucky had been free roaming during a routine walk, it wouldn't have provided the perfect moment to take a perfect photo.

After the photo op, Lucky rolled on the grass and the Prime Minister knelt down and began petting the gleeful mutt, while Reagan kept holding the red leash. I walked up, stood next to them and continued taking pictures. The president said to me, "Nice to see you again."

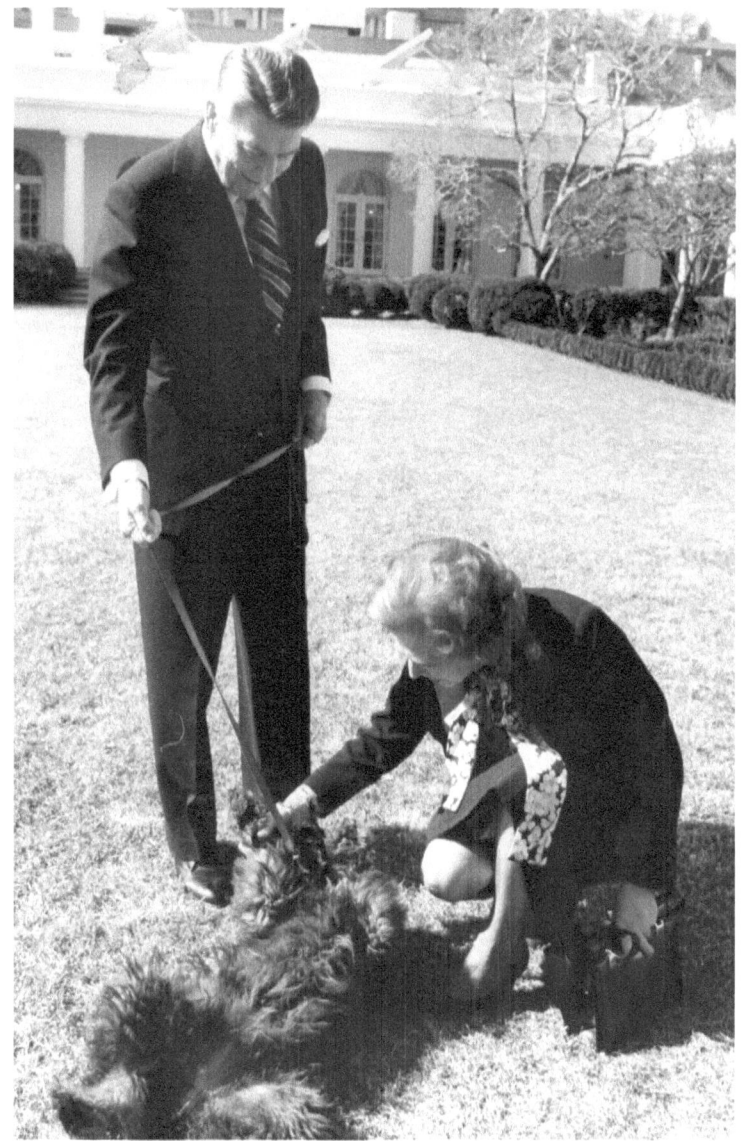

Margaret Thatcher pets Reagan's dog Lucky in Rose Garden 1985

"Thank you, Mr. President. Lucky is a cute dog."

"Meet Prime Minister Thatcher."

"Hello ma'am, nice to meet you." She smiled and said, "Thank you. Lovely day isn't it."

It was, and I knew for years later that in part, I had just gotten lucky.

OLD TIME RELIGION

Evil's so passé, some say, but it deserves a closer look. But another fundamental disconnect I have with believers in secular dogma is that they idolize humans. They place humans at the top of the pyramid, instead of God, or at least instead of something greater than mankind. They have faith that humanity can resolve man's problems, and that people can prove all matters of existence through wise, reasoned and scientific brains. I do not share those beliefs.

Witnessing human behavior throughout the world, over the years, has provided me with more than just belief to back up my view that mankind can't do this alone, and won't have enough to answer the deepest questions. The Bible offers the story I believe. The Bible instructs in Proverbs 1:7, "The fear of the Lord is the beginning of knowledge, fools despise wisdom and instruction."

An op-ed in *The New York Times* caught my attention one day; it was titled, "Liberalism and Secularism: One and the Same," and by Stanley Fish. He wrote, "I am not criticizing liberalism, just explaining what it is. It is a form of political organization that is militantly secular and incapable, by definition, of seeing the strong claim of religion— the claim to be in possession of a truth all should acknowledge—as anything but an expression of unreasonableness and irrationality." He went on to say, "In liberal thought, 'reasonable' is a partisan, not a normative notion. It means 'reasonable' from our perspective." Fish cites Georgetown University professor Jacques Berlinerblau, who asks, "Can an atheist or agnostic commentator discuss any aspect of religion for more than thirty seconds without referring to religious people as imbeciles, extremists, mental deficients, fascists, enemies of the public good, crypto-Nazis, conjure men, irrationalists... authoritarian despots and so forth?" Good question.

Secular liberals often wrap themselves in other garments, like moral relativism and political correctness. The combination of secular, liberal, moral relativism and political correctness can sometimes be toxic, or even dangerous. It leaves, I fear, the believing person deaf, dumb and blind. In other words, it can put you out of touch with reality. More alarming, you can lose the capacity to distinguish fundamental moral issues of right and wrong, good and evil. Moral relativism can lead you astray when it refuses to call evil what it is, which in turn feeds a concurrent willingness to denigrate truth, if truth requires that you notice evil. Is it acceptable to call an evil act "wicked?" I prefer to call it evil.

Every human has the capacity for both good and evil, though sometimes individuals have a higher octane for one or the other. The brothers who bombed the Boston Marathon were running on high-octane evil, as was the Fort Hood psychiatrist, a terrorist who ended the lives of thirteen people. In both cases the individuals had years earlier come to the attention of counter terrorism agencies, yet slipped through the cracks, perhaps because of PC culture. Adam Lanza, too, the murderer of twenty children and six adults, was a disturbed man of horrifying evil, as was James Holmes and the Castro brothers, too—all men who were Americans and neighbors, perpetrators of vicious evil who had for years shown warning signs which only went unheeded.

The New York Times reported recently on anti-Jewish comments during speeches by Egyptian President Mohamed Morsi, a longtime prominent member of the Muslim Brotherhood. He said, "We must never forget, brothers, to nurse our children and our grandchildren on hatred for them: Zionists, for Jews." He said that Egyptian children "must feed on hatred; hatred must continue. The hatred must go on for God and as a form of worshipping him…[Jews are] bloodsuckers, and descendants of apes and pigs." Egypt, with 82 million people and decades of military dictatorship, is considered a US ally and regularly receives some of our newest and most expensive toys of war.

Another op-ed piece, "Raised on Hatred," written by Ayaan Hirsi Ali, sparked my attention in January 2013. He wrote, "Millions of Muslims have been conditioned to regard Jews not only as the enemies of Palestine but as the enemies of all Muslims, of God and of all humanity. Arab leaders far more prominent and influential than Morsi have been tireless in 'educating' or 'nursing' generations to believe that Jews are 'the scum of the human race, the rats of the world, the violators of pacts and agreements, the murderers of the prophets, and the offspring of apes and pigs.'" (These are the words of Saudi sheik Abdul Rahman al-Sudais, imam at the Masjid al-Haram mosque in Mecca.)

HBO's fiery, atheist host Bill Maher, on the other side of the world, debated guest Brian Levy, the director of the Center for the Study of Hate & Extremism at California State University in San Bernardino, about the Boston Marathon bomber's faith and terrorism. "It's not like people who are Muslim who do wacky things have a monopoly on it," Levy claimed. "We have hypocrites across faiths, Jewish, Christian who say they're out for God and end up doing not so nice things." Maher, responded, and said his premise was "liberal crap": "I mean, yes, all faiths, they're not as dangerous. I mean, there's only one faith, for example, that kills you or wants to kill you if you draw a bad cartoon of the prophet. There's only one faith that kills you or wants to kill you if you renounce the faith. An ex-Muslim is a very dangerous thing. Talk to Salman Rushdie after the show about Christian versus Islam. So, you know, I'm just saying, let's keep it real."

• • •

Although Christ is considered a prophet by Muslims, Christianity and Islam are not even close to being on the same page. Secular, moral and cultural relativists preach that all religions are the same, but the differences are not only present but extremely important. Contrast, for instance, the lives of the central figures of each faith, Jesus versus the prophet Muhammad, or even Buddha for Buddhists. Buddhism blurs the lines between philosophy, religion, and even atheism, and I would argue that many Buddhists approach the latter and have very little in common with the other major faiths. For all practical purposes, they are atheists.

Muhammad spent his last ten years, from 622 to 632 AD, in Medina, western Saudi Arabia, and was buried there. He had established an ideology with revolutionary implications, and it proved attractive to Arabs who lacked status. He waged war against his contemporaries and Islam itself became a means of recruiting followers, who formed part of his new kind of Arab community, which used faith as its center yet provided for an expanded scope of military conflicts and highly restrictive social structures.

Contrast Muhammad's life with Jesus, for which the Sermon on the Mount, serves as a pithy summary. Take note, Jesus said:

Blessed are the poor in spirit, for theirs is the kingdom of heaven.

Blessed are those who mourn, for they will be comforted.

Blessed are the meek, for they will inherit the earth.

Blessed are those who hunger and thirst for righteousness, for they will be filled.

Blessed are the merciful, for they will be shown mercy.

Blessed are the pure in heart, for they will see God.

Blessed are the peacemakers, for they will be called sons of God.

Blessed are those who are persecuted because of righteousness, for theirs is the kingdom of heaven.

Even a strident atheist like Bill Maher recognizes the differences between a religion of peace and one with an origin story riven by bloodlust. As he said, "Talk to Salman Rushdie after the show about Christian versus Islam." Contrast the efforts of radical Islamists with those of radical Christians.

And just what is a "radical Christian?" Some might call them "Jesus Freaks." They plant churches, feed the poor, heal the sick; they open orphanages and pregnancy resource centers; they visit prisoners and deliver the oppressed; in other words, they have sold themselves out to be the hands and feet of the One they worship.

Radical Christian and Habitat for Humanity founder Millard Fuller and his wife, Linda, started an organization "that has helped build or repair more than 600,000 houses and served more than 3 million people around the world." Meanwhile, Muslims in Pakistan recently burned nearly 200 Christian homes over the *alleged* blasphemy against Muhammad by a Christian sanitation worker.

Radical Christians build hospitals; radical Muslims have filled them up. Christians have led the world in caring for the sick and dying, and with the spread of Christianity, hospitals grew as part of the church's mission, eventually becoming part of the community. The Catholic Church alone operates over 1,100 hospitals and long-term health care facilities in the US.

Radical Christians build schools. The world's first university, birthed in 1088, was the University of Bologna, in Italy, founded to teach canon (church) law. The second-oldest university, the University of Paris, grew out of the cathedral schools of Notre Dame and soon became a great center for Christian orthodox studies. Dr. Alvin J. Schmidt, in his book *Under the Influence: How Christianity Transformed Civilization*, points out that every college established in colonial America, except the University of Pennsylvania, was founded by some denomination of Christianity.

Radical Muslims have attacked young girls who merely wanted an education. In 2012, Taliban forces in Afghanistan were responsible for what was described as "an intentional act to poison schoolgirls." According to the UN, there were nearly 200 attacks on schools and hospitals in Afghanistan in 2011. As the word implies, "extremism" exaggerates the qualities of a faith or ideology. The world has millions of Muslims who do not embrace the worst characteristics, but the few that do have inflicted terrible pain on others. The few Christians who have taken it upon themselves to amplify the traits of Christ in their own lives have helped millions in turn. When it comes to comparing radical Christians to radical Islamists, there is no comparison. I want to count myself a radical Christian.

• • •

In need of a break from completing the final pages of my book today, I took my daughter Sofie to the Santa Monica Promenade to shop for a skirt. I had been working feverishly to complete the last chapter and send to the publisher next week. I hadn't been able to focus my mind on writing since news of the Boston Marathon terrorist bombing broke. It was a riveting, emotional story, and I couldn't stray far from television reports and updates. Like millions of Americans, I reacted emotionally, and felt lacerated by human evil and terrible sadness for the victims.

I sat on a fixed metal chair outside the store she had entered. I noticed two young men handing out pamphlets and wearing matching T-shirts. They approached pedestrians the words were apropos, reading: "Fighting evil, Teaching Tolerance, Seeking Justice." I wanted to talk with them and noticed smaller words on their shirts,

"Southern Poverty Law Center" (SPLC), and realized they were under the tutelage of the law center. I agreed with some of their principles but disagreed with others, as in some regards they were de facto secular, liberal, PC, moral relativists. But more importantly, they preached tolerance—except for religious groups, and particularly Christians. They did though seek tolerance for Muslims. Ken Silverstein, in a piece for *Harper's Magazine*, wrote about them and their founder Morris Dees in a piece titled, "The Church of Morris Dees." The story's subtitle read: "How the Southern Poverty Law Center profits from intolerance." Silverstein's piece described Dees as cofounder of SPLC, a civil rights lawyer cum direct-marketing millionaire in 1971 Alabama. The story cast him as the Jim and Tammy Faye Baker of the civil rights movement.

Today, the SPLC spends most of its time—and money—on a relentless fund-raising campaign, peddling memberships in the church of tolerance with all the zeal of a circuit rider passing the collection plate. The Center earned $44 million last year alone—$27 million from fund-raising and $17 million from stocks and other investments—but spent only $13 million on civil rights programs, making it one of the most profitable charities in the country.

When I walked up to them I threw a curve ball. Instead of asking about the SPLC I asked, "Are you from a religious group?' In chorus they responded, "No we're secular."

"Are you also liberal?" They seemed nervous.

"Yes, I suppose."

"Do you know that millions of people hate you?"

"Huh?"

"You're Americans, and so you're hated, perhaps by millions of people, especially by those in the Middle East who lump us together with Israel. First they hate Israelis, then the Jewish people in general, and third they hate the infidels on the soil and streets of the USA."

One of them responded, "Hey, I agree, and understand what you are saying—I'm Jewish." I'd just been reading and writing about the opposite extremes of Morsi and the secular, liberal, PC, moral relativism, but I realized I shouldn't give in to my own combative impulses, and turned and walked away. Knowing the differences between good and evil, love and hate, is vital, as is the internal peace and control to choose one over the other.

When I returned home, I read a story in the *Los Angeles Times* in which a counter-terrorism expert explained the difficulties of the war on terror. The expert asked rhetorically, "Who knows how many people out there are disenchanted with their lives, and are considering taking violent action?" My guess would be a few billion, if you counted all the old, white conservative men in the US who blamed the left for their problems, and who liberals blamed for their own. He explained, "There is no way law enforcement can take on those numbers of individuals and investigate all those leads. We understand better how to go after and dismantle an organization with clear ideology like Al Qaeda. There is no X-ray that looks into a man's soul." God does without X-rays.

Two days after the Boston bombings, I sat before my class at USC. The course, titled "Visual Communication of Death in the Digital Age," required students to analyze current photos and video depicting death or near death in media. I began the class by showing coverage from Boston on a large screen. We spent an hour viewing photos and video from Boston's horror, and several students considered the pictures too horrific and turned away. Then I showed historic photos to contrast the images of death from the decades before the Internet age. It turns out that images of death published in media relate to a nation's dominant religions, values, race and geographical distance from other countries and cultures.

Carved in my mind were images I had taken on numerous assignments featuring terrorism, death and carnage. One example I remembered was the day I had spent over twelve hours photographing the Munich massacre during the 1972 Olympics. I photographed the hooded terrorists who had just slaughtered athletes inside as they walked onto the apartment's balcony. They peered at us photographing them. The terrorist attack images from Boston's mayhem and carnage were affecting me similarly, though I was not personally at the scene. The story was in some ways causing psychic damage to Americans, and all of it was making me and some of my students both angry and sad.

When news was released that the Boston bombers had immigrated to the US from Chechnya, I remembered the Belsam School Massacre. During my next class I displayed gruesome images from the 2004 atrocity in Russia. Muslim terrorists from Chechnya took 1,100 people hostage in the school, including 777 children. Many of the girls and women were raped before being murdered by the terrorists, and the three-day siege ended with the death of over 380 people, 186 of them children. The Tsarnaev brothers were no doubt aware of, perhaps, influenced by that event in Belsam, yet my students had never heard of the tragedy. The enormity of evil that humans have committed against each other boggles and agonizes the mind.

One of the most celebrated and reverently esteemed figures in modern literature, Gilbert Keith (GK) Chesterton, was asked by a newspaper reporter what was wrong with the world. He skipped all the expected answers. He said nothing about corrupt politicians or ancient rivalries between warring nations, or the greed of the rich and the covetousness of the poor. He didn't mention street crime and unjust laws and inadequate education. Environmental degradation and population growth overwhelming the earth's carrying capacity were not on his radar. What's wrong with the world? Chesterton responded with two words: "I am."

When family and friends were interviewed by media about the Tsarnaev brothers, one parent said, "He's an angel," and the other said, "He has a heart of gold." We also know that the seeds for evil in the brothers' hearts, like seeds for grass, had taken root.

The Beginning

Since the Boston atrocity the subject of human nature went viral. Like bumper-to-bumper traffic on the 405, media and bloggers have been pondering and posting on what human nature is really like. What's in our hearts and souls?

"If only the world could rid itself of evil people," said Russian writer Aleksandr Solzhenitsyn. He wrote, "If only it were all so simple! If only there were evil people somewhere insidiously committing evil deeds, and it were necessary only to separate them from the rest of us and destroy them. But the line dividing good and evil cuts through the heart of every human being. And who is willing to destroy a piece of his own heart?"

On the topic of atheism Solzhenitsyn offered, "Over a half century ago, while I was still a child, I recall hearing a number of old people offer the following explanation for the great disasters that had befallen Russia: 'Men have forgotten God; that's why all this has happened.' Since then I have spent well-nigh 50 years working on the history of our revolution; in the process I have read hundreds of books, collected hundreds of personal testimonies, and have already contributed eight volumes of my own toward the effort of clearing away the rubble left by that upheaval. But if I were asked today to formulate as concisely as possible the main cause of the ruinous revolution that swallowed up some 60 million of our people, I could not put it more accurately than to repeat: "Men have forgotten God; that's why all this has happened."

But let's journey back thousands of years to the stories from the Bible. As it is an unrivaled resource for understanding all of humanity, it helps us understand ourselves. After only the first few chapters in Genesis, we discover that the heart of sin, evil, is the desire of the self to be God. The human heart is hopelessly incorrigible: God created kings and slaves in his image, democratizing all humans, but humans instead perceived themselves as higher and lower than each other, missing the point entirely. All are equal. Never has there been in a religious book offering a more majestic tribute to humans. In Genesis 1:27: "So God created man in his own image, in the image of God he created him; male and female he created them."

In a dramatic turn of events from Genesis 6:5-14: "The Lord saw that the wickedness of man was great in the earth, and that every intention of the thoughts of his heart was only evil continually. And the Lord regretted that he had made man on the earth, and it grieved him to his heart. So the Lord said, 'I will blot out man whom I have created from the face of the land. For I am sorry I have made them.'

"Now the earth was corrupt in God's sight, and the earth was filled with violence. And God saw the earth, and behold, it was corrupt, for all flesh had corrupted their way on the earth. And God said to Noah, 'I have determined to make an end of all flesh, for the earth is filled with violence through them. Behold, I will destroy them with the earth. Make yourself an ark of gopher wood. Noah did this; he did all that God commanded him."

It is startling that God grieved like a parent who loses a child. Hardly equivalent, but I knew the depths of personal grief when I suddenly lost my daughter. For God it was grief for everything living on earth, a loss incomprehensible and unimaginable.

Albert Camus said, "What we learn in time of pestilence: that there are more things to admire in men than to despise." You can see his point in the first responders risking their lives on 9/11 and in the aftermath of the Boston bombings.

What was startling was the Bible's description of wickedness, which can be summarized as relaying that the heart of sin lies in the desire to make the self into God. So what dominates humans—good or evil? "The Lord saw that the wickedness of man was great in the earth, and that every intention of the thoughts of his heart was only evil continually."

God's love and grace for humankind shone in Genesis 8:21, in God's covenant with Noah after the flood. God said, "I will never again curse the ground because of man, for the intention of man's heart is evil from his youth. Neither will I ever again strike down every living creature as I have done."

Almost every ancient civilization, from one continent to the next contains a story of a great flood, wiping out nations and life save for a handful of survivors. How could it be that the stories of all people's align, that each ancient culture tells a story of evil, terror and a calamity of unimaginable proportions, followed by forgiveness, resurrection and a way forward for the whole human race? From where does it all come, and from where do we find the strength and love to contend with the senselessness and hate that remain with us, and in us? The answer is there, too—in each other and in the depths of love and awe that always exist in our lives, even in the darkness. We call it God.

AFTERWORD

And thank God I've figured out how to end my book. A story about life, work, and a faith journey. But a gnawing, perplexing issue remained I needed to work through. It has to do with contempt toward others. I thought about how I am commanded to love my neighbor. I held contempt for my neighbor who was recently charged with fourteen felonies for sexual crimes against children. Add to the list fundamentalist atheist minister Richard Dawkins and others. Can I love them but hold onto contempt? Probably not. Minimally that would wound my connection to God. I will continue praying and listening for God's wisdom in this area of my inner life.

Sad news arrived when I heard about the passing of USC colleague Dallas Willard. I emailed him a few months ago requesting a meeting but did not hear back. He was already ill. His books touched and informed my life and thousands of disciples and ministers around the world. A close friend of his wrote that Dallas struggled with the problem of harboring contempt for people. I sighed a breath of relief. My struggle was not unique. If a giant like Professor Willard had difficulty with disgust for others, who was I, a former Weaver's Ranger, to be exempt from such a struggle?

An email arrived late the same afternoon I would send the manuscript to my editor for a final edit before publication.

> *Hi Jim,*
>
> *My name is Kelli Beyer, contacting you on behalf of the Homeless Children's Playtime Project. As our name suggests, we work directly with children experiencing homelessness living in shelters and transitional housing programs throughout the District of Columbia. Similar to your experience*

*with homeless children when you founded Shooting
Back, I've discovered that in trying to take photos
of the children, the youth have the strong desire and
curiosity to look through the lens themselves. We
would love to empower our children to photograph
their world and shed light on the childhoods they
experience while living in shelters in DC. Do you
partner with organizations to bring photography to
children or can you recommend ways in which we
can start a similar project among our children and
volunteers?*

Thank you, Kelli

A quarter century after I began working with homeless children
in the nation's capital, someone had noticed what I had. The children
wanted to look through the lens and take their own pictures. Kelli later
explained that the residents of the greater Washington metropolitan
area had little regard for the homeless and ignored them—not unlike
1987, or the themes mentioned in over 2,000 verses in the Bible about
the poor.

My book's title, "Shooting Back From the Heart," describes two
facets of my life. First, my operative praxis: I had attempted to use my
skills with a camera to serve God by highlighting the least amongst us,
and to raise awareness of their plight. God showed me the enormity
of the broken condition of humanity through my travels as a news
photographer. I saw and met some of the millions of sick, needy and
afflicted across the earth for whom I had prayed as a child.

I didn't do this perfectly, but the Shooting Back idea had been
inspired by prayers with my mother, the Bible and through my studies
at the seminary. The president of Wesley once told me that about my
photography: "That is your ministry." Each of us can have a ministry
as unique and creative as our personalities, if only we let ourselves be
open to the task of God's work.

I am thankful to God for directing and challenging me to use
photography as a tool for ministry, and for my life, which has been
wonderful. I was sure I would be dead before I reached twenty, and
who was I to question my high school principal. God, for some
unknown reason, let me live much longer, and even blessed me with

a rich life in which I have too often made poor decisions. For all my wrongs I am forgiven, and I try every day to remember the countless things for which I'm grateful.

Secondly, and more importantly, I am shooting back toward having relationship with God and surrendering completely to Him. In Psalm 34: "I sought the Lord, and he answered and delivered me from all my fears. Those who look to him are radiant, and their faces shall never be ashamed." This is the story I am guided by. We all decide the story we believe in, and it becomes our guiding light. I began to understand that righteousness is a Godly life, and it is in complete conformity to His will. The opposite of faith is self-reliance, and to that I confess my error. The most common demand in the Bible is "Fear not." I tapped into fear and felt relief. I was persuaded to abandon my fears. Faith in God reforms the soul—faith creates and renews trust, and trust is hope.

Praying each night with my mother at my bedside was a gift far greater than silver or gold. She taught me to pray for others, never for myself. Prayer is for One to control, guide and use the self, and it has therapeutic or healing value only if it frees you from self-preoccupation, and gets you interested in something outside yourself. The self is lost in others and found again through them, in itself. The art of prayer must be learned, for reservoirs of power are at our disposal within it; it's a skill just like playing a musical instrument, and like a piano performed with enough skill, it can create an almost magical beauty that also has the power to change. But it takes practice, and a lot of it.

I am eternally grateful for having been blessed with four beautiful daughters. My daughter Priya works in public relations and has that special charm that ensures success. Hanna runs a daycare and her warm, quiet personality is perfect for nurturing and caring for children. Hanna's sons, Aiden and Dylan, are lucky Hanna is their mom. Hanna shares life with her wonderful husband David Gusse. Sofie is an aspiring actress and her magnetic persona leaps off the stage. She's a natural. And of course, I am grateful to Lynn, who has challenged me is so many ways. I love her, and the obstacles we have faced together have made us work toward love. I pray daily for my daughters, grandsons, my brother, his wife, their son. My brother Paul has been missing for forty-four years. I pray for him even though I do harbor some lingering resentment for the pain he caused our mother.

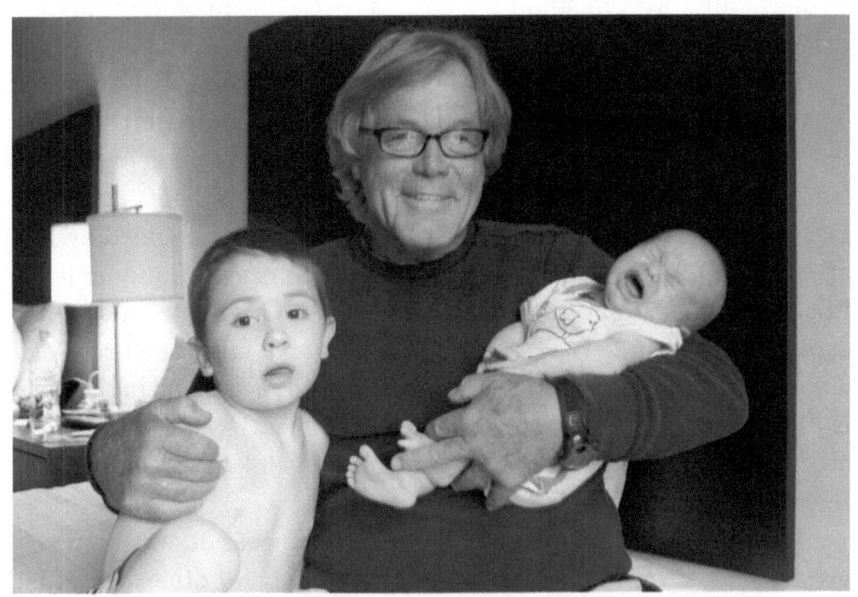

Me and my grandsons Aiden (L) and Dylan 2012

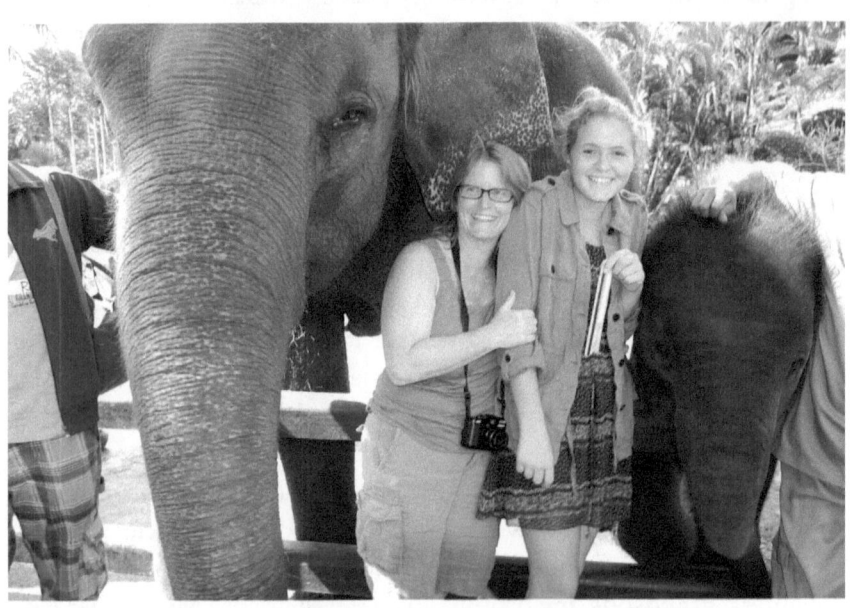

Lynn and Sofie in Bali 2011

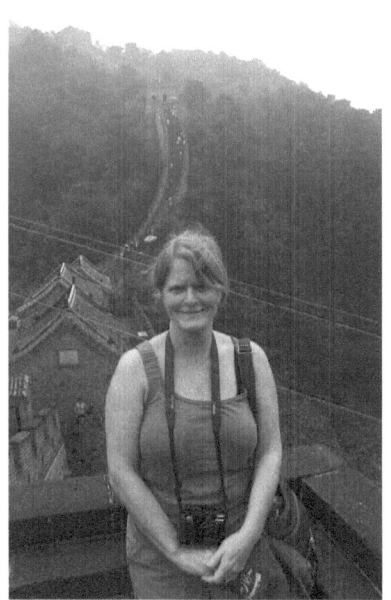

Lynn at Great Wall 2011

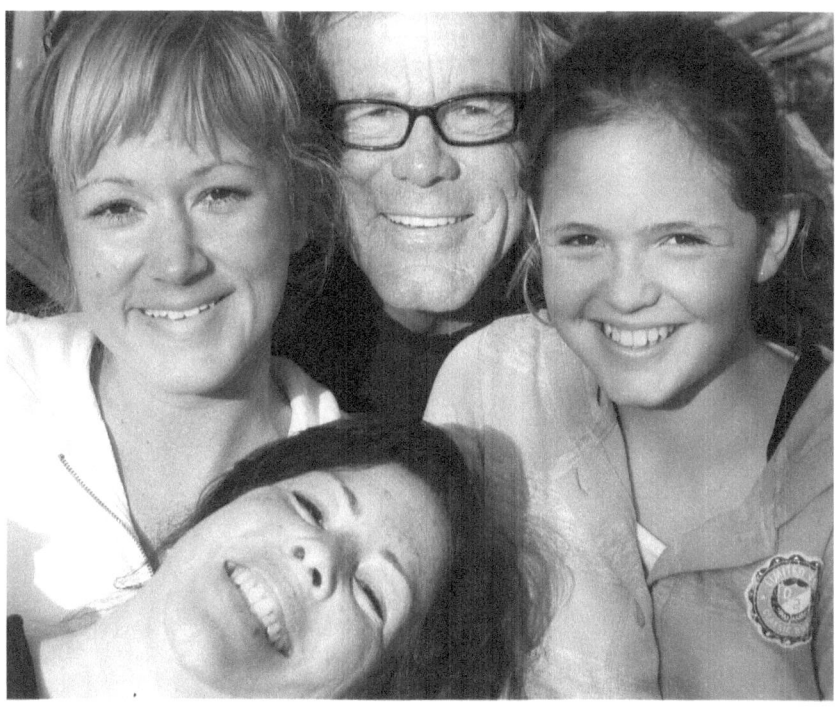

Jim with daughters Hanna(L), Sofie (R) and Priya (lower left), 2010.

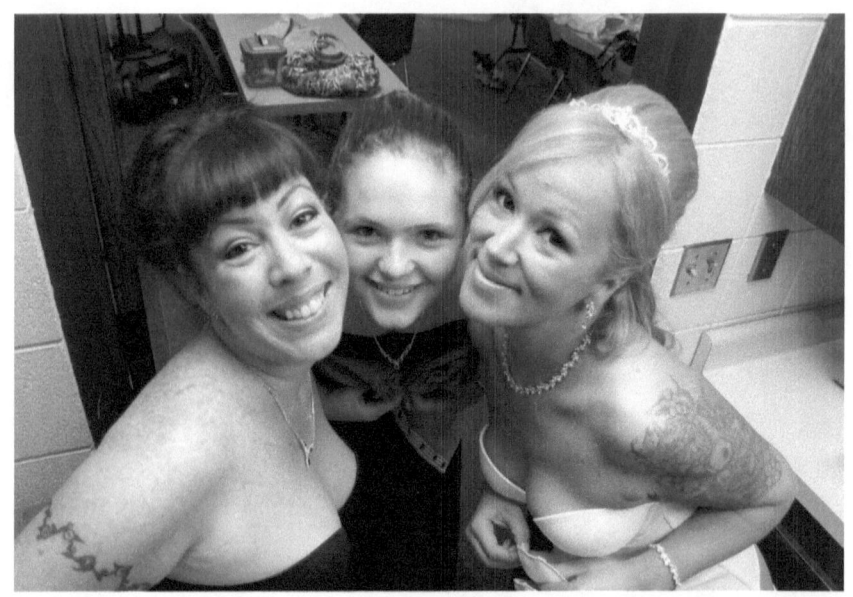

Daughters Priya(L)Sofie and Hanna (R)

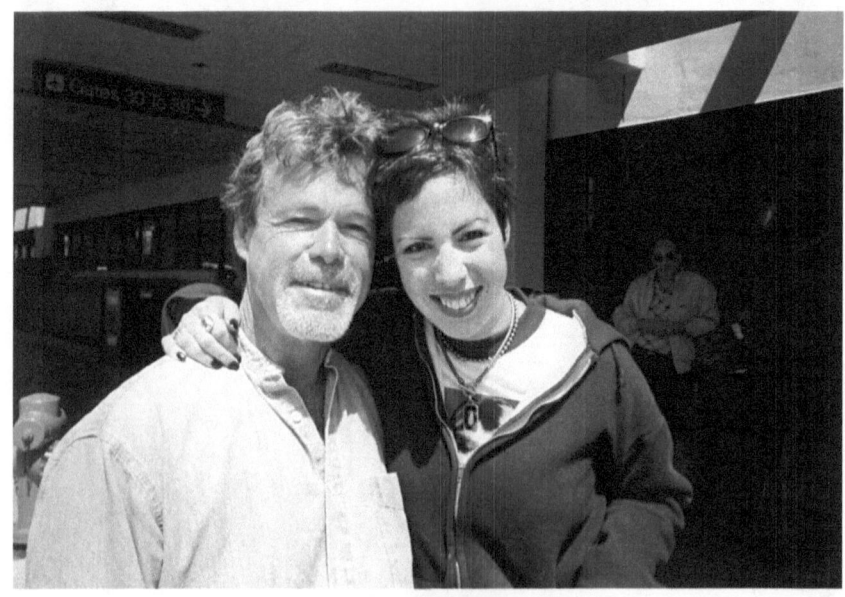

Jim and Priya

My Firstborn Brijjie, my mom, dad and many other loved ones have hopefully crossed to the other side, into the heavenly Kingdom of God. I fervently want everyone I love to be there, with their names written in the Lamb's Book of Life.

My grandfather, Papa Bohannon, wrote in his 1954 song, "When the toils of life are over and we cross the stream of death, Oh what sorrow it will bring to those that stand around our bed; But just over on the other side is sunshine, love and smiles, For Christ the Lord will meet us there and lift us to the skies."

The secularist story offers an eternity in a black hole after being buried or incinerated. That narrative is beyond depressing and patently false. The gospel (Good News) offers eternity in the Kingdom of God.

The continuing faith journey requires I practice the little faith I have today and pray, "Lord, you are my strength." More will be revealed, so long as I keep to Mark 9:24: "I believe and I need help."

And above all else, the worth of my cherished belief in God, I return to Pascal: "But is it worth the price? What must be given up to wager that God exists? Whatever it is, it is only finite, and it is most reasonable to wager something finite on the chance of winning an infinite prize. Perhaps you must give up autonomy or illicit pleasures, but you will gain infinite happiness in eternity. Pascal had said: belief in God provides, purpose, peace, hope, joy, and the things that put smiles on the lips of martyrs, here, now and for eternity, in Heaven and in this life.

My faith journey has yielded from the Old Testament's Prophetic Books, Isaiah 12:2, "Behold, God is my salvation; I will trust, and will not be afraid; the Lord God is my strength and my song, and He has become my salvation."

An example of what I love about reading God's word is a nugget I often ponder from 1 Corinthians 1:27-29, "But God chose what the world thinks foolish to shame the wise, and God chose what the world thinks weak to shame the strong. God chose what is low and despised in the world, what is regarded as nothing, to set aside what is regarded as something, so that no one can boast in his presence.

Sigmund Freud said, "You only believe in a God like that because you need to believe in a God like that." C.S. Lewis pointed out Freud's flawed reasoning in turn, "And you only disbelieve in a God like this because you need to disbelieve in a God like this to live the life you want to live."

JIM HUBBARD BIO

http://www.jimhubbardphoto.com/
http://www.shootingback.net/
email jim@venicearts.org

Jim Hubbard is an acclaimed documentary photographer who, in 2007, was the first photographer to be the recipient of the prestigious Lewis Hine Distinguished Service Award given by the National Child Labor Committee. He also won the Leica Award for Excellence in 1988 for series on Homeless in America. Named a Fellow in 2007 at the USC Annenberg School for Communication and Journalism and a co-founder of the USC Institute for Photographic Empowerment (IPE) he joined USC's Adjunct Faculty in the Annenberg School in 2008 and teaches a class titled Visual Communication and Social Change and another Visual Communication of Death in the Digital Age. Jim has been nominated three times for the Pulitzer Prize for his homelessness series 1987, Rapid City 1972, SD flash flood and Wounded Knee coverage 1973, and has won over 100 awards from the National Press Photographers Association (NPPA), White House News Photographers Association (WHNPA) and United Press International (UPI). His work has been exhibited nationally and internationally, featured in print and television media.

Jim began his career as a photojournalist in Detroit during the tumultuous 1967 Detroit riots one of the first major international stories he covered. Jim's photographs have been published in most of the world's major print publications and he has covered many of the world's major stories including the 1972 Munich Olympics and massacre, the 1979 Cambodian genocide by the Pol Pot regime, the death of 10,000 people in 1971 during a cyclone near Calcutta, India, and the Wounded Knee siege in 1973. Jim also served with the White House Press Corps during his 16 year staff position with United Press

International (UPI) and has photographed five U.S. presidents and numerous presidential campaigns including traveling with Bobby Kennedy shortly before his death in 1968.

After 25 years as a professional photojournalist, Hubbard founded Shooting Back in Washington, D.C. to empower disenfranchised homeless youth with the ability to describe their world: with the camera they "shot back" as the experts of their lives rather than the subjects of a professional's work. The inspiration for Shooting Back came while Jim was studying for a three year Master of Divinity (M Div) degree at Wesley Theological Seminary (WTS) in Washington, D.C.

The pioneering nature of Jim's methodology, often referred to as participatory photography (PP), has been cited in a wide range of literature and academic journals on photography, visual sociology and contemporary art. Hubbard also authored four books: American Refugees, Forward by Jonathan Kozol, University of Minnesota Press (1991). *Shooting Back,* Forward by Dr. Robert Coles, Chronicle Books (1991) *Shooting Back from the Reservation*, Forward Dennis Banks, The New Press (1994) and Lives Turned Upside Down, Simon&Schuster (1996).

Jim holds both Master of Arts and Master of Divinity (MDiv) degrees. He is the father of four daughters and resides in Los Angeles, CA with his wife Lynn Warshafsky. Jim is a member of Pacific Crossroads Church (PCC) in Santa Monica, CA.

www.ingramcontent.com/pod-product-compliance
Lightning Source LLC
Chambersburg PA
CBHW031821170526
45157CB00001B/138

* 9 781452 577678 *